D0073480

ENTHUSIASM

Enthusiasm

A STUDY IN SEMANTIC CHANGE

SUSIE I. TUCKER

Sometime Reader in English Language,
University of Bristol

'Dark ambiguous word'

JOHN WESLEY, *Sermon on*
the Nature of Enthusiasm

CAMBRIDGE

AT THE UNIVERSITY PRESS

1972

Published by the Syndics of the Cambridge University Press
Bentley House, 200 Euston Road, London NW1 2DB
American Branch: 32 East 57th Street, New York, N.Y.10022

© Cambridge University Press 1972

Library of Congress Catalogue Card Number: 79-161296

ISBN: 0 521 08263 3

Printed in Great Britain
at the University Printing House, Cambridge
(Brooke Crutchley, University Printer)

CONTENTS

CONTENTS

PREFACE

Why should anyone set out to write the history of such a set of words as *Enthusiasm, Enthusiast, Enthusiastic, Enthusiastical(ly)*? They are all very much alive (except *enthusiastical*) so it is not a matter of resurrecting and studying an archaism, unknown to the modern reader or speaker, and therefore opaque. It is, indeed, precisely because the set is still on everyone's lips that it is interesting. For it can be misleading, a veritable collection of false friends. When we meet any of these words in older literature, we think at first sight that we know its reference, its atmosphere, its overtones, only to find as we read further that we have misunderstood it, or at best lost some of the sense.

In two recent books, the word *Enthusiasm* is glossed as a technical term: one is a study of Dryden's critical vocabulary,[1] the other a study of Bunyan's theology.[2] Certainly, in the seventeenth century, these are the only areas where the word is in use. Because it is a technical word, it can cause difficulty or discomfort to the general reader for whom *Enthusiasm* is the abstract noun which sums up the more or less laudable qualities of keenness and verve to be expected in any walk of life. So when we are confronted by seventeenth- or eighteenth-century denigration of Enthusiasm in the religious sphere it is all too easy either to laugh at the odd ideas of our ancestors, or to comment that such an attitude was to be expected then. After all, the eighteenth century is still too widely held, especially by undergraduates, to have been prosaic and artificial in its poetry (by contrast with the exuberant and

vii

natural Romantics) and lukewarm in its religion (until the Evangelical Revival restored that warmth of heart which the Catholic Middle Ages also experienced). People of the age of Enlightenment and Deism felt that this connection between Methodism and Catholicism was no recommendation to either, and we shall be deaf to the strength of contemporary criticism if we do not hear the vituperative overtones of *Enthusiasm* and *Enthusiast*.

On the other hand, from Dryden's time onwards, Enthusiasm in poetry was considered essential: the meaning of the word is clearly different from its meaning in religious controversy. But even in poetry, enthusiasm could be false – in religion, most people assumed that, in modern times at least, it normally was.

This attitude towards religious enthusiasm (in the derogatory technical sense of false inspiration) persists well into the nineteenth century, when theologians were still trying, though in vain, to restrict the word to religious contexts. In the twentieth century, the last thing we think of is religion or controversy, or even poetry, when we hear the word. Though anyone can be an enthusiastic churchman or controversialist, the adjective merely implies great keenness, not a specific theological stance, and the controversy might as well be political.

It seems, however, that to be described now as *enthusiastic* cannot always be taken as unalloyed compliment: there is often an implication of more heat than light, and not the heat that generates power at that. The word is still slippery.

This study might be described as an extended series of illustrations of the *Oxford English Dictionary*'s notes on the

main words of the set. I have tried to make a readable
narrative of their vicissitudes according to the areas of life
with which they are concerned – not as a contribution to
the history of religious controversy, literary criticism, or
social development, but simply to show how one set of
words can reflect changing human attitudes and interests,
deducing these attitudes from definitions (mostly evaluative), formal or implicit, or from the contexts in which the
words occur.

I owe a deep debt of gratitude to the many friends who
have encouraged my enthusiasm (in the modern sense) for
Enthusiasm in its older senses, particularly to Dr C.
Diffey and Dr T. Diffey, Professor C. H. Gifford, Professor L. C. Knights, Mr C. B. Knights, and Miss D. M.
Skews who have filled many a gap in my own reading;
to Dr J. A. Newton and Professor K. Grayston for help on
particular points; to the Bodleian Library, the Library of
the University of Bristol and the British Museum Library;
to the Syndics of the Cambridge University Press, its
other authorities and its referee for their careful presenta-
tion and constructive criticism without which the book
would be even less worthy of their imprint than it is.

Bristol   SUSIE I. TUCKER
July 1971

1

THE PROBLEM

It may be useful to list the main senses of the words
Enthusiasm, Enthusiast(ic), Enthusiastical(ly) before demon-
strating by a series of examples from the seventeenth
century to the twentieth, some of the problems posed by
these words for modern readers who may not have noticed
how many and varied are the overtones and implications
of these words even now.

The *Oxford English Dictionary* shows that *Enthusiasm* has
had three main senses: (1) Divine inspiration, which may
manifest itself in both religion and poetry, (2) the delusion
that one has such an inspiration, or a false claim to it,
(3) ardent zeal for any person, cause or principle. It is in
the transition from one to the other or the co-existence of
old and new meanings in people's minds, that both interest
and difficulty lie. *Enthusiast* has the sense-pattern of its
abstract noun, though the sense of 'one suffering from
delusion' comes earlier. The meliorative sense of 'ardent
supporter of anything' comes after the mid-eighteenth
century according to the Dictionary (we shall see that as
a matter of fact it developed earlier) and is still the main
one. The disparaging sense of 'self-deluded person' continued, and the Dictionary thinks it is still current, and
more likely to be carried by *Enthusiast* than by *Enthusiasm*
or *Enthusiastic*. The E–volume of the Dictionary was
published between 1888 and 1893, so we must ask whether
this is still true - there is no further comment in the first

supplement. The adjective *Enthusiastic* goes with the various senses of *Enthusiast*, though it is found earlier – Philemon Holland uses it in 1603. The sense 'deluded in religion' is implied in Sir William Temple's *Essay upon Heroic Virtue* in 1690. Dryden appears to be the first to imply general irrationality (in 1692, translating St Evremond's *Essays*) and the meliorative extension to 'strongly manifesting zeal' follows in the eighteenth century.

Enthusiastical, says the Dictionary, has been rarely used implying the basic sense of 'divine possession' – there is one example quoted from 1652. Otherwise, it is merely a longer alternative for *enthusiastic*, meaning 'deluded in religion' or 'moved irrationally'. In the later approving sense it is little used and felt to be archaic. It does not figure in the latest *Pocket Oxford Dictionary*, the *Oxford Dictionary of Current English* or the *Concise Oxford Dictionary*. The adverb *enthusiastically*, however, which is obviously based on it, is the accepted form. It follows *enthusiasm* in its pejorative sense in reference to religion during the seventeenth century, and in the extended approving sense in the late eighteenth. A note on etymology should perhaps be added.

The abstract noun, says the *Oxford English Dictionary*, comes from later Latin *enthusiasmus*, itself from Greek ἐνθουσιασμός, a noun based on the adjective ἔνθεος which gave rise to the verb ἐνθουσιάζειν from earlier ἐνθουσία. In English *enthusiasm* first appears in its Greek guise, in E.K's notes to the October Eclogue of *The Shepheardes Calender* (1579). The transliterated form comes in Joshua Sylvester's translation of Du Bartas's *La Semaine* (1608), and *en-*

thusiasme in Philemon Holland's translation of Plutarch's *Moralia* (1603). Dr Onions, in the *Oxford Dictionary of English Etymology*, suggests that it may have come from French. Obviously, E.K. and Sylvester took it direct from Greek, but in Renaissance culture it could have been borrowed by any scholar from any of these languages.

Classicists have argued whether ἔνθεος, the basic word, refers to God possessing Man or Man caught up into God.[1] This is a matter for experts in Greek linguistics, mythology and philosophy. In the earlier English usage, *Enthusiasm* always referred to religious experience, whether of possession or ecstasy, and whether the deity was conceived as a false god, the Christian God, or – more often – the Christian God mistakenly worshipped. We could maintain that the wider uses of the word might be thought to refer to our private idols or to the idols of the market-place; but it is true that a man could now be described as an 'enthusiastic atheist'[2] without any sense of linguistic impropriety, except for the intransigent etymologist who would disapprove on the same ground, and with as little justification, of a 'dilapidated wooden fence' or 'twenty days' quarantine'. There is no linguistic impropriety by the strictest standards in saying that a man is an 'enthusiast for Deism', but we can see why a critic who used the phrase added 'if I may thus speak', when he extended the word to include Scepticism.[3]

How then does the word stray from the religious sphere to the non-religious, whether anti-religious or merely secular? How does it change from technical term to emotive, from smear-word to word of commendation, and to its present standing on slippery ground? At first,

Enthusiasm is a historical term for certain religious manifestations in the classical past;[4] in the later seventeenth
century and throughout the eighteenth, it is mainly a
technical term for religious manifestations in the present;
it could be used in this way even in the nineteenth century,
when its wider uses were current; and it now presents a
special problem to the historian or critic who wishes to
describe the past in its own language. He must begin with
a definition,[5] and after that he may put us on our guard by
capitalising the word when used historically, or by putting
it in inverted commas. He would be well advised not to
use the word in its modern commendatory sense anywhere
near its misleading twin.

Here is the obvious difficulty, since what was once
technical is now general, and, which is worse, is often a
compliment instead of a disapproving label or signal. True,
the modern word is one that needs some careful handling,
for whereas the eighteenth-century writer of a testimonial
was apt to begin with some such formula in mind as 'He
is good but enthusiastic', we tend to reverse the order and
write 'He (more likely *she*?) is enthusiastic but good'.[6]
This set of words has played so many parts that we are still
not quite sure what to make of it. The nineteenth-century
coinage of that tell-tale back-formation *to enthuse* suggests
that enthusiasm can be excessive still, though there are now
some signs that this verb is becoming a word of approval.
For most people in the seventeenth and eighteenth centuries, *enthusiasm*, except in poetry, meant something
'excessive' by definition. We have changed the word in
degree of strength as well as in sphere of application.

The history of *Enthusiasm* in its religious sense can be

read in Ronald Knox's study and in earlier writings.[7] The poetical and nature-loving Enthusiast has been defined.[8] The medical,[9] political, social[10] and philosophical[11] aspects of the matter have been treated in depth; and Frank E. Manuel has devoted a chapter to the 'Psychopathology of Enthusiasm'.[12] I do not wish to re-assemble the arguments or to try to glean in such well-reaped fields, but rather to take a tentative look at the *word* – to consider its definitions historically given, to deduce from the linguistic company it keeps how people regarded the things it stood for, to see how far the dictionary definitions are expanded in tabulated form or by contextual implication,[13] to find how figurative language reflects attitudes of mind, to record the dates when changes of tone and reference have become plain, to note attempts to stabilise or restrict the word's reference, to notice late appearances of older senses, and to ask what is the state today of this multifarious abstract noun and its relatives.

Historically, we can see the problem in miniature when we find very diverse writings all carrying *Enthusiast* in their titles. In 1744, Joseph Warton published a poem which he called 'The Enthusiast: or the Lover of Nature', which concerns a lover of solitude and picturesque scenery. In 1788 was published a novel entitled *The Amicable Quixote*, subtitled 'the Enthusiast of Friendship', the story of a man who made 'friends' without discretion; in 1796 comes *Modern Novel Writing, or The Elegant Enthusiast,* which is William Beckford's prolonged skit on Gothick horror novels and sentimentality; and in 1962 comes Arthur Calder-Marshall's biography of Joseph Leycester Lyne called simply *The Enthusiast* – and this uses the word in its precise technical sense but with some overlay of modern approbation. In the same year also, Professor Pinto's biography of Rochester came out describing him in the seventeenth-century phrase 'Enthusiast in Wit'. Less serious than any of these is *The Enthusiast, or Spiritual Mountebank*, the title of an alleged 'pious farce' to be played in Bristol in 1756. This was a fake playbill satirising Whitefield and Wesley.[14]

That the word *enthusiasm* can be a worry in both its older technical sense and its present variety of senses can be demonstrated by various examples. The classic eighteenth-century discussion of religious Enthusiasm is *The Enthusiasm of Methodists and Papists Compar'd* by George Lavington, Bishop of Exeter. The monument erected to him still stands in the south choir-aisle of his Cathedral, and the reaction of visitors reading it is worth consideration. It eulogises him as a man

> Endowed by Nature with superior Abilities,
> Rich in a great variety of acquired Knowledge,
> In the study of the holy Scriptures consummate,
> > He never ceased to improve his Talents,
> > Nor to employ them to the noblest Purposes;
> An instructive, animated & convincing Preacher,
> A determined Enemy to Idolatry & Persecution,
> A successfull Exposer of Pretence & Enthusiasm.

As Ronald Knox says, 'was there really an age when [Enthusiasm] could be bandied about as a term of reproach?'[15] The puzzled face of the tourist shows how real the difficulty can be. Knox dislikes Lavington's book, as well he might, for its 'thin-blooded' Christianity as well as for its unfairness, and he puts his finger on the reason for our modern bewilderment when he adds that the 'very word enthusiastic is a compliment', though sometimes a 'guarded' one now.

But that we are also troubled by too many senses instead of one bad sense, can be illustrated by a look at three occurrences of the word in Irving Howe's *Politics and the Novel* of 1961. He refers to a 'pure enthusiast' who can always be 'led by the nose' by 'the latest apostle of the most advanced ideas' – no compliment to the enthusiast's common sense. One of the oldest complaints against enthusiasm of any sort is that it defies reason and dispenses with thought. Again, Professor Howe comments on a 'revolutionist of enthusiasm' who cannot see that enthusiasm may result in murder – the eighteenth century, looking back on the Civil War of the seventeenth century or at the French Revolution of its own time, could have provided plenty of evidence for such a conclusion. But on the other hand, Howe comments that the rulers of George Orwell's Oceania had 'probably read enough history to know that in the Protestant era', enthusiasm could turn into individualism – and in that drab, depersonalised world of *1984*, enthusiasm of that sort would obviously have meant sanity and political salvation. It is not surprising that Howe speaks elsewhere of 'large enthusiasm', coupling it with 'animating idealism'. It is clear that interpretation depends on context.

It is possible to use the group with its modern connotations throughout a book, and yet to introduce the old technical sense without warning. The author of *The Fifth Monarchy Men* writes his book, he explains, because of a renewal of earlier 'enthusiasm' for the subject;[16] he speaks of the Fifth Monarchy men looking forward to an assembly with 'much enthusiasm' and tells us how this quality coupled with initiative made up in their Parliamentary group for what they lacked in numbers. But he quotes from Evelyn's diary of 6 August 1657 a reference to 'a sort of Enthusiasts and desperate Zealots call'd the fifth Monarchy-men'. Obviously Mr Rogers and Mr Evelyn are not using the words in the same sense.

Michael Walzer, on the other hand, can employ the set partly in a purely modern style even though this subject is *The Revolution of the Saints* and therefore religio-political – and partly in ambiguous contexts.[17] His Puritans engage in 'enthusiastic and purposive activity', his Renaissance writers 'enthusiastically praise' Roman military methods. We can understand that 'Radical enthusiasm' could be used by any politician (pro or con), and 'revolutionary' enthusiasm, whether of Puritan saint or Bolshevik poet, is in like case. But when we read that Prynne was 'carried away by the millenarian enthusiasm of the early 1640s',[18] is this the voice of a modern recognising the fervour of that time or the voice of the modern speaking as a seventeenth-century critic would have spoken – or as the technical historian speaks?

Historians – particularly Church historians who are treating the phenomenon in its strict sense – are careful to define their terms in the light of past semantic development; they are of necessity more aware of the misleading possibilities. Dr Parr, his biographer tells us, was jealous in 'preserving his little flock from the rival contagions of "infidelity", "enthusiasm" and "bigotry"',[19] and the modern writer ironically interprets Parr's phrase 'methodistical enthusiasm' as 'devout Evangelical piety'.[20]

An article entitled 'Swift and some Earlier Satirists of Puritan Enthusiasm' might be referring to the same sort of thing, but its author, C. M. Webster, is careful to remind us that in the seventeenth century 'enthusiasm, and especially the religious variety, was a state of mind to be avoided'.[21]

There was in Swift's time so little use of the term for varieties other than religious that the word hardly needs restriction: but Webster was speaking as a modern when, in an earlier article, after describing the *Tale of a Tub* as a 'very brilliant analysis...of religious and sectarian enthusiasm',[22] he goes on to acknowledge that Swift 'at times forgot the brothers and wrote of all men as they struggle and are enthusiastic'.[23]

A particular difficulty confronted Arthur Calder-Marshall when he set out to write the life of Joseph Lyne, alias Fr Ignatius. For Lyne was what in modern terms would be called an enthusiastic Anglo-Catholic - colourful ritual and the revival of monasticism appealed to him; he was full of zeal, and his biographer sees the bright side of his life in that 'conspicuous quality the purity of faith which was the essence of his enthusiasm'.[24] But Mr Calder-Marshall is at times more ambiguous for he describes Fr Ignatius as a man 'certain of his divine guidance', 'a man possessed' - 'but less by God than by powers which he was unable to identify or control',[25] which fits the old definitions. To what, therefore, does 'his stormy and enthusiastic life' refer?

For the modern reader who dips into - for example - Laurence Sterne's sermon on Enthusiasm,[26] the portrait there painted of 'the mistaken enthusiast' will be a puzzle.

For Sterne depicts a sanctimonious precisian who regards cheerfulness as criminal, ejaculates 'pharisaical' pieties in unsuitable places, and boasts of 'extraordinary communications with the God of all knowledge,...at the same time offending against the common rules of his own native language'. The word that springs to modern lips is 'Puritan', not 'Enthusiast': the former may well be unfair, but the latter is quite out of place nowadays.

Even in the nineteenth century the old technical meaning could survive, even if with an overlay of more modern connotation, and an extension to politics. And this may pose a problem for the modern historian's reader if he is presented with the word without comment. In November 1868, Disraeli was trying to dissuade Queen Victoria from appointing Bishop Tait to the throne of Canterbury. 'There is in his idiosyncracy a strange fund of enthusiasm', he wrote, 'a quality which ought never to be possessed by an Archbishop of Canterbury or a Prime Minister of England.'[27] A few weeks before his death (the letter was written in January 1881), Disraeli was writing that he found it easier to settle affairs with Palmerston than with Gladstone, because in the latter he had to deal with 'an earnest man, severely religious and enthusiastic', and so 'every attempted arrangement ends in unintelligible correspondence and violated confidence'. He preferred 'a man of the world...governed by the principle of honour'.[28] This is an astonishingly late persistence of the old abusive use of the adjective in a religio-political context.

Disraeli's biographer catches the tone when he notes that Disraeli found Gladstone's 'enthusiasm' and his 'other-worldly indifference to the London drawing rooms almost as annoying as his politics'.[29]

Without Disraeli's own words, the modern reader is unlikely to see any connection between enthusiasm and other-worldliness. Disraeli, elsewhere, shows that in the nineteenth century the word could be derogatory or commendatory according to content in political contexts or to indicate an excessive keenness on a trivial occasion.

In *Sybil* he describes a Chartist delegate whose votaries had 'nothing but enthusiasm to recommend them'.[30] It was all the poor and unprivileged had. Again, a crowd of trade unionists, left leaderless because their leader had been imprisoned, demonstrate an enthusiasm that was 'earnest and deep'.[31] Surely here Disraeli approves. And any party leader who can inspire enthusiasm possesses a divine faculty,[32] he considers.

But he has no approval for those enthusiasts who have told their candidate 'twenty times a day for the last fortnight, that they would get up in the middle of the night to serve him and then have to be chased to the poll on election-day'.[33] And no more for the dandy Captain Grouse who is teaching a spaniel to beg 'with a zeal amounting almost to enthusiasm'.[34]

These instances present no difficulties, they merely demonstrate the chameleon nature of the word. But what are we to make of Egremont's musings about Sybil, who has a tone 'so lofty combined with such simplicity'? For 'there is no affectation of enthusiasm about her; nothing exaggerated, nothing rhapsodical'.[35]

Clearly, *enthusiasm* by implication means exaggeration, and it is worth noting that Sybil is a Roman Catholic who might have been given to enthusiasm in the religious sense.

Sybil was published in 1845, *Coningsby* in 1844. Some score of years earlier, William Cobbett was using the word with the sense normal in the twentieth century and also in the religious sense of the eighteenth. Again, context is the determining feature. In 1821, he comments amusingly that the girls of Rochester and Chatham do not seem 'so pretty' as they were when he was a lad. Has the passage of time corrected his taste, he wonders – or does he now look at them with the 'solemness' of a 'Professional Man', and not with the 'enthusiasm' and eagerness of an 'amateur'?[36]

But a year later, visiting the Hampshire villages of East and West Stratton, he met a dozen little girls in their Sunday best, carrying books, one of whom told him that Lady Baring had provided the clothes, 'and had her taught to read and to sing hymns and spiritual songs'. This kind of teaching strikes Cobbett as hypocrisy, even if 'done with a good motive'. For, he assumes, the rich educate the poor merely to 'insure their own safety... though in this particular case, perhaps, there may be a little enthusiasm at work'.[37]

The religious overtones are clear, when he goes on to say that when people are 'glutted with riches... when they are surfeited of all earthly pursuits, they are very apt to begin to think about the next world' and to start considering the celestial balance-sheet. Cobbett, from social indignation rather than religious, was making the same charge of 'enthusiasm' that was levelled at Hannah More when she tried to educate her poorer neighbours in Somerset during the period 1800 to 1804.[38]

George Eliot in *Adam Bede* illustrates at once the lingering religious values of *enthusiasm* together with its extension to poetry, and indeed puts it in its original classical context.[39] Her 'Epicurean' rector Mr Irwine is 'one of those large-hearted sweet-blooded natures that never know a narrow or a grudging thought'. He has 'no enthusiasm, no self-scourging sense of duty'; nor has he any 'lofty aims' or 'theological enthusiasm' (the adjective two hundred years earlier would not have been necessary). He is a practical pastor rather than a theoretical dogmatist. He loves the pagan classics – indeed his 'reflections of a young enthusiasm were all associated with poetry and ethics that lay aloof from the Bible'.

It is difficult to see whether – or how far – his creator disapproves of him. The tone of the word is uncertain in 1859. It is accordingly difficult at times for the twentieth-century critic to be sure of his ground. An example of this occurs in *Mansfield Park*. It has been suggested recently that when Fanny expresses her responses to beautiful scenery, she incurs a rebuke from Edmund because to show *enthusiasm* (his word) is to be out of step with Mansfield Park attitudes and to connect oneself with the attitudes of lower-class Methodists.[40] But Edmund says he *likes* her enthusiasm, which may be playful, but is certainly not derogatory.[41] It is historically evident that by the time the novel was being completed (1812–14) there is no necessary connection between religion of any sort and this word.

2

DEFINITION

As late as 1794, a correspondent wrote to the *Gentleman's Magazine* asking for a definition of the word *Enthusiasm*.[1] It would be acceptable, because he had not been able 'to find anything satisfactory thereon'. We can only wonder how far his researches had taken him, for a large number of people very various in their outlook had done their best. His complaint has been echoed in our day by Ronald Knox. But lexicographers, philosophers, satirists, journalists, poets, politicians and preachers had all at least tried.

The definition of the word of course lies in one's conception of the nature of the thing – and that, said Shaftesbury, is 'wonderfully powerful and extensive...it is a matter of nice Judgment, and the hardest thing in the world to know fully and distinctly; since even Atheism is not exempt from it'.[2] So the word remained, as Wesley assessed it, 'dark' and 'ambiguous'.[3]

Its origin in religion, even if it could be applied to the denial of religion, was regularly recognised. Even a non-specialist like Defoe points out that its base is Greek,[4] and some sixty years later, James Usher remarks that however it is applied, 'it originally belongs to religion and must perish when religion is lost' – which is not true.[5]

The enthusiast for Communism regards religion as undesirable and the sporting enthusiast can reasonably regard it as irrelevant to his interest. Nor is religion the first thing we think of when we hear the word and its congeners.

14

We may well begin with a brief consultation of the old standard dictionaries.

Thomas Blount[6] in 1656 connects *Enthusiasts* historically with the 'Anabaptisticall Sect' of Nicholas Stork of Silesia [correctly, Niklas Storch] in the early sixteenth century, and therefore considers it to mean 'a sect of people that thought themselves inspired with a Divine spirit, and to have a clear sight of all things which they believed'. *Enthusiasm* or *Enthysiasm* means 'an inspiration, a ravishment of the spirit, divine motion, poetical fury'. His adjective is *Enthysiasmical*, 'pertaining to an inspiration'.

Edward Phillips in *The New World of Words* of 1658 says that *Enthysiasts* (the form he prefers) are a 'certain Sect of people which pretended to the Spirit and Revelations'. This is repeated in 1662 and in 1671 (except that here *pretended* has been changed to *pretend*, so that one feels it is not all past history). By the 1720 edition, issued some quarter of a century after Phillips's death, *Enthusiasm* has become 'Fanaticism, a making shew of Divine Inspiration'. An *Enthusiast* is 'one that pretends to be so inspired, or transported with imaginary Revelations'.

In 1696, Edward Coles defines *Enthysiasm* (*Enthusiasm*) as 'the doctrine or principles of an *Enthusion*' (or *Enthusiast*) who is 'one pretending to divine revelation and inspiration'.[7]

This is repeated in Cocker (1704).[8] In 1707, *Glossographia Anglicana Nova* is surprisingly non-committal. Is it thinking of religion or literature when it defines the abstract noun as 'an Inspiration, whether real or imaginary; a Ravishment of the Spirit, a Poetical Fury'? It may therefore be a good thing, genuine in its source – but not so Enthusiasts, who are described as

those People who fancy themselves inspired with the Divine Spirit, and consequently to have a true sight and knowledge of things.

In other words, although the inspiration may be true, nobody really has it!

In 1721, Nathaniel Bailey expands *Glossographia* for the abstract noun and quotes it in part for the personal, again with an agnostic attitude of non-committal, since *pretend* need mean no more than 'claim'; and he has no objection to enthusiastic poetry.[9] *Enthusiasm* means

a prophetick or poetical rage or fury, which transports the mind, raises and inflames the imagination, and makes it think and express things extraordinary and surprising.

The Enthusiast is

one who pretends to be inspired by the divine spirit, and to have a true sight and knowledge of things: one who is transported with imaginary revelations.

Dyche and Pardon[10] have made up their minds, and for them 'pretend' surely means what it does to us. After quoting Bailey's definition of the abstraction, they continue:

but the word is generally applied to those persons, who pretend to have divine revelation to support some monstrous, ridiculous, or absurd notions in religious matters, and thereby takes away both reason and revelation, and substitutes in the room thereof the groundless fancies and obstinate result of self-willedness, by using extravagant gestures and words, pretending to things not only improbable but also impossible.

Enthusiast commonly means a person poisoned with the notion of being divinely inspired, when he is not, and upon that account commits a great number of irregularities in words and actions.

Enthusiastic(al) means wild, irregular, something belonging to, or acted by, the spirit of enthusiasm, delusion or madness.

Martin in 1749 equates Enthusiasm with fanaticism (which means 'pretending to inspiration') and explains *fanatical* as both 'inspired' and 'mad, frantic, beside himself'.[11] Wesley in 1764 limits Enthusiasm to 'religious madness, fancied inspiration', and agrees that *fanatic* means mad.[12] The greatest lexicographer of the age, Dr Johnson,[13] is more generous in his recognition that the group need not be limited to religion or necessarily imply insanity. Enthusiasm for him is

(1) A vain belief of private revelation; a vain confidence of divine favour,

(2) Heat of imagination; violence of passion,

(3) Elevation of fancy; exaltation of ideas.

Enthusiast and *enthusiastick(al)* are defined in the same senses, though it is noteworthy that for *Enthusiastick* (1) he writes 'Persuaded of some communication with the Deity', which at least casts no aspersions on the honesty of the Enthusiast.

Discussion of Enthusiasm in religion for the whole of the eighteenth century – and sometimes into the first half of the nineteenth – can be regarded as an enlargement of Dyche and Pardon's summary in all its details. Most people granted a place – if not always the highest one – to it in poetry, which this dictionary seems unwilling to recognise.

The phrases of the early dictionaries are still being parroted in 1819 by Abraham Rees's *Cyclopaedia, or Universal Dictionary of Arts, Sciences and Literature*, where *Enthusiasm* is defined as

a false or prophetic rage or fury, which transports the mind, inflames and raises the imagination, and makes it conceive and express things extraordinary and surprising.

17

One of the most interesting attempts at definition comes from the *Grub Street Journal* of 1735,[14] for this runs counter to both the original religious application of the term and to our modern mainly eulogistic tone:

Enthusiasm is any exorbitant monstrous Appetite of the Human Mind, hurrying the Will in Pursuit of an Object without the Concurrency or against the Light of Reason and Common Sense.

It is noteworthy that there is nothing here specifically related to religion, or even to poetry. It both recognises a wider incidence of Enthusiasm than usual at that early date and disapproves of it wherever manifested: as a definition it seems out of step with both its own time and ours.

The earlier eighteenth century is concerned to distinguish Enthusiasm from Superstition, the later from Fanaticism, though for some – as some dictionaries imply – Fanaticism is merely another word for it. Pastor Stinstra's translator writes of Fanaticism in precisely the same terms as others had written of Enthusiasm.[15] The famous bookseller James Lackington, who may stand for the ordinary intelligent literate man, notices that the two are closely related: he reflects in his autobiography:

Was it possible to keep the enthusiast at all times from fanaticism, I believe the mischief to society would not be so great, as in that case, enthusiasm would be a more harmless madness; but it seems impossible to keep the two characters separate. Which is the reason the terms are often used by writers indiscriminately.[16]

One writer who tried to distinguish was Thomas Ludlam, who says that both words imply 'an *unsupported* claim to *immediate sensible* intercourse with God'. The

enthusiast, however, supposes himself in possession of *knowledge*, the fanatic of *directions*, immediately (and miraculously) communicated to him from *God* himself; but neither of them produce any credentials to establish their claim.[17]

Coleridge, too, tried to keep the words apart. He couples 'Fanaticism and visionary Enthusiasm' and after saying that Behmen had many gross delusions, continues to describe him:

A meek and shy quietist, his intellectual powers were never stimulated into fev'rous energy by crowds of proselytes or by the ambition of proselyting. He was an enthusiast in the strictest sense, as not merely distinguished, but as contra-distinguished from a fanatic.[18]

After which, it seems hard that, if we look up *Enthusiasm* in the index to the modern edition, we are instructed to 'see Fanaticism'.

Coleridge's attitude is modern rather than in line with eighteenth-century or early nineteenth-century thinking. He writes in *The Friend*:

If we would drive out the demons of fanaticism from the people, we must begin by exorcising the spirit of Epicureanism in the higher ranks, and restore to their teachers the true Christian enthusiasm, the vivifying influence of the altar, the censer, and the sacrifice...they must not seek to make the mysteries of faith what the world calls rational.[19]

The eighteenth century was inclined to believe that when mystery came in, religion went out. Coleridge adds a footnote reminding his readers that the Greek *Enthousiasmos* originally meant 'the influence of the divinity such as was supposed to take possession of the priest during the performance of the services at the altar': he clearly believes that the same afflatus can properly inspire the worshippers at the Christian altar.

Isaac Taylor works out the contrasts between Enthusiasm and Fanaticism, as he sees them, in full, publishing his

Natural History of Enthusiasm in 1829 and his *Natural History of Fanaticism* in 1833. We have come a long way since the *Critical Review* in 1769, which said that *Fanaticism* is an arbitrary word, and generally carries with it an idea of ridicule.[20] This comment is wedged into an account of *Enthusiasm* which shows that the word is on the way to its modern sense. The reviewer admits the derogatory meaning, but insists that there can be a commendatory one:

The martyr who dies for the purity of religion is an *enthusiast* for truth; the matron who bleeds rather than suffer pollution, is an *enthusiast* for virtue...*Enthusiasm* has a precise determined meaning, and brings with it ideas of awe, admiration, or horror. Mr. Pope, somewhere speaking of Dr. Arbuthnot's brother, says he had about him the enthusiasm of honesty.

I doubt whether awe or horror enter into the modern connotation, but admiration frequently does.

Thirty years later, there were people who would have been far from agreement with the *Review*. In 1799, Joseph Entwistle, defending Methodist preachers from the charge of being 'Fanatics and Enthusiasts', points out to the author of the offending anonymous treatise,

Your readers, in general, it is probable, have no determinate ideas affixed to these terms; only they understand that they mean something very ridiculous.

He turns the tables on those for whom Enthusiasm is irrational by commenting that

it is very common when anything is said about the influence of the Holy Spirit, for some persons to exclaim 'Enthusiasm! Enthusiasm!' And this is to stand in the place of reason and judgment.[21]

So true is it that response to *Enthusiasm* varies in its connotation according to the state of the religious barometer.

We may recall George III's remark on the 'Methodist' Lord Dartmouth – 'he says only what any Christian ought to say'.[22]

Duff, in his *Essay on Original Genius*, notes that words

degenerate through accident, custom or caprice. Sometimes expressions, which have been anciently taken in a good sense, are, by a strange perversion of language, used in a bad one, and by this means they become obnoxious upon account of the ideas which, in their common acceptation, they excite. This is the case with the word *Enthusiasm*, which is almost universally taken in a bad sense: and, being conceived to proceed from overheated and distempered imagination, is supposed to imply weakness, superstition, and madness. *Enthusiasm*, in this modern sense, is in no respect a qualification for a poet; in the ancient sense, which implies a kind of divine *Inspiration* or an ardor of Fancy wrought up to Transport, we not only admit it, but claim it an essential one.[23]

He adds that etymology will put us right on the meaning – yet that is obviously what it will not do at this period or nowadays. The Greek implies real possession by a god, or at least 'an intercourse with Him' in Dr Johnson's words. But the seventeenth- and eighteenth-century critics (and their nineteenth-century followers) believed that such a state never existed – it was always a false, vain, confidence. As for us, in a different kind of departure from the source *enthusiasm* need have no divinity in it, for our absorbing interests are frequently matters not specially religious at all.

Shaftesbury is willing to grant that '*inspiration* may be justly call'd *Divine Enthusiasm*; for the word itself signifies *Divine Presence* and was made use of, by the Philosopher whom the earliest Christian Fathers call'd Divine'.[24]

It was all very well for Plato, but Daniel Defoe, though he too knows 'the true and original meaning of the word Enthusiasm' was Divine Inspiration, claims that he is 'no

Enthusiastick'. For he knows the current connotation – he is not one 'of those that are apt by poring on Futurities, to fill [their] Head with Whymsical Notions, that Dream of Inspirations, and fancy themselves on the other side of Time; that call strong Imagination Revelation, and every Wind of the Brain an Impulse of the "Spirit"'.[25]

The eighteenth century was not unduly given to the sort of etymological fallacy which holds the original meaning to be the only one to be taken into account. The modern developments may be deplored, but they are fully acknowledged. Isaac Taylor, in the early nineteenth century, gives us explicit warning on this matter:

Preposterous... would be the pedantry of a writer, who in discoursing... of Superstition or Enthusiasm, should confine himself to such a definition of those terms as might comport with the senses they bore centuries ago, in the minds of Lucian, Plutarch, Epictetus or Aristotle.[26]

So Dr Chauncy states the etymological starting-point which 'carries in it a good meaning', but goes on to say it is

more commonly used in a bad sense, as intending an *imaginary*, not a *real* inspiration: according to which sense, the *Enthusiast* is one who has a conceit of himself as a person favoured with the extraordinary presence of the *Deity*. He mistakes the workings of his own passions for divine communications and fancies himself immediately inspired by the *Spirit* of *God*, when all the while he is under no influence than that of an overheated imagination.[27]

Opinion was agreed on both sides of the Atlantic.

Enthusiasm in religion was always false, but whether it was self-deception or imposture depended on the enthusiast. According to Clarendon, Sir Henry Vane the younger

was not to be described by any character of religion; in which he had swallowed some of the fancies and extravagances of every sect and faction; and was become (which cannot be expressed by any other language than was peculiar to the time) a *man above ordinances*, unlimited and unrestrained by any rules or bounds prescribed to other men, by reason of his perfection. He was a perfect enthusiast, and, without doubt, did believe himself inspired, which so far corrupted his reason and understanding, (which in all matters without the verge of religion was not inferior to that of other men) that he did at some time believe, he was the person deputed to reign over the saints upon earth for a thousand years.[28]

Not every enthusiast had such an exalted opinion of his destiny, but it is a constant complaint that such people are sure of their own rightness whatever the evidence to the contrary. The new scientific approach - in religion as well as learning - is clear in two statements made in *The Nature and Consequences of Enthusiasm Consider'd*.[29] The first is a warning against

This Certainty in Matters of Faith, Opinion, or Persuasion, this immoveable Confidence, or Invincible Adherence to a Thing beyond its just Degree of rational objective Evidence, which is the great Foundation of and last Refuge of all Bigotry and Enthusiasm.

The other is a definition:

The pretending to Knowledge and Certainty in Matters which are incapable of such Evidence, mistaking the strength of Persuasion for the Certainty and Evidence of the Thing, is the proper nature of Enthusiasm.[30]

It is noteworthy that the latest edition of the *Concise Oxford Dictionary* (1964) defines *Enthusiasm* merely as 'ardent zeal' but it also allows that an enthusiast may still be a 'visionary, self-deluded person'. Why should there be a disapproving attitude to the man, but not to the idea? Or does the idea take all its colour from the thing for which the ardour is felt?

Modern philosophers, facing the problem of definition, would talk of *real* definition,[31] when one tries to define the actual thing to which the word refers. Obviously this is difficult with abstract nouns, as Shaftesbury and Wesley saw. Blount, with his historical note, comes as near it as he can. A second kind is *ostensive* definition, when one points out something to which ordinary usage applies the word, or when one can explain what to do in order to produce that to which the word will be properly applied. It has been said, for example, that the ostensive definition of *pudding* is the recipe for a pudding. I hope it can be seen that many of the definitions of *enthusiasm* and *enthusiast* – Bailey's, Dyche and Pardon's – are ostensive in the latter sense, for they tell us what are the characteristics summed up in the words. The trouble here, naturally, is that different people choose different ingredients as times change. What strikes us now is that our forefathers were often describing an unpalatable mixture that was usually bad for the health of the soul, and often for that of the body too, whereas we describe an appetising mixture, even if our pudding, because of its light-weight nature, is sometimes more like a soufflé.

We shall see that the ostensive definition of *enthusiast* is easy - you just point out people who deserve the name. But again, they are not always the same sort of people: indeed, the same person may be disparaged by the term in one age and complimented in the next, as, for instance, St Francis of Assisi.

All these definitions other than the 'real' are evaluative and therefore 'persuasive'.[32] They are evaluative because they tell us in what esteem enthusiasm and enthusiasts were held: they imply attitudes of disparagement or approval and are consequently persuasive, for in earlier times they often imply that we should not be enthusiasts and later they frequently imply that we should.

Bailey, the *Grub Street Journal*, Dyche and Pardon, and Rees, are firmly persuasive beyond the duty of a diction-ary. We have only to look at their adjectives – *wild, exorbitant, false, vain, extraordinary, surprising, monstrous, ridiculous*, or such a verb as *inflame* – to see how much they are trying to influence us out of the strength of their feelings. Coleridge, with his *true Christian*, marks a change of persuasive attitude in the religious sphere – the old focus for abuse.

3

CONNOTATION

In the seventeenth century, the set is usually religious in reference, though Milton's comment about *Enthusiastarum deliriis*[1] has a political context. This is from the *Defensio Prima*, against Salmasius, and later we find that Salmasius calls the English *Enthusiasts*. The next century was inclined to agree, taking the word in its technical sense. Its derogatory tone is implied in the phrase *enthusiastarum omnium amentissimus*,[2] which suggests that all enthusiasts are mad, though some are madder than others. Such people existed among the pagans, and claimed direct inspiration 'sometime one way, sometime another, whereof they had no notice or apprehension'. Their prophets were moved by the devil, and they were 'enraged with vapours, fumes, water, ayre, formerly infected and troubled by spirits'.[3] Their modern counterparts were 'mechanick' and 'upstart Enthusiasts',[4] who uttered unwarranted, schismatical and seditious prayers.[5] The whole point of Meric Casaubon's *Treatise* was to demonstrate that Enthusiasm 'is an Effect of *Nature*', but mistaken by men for either Divine Inspiration or Diabolic Possession.[6] He points out that 'private inspirations and Enthusiasms began to be out of request' as men became 'more rational'.[7] They are a result of ignorance of natural causes.[8] No doubt this kind of enthusiasm could be innocent, he admits – but the belief in divine revelation can lead to the modern repetition of the 'horrid rites and mysteries' of the ancient world.

It is the private revelation that worries the theologians. Henry Hammond,[9] a Biblical and textual critic, is by the nature of his scholarly work concerned about these pretensions. Obviously, if you can understand Scripture by inspiration, his work is in vain. People who claim this power are Enthusiasts: the ordinary means of study are needed as well as God's blessing. (Any scholar might express the same view adapted to secular texts.) Further, the Enthusiasts for the 'new light' hold that whatever they teach is as true as Scripture itself; they indulge in additions and subtractions, and conclude that the Scripture, where it differs from the Enthusiasts' fancy, is 'pernicious and mortiferous'.[10]

So in 1763 Martin Madan says:

To equal the *imaginations of men* to the *holy scripture of God*, and think them as much the *inspiration of God*, as what was dictated as such, to the *holy prophets* and *apostles*, is strictly and properly *Enthusiasm*.[11]

Private inspiration can result in opposition to normally accepted regulations and so become antinomianism. This is where Enthusiasm can become a political and social problem. Samuel Parker in 1670 states it fairly, though we may doubt whether the Restoration authorities were either so spineless or so tender:

Superstition and Enthusiasm have out-faced the Laws...Confident men have talked so loudly of the inviolable Sacredness and Authority of their Conscience, that Governours, not thoroughly instructed in the nature and extent of their Power so lately restored to them, have been almost scared from intermedling with any thing, that could upon this score plead its Priviledges and Exemption from their Commands.[12]

He goes on to attack the sectaries who regard moral goodness as the greatest hindrance to conversion:

they have brought into fashion a Godliness without Religion, Zeal without Humanity, and Grace without Good Nature or good Manners, have found out, in lieu of Moral Vertue, a Spiritual Divinity that is made up of nothing else but certain Trains and Schemes of effeminate Follies and illiterate Enthusiasms.[13]

So John Owen (a Congregationalist) distrusts raptures, ecstasies and 'Enthusiastick Inspirations':[14] the Holy Spirit 'works on the Minds of Men in and by their own *natural Actings*', not by 'any *Enthusiastical* Impressions'.[15]

The world-wide nature of Enthusiasm was noted by William Hubbard when, in 1677, he described the troubles of the settlers in New England with the Indian chief Squando, 'that *Enthusiastical,* or rather *Diabolical Miscreant*'.[16] He had put on '*a garbe of Religion*' but was 'supposed to have very *familiar Converse with the Devil*'. It is characteristic that Hubbard suspects that Squando has had some help from the 'Papists' – whom Lavington was to couple over seventy years later with the Methodists as fellow-enthusiasts. There was good reason for William Darrel to lament in 1688 that the very 'Imputation of Enthusiasm would raise the Hot-headed Mobile against us', when as a Jesuit priest he published *A Vindication of Saint Ignatius...from the Calumnies...in a late Book*,[17] and there was still need for such defence in the middle of the next century.

The 'late Book' was an attack by Henry Wharton, *The Enthusiasm of the Church of Rome* (1688). Her most eminent Saints were 'extravagant enthusiasts', distinguished by merely 'the exercise of a blind Enthusiasm', given to follies and whimsies. Such dangers and follies could be prevented by learning. He stigmatises the 'delusions of designing or ignorant Enthusiasts'; they have frenzied brains. 'The great Engines of these religious Juglers were ever Enthusiasm, and the pretence of Miracles'[18] – and as miracles have now ceased, the Papists must depend on Enthusiasm as manifested in the doctrine of the Inward Light. (Since this was commonly held to be the essential Quaker doctrine, here extremes meet, with a vengeance !) Romanist 'Enthusiasm debaseth the Reason and Understanding of Mankind, and exposeth both to the scorn and derision of the most judicious and intelligent Word...as if none but Fools and Idiots could be perfect Christians; and the highest degree of madness were the most certain mark of piety.'[19] Wharton is not being complimentary when he credits Rome's special doctrines and present prosperity to the Enthusiasm of her followers.[20]

Monks were fanatical enthusiasts, and the doctrines of Purgatory and Transubstantiation are based on their 'Enthusiastick Visions and Revelations'.[21] It is folly and 'impertinence' (i.e. inappropriate proceeding) inspired by Enthusiasm to deny oneself the common benefits of life. St Ignatius was a 'most extravagant Enthusiast' and there was no greater or 'more extravagant Enthusiast' than St Francis of Assisi, 'if we except his Ape, Ignatius'.[22] It is obvious from Wharton's choice of exemplars that a judicious modern might well disagree with him, though both Wharton and Lavington would certainly have been ready to echo the comprehensive phrase used by Thomas D'Urfey in 1709 about the activities of the 'French prophets', which he summed up as 'the abominable Impostures of those craz'd Enthusiasts'.[23] Wharton speaks later of Thomas à Kempis as an unintelligible Enthusiast.[24] Presumably, those who publish versions of the *Imitatio Christi* in paperback format do not suppose that the general public would second this judgement. Both vocabulary and sentiment may well strike the modern as uncalled for, when Wharton flatly declares that 'the Church of Rome is in the highest degree guilty of Enthusiasm; and that Ignatius and (whom he imitated) Saint Francis were the greatest and most foolish Enthusiasts of any age [and ought to be] placed one degree beneath Fools and Madmen'.[25] Bishop Lavington over sixty years later was willing at least to admit that St Francis was well-meaning – though he considers him 'weak'[26] – but he is still harping on the 'wild and pernicious Enthusiasms' of some of the 'most eminent *Saints* in the *Popish Communion*'.[27]

For George Hickes, in 1680, the enthusiastic spirit is a Spirit to be exorcised: unless God in his mercy rebukes it, as it is 'gone out amongst us in these Three Kingdoms, we may have as many *Legends* from some sort of Protestants as we have formerly had from the Church of Rome'.[28]

In view of Dr Hickes's knowledge (and interpretation) of ecclesiastical history, it says much for his sober Anglican faith that he can assert that however much Christianity 'hath suffered, and still suffers by some Mens Enthusiastical Notions and Pretensions; yet...it really is the most rational, sober, and regular Institution that [God] could have given to the sons of men'.[29] By implication, Enthusiasm is irrational, wild and irregular, and the usual charge against both sectary and papist is that they deviate, if in two different ways, from the high road of the Anglican *via media*. It could not be put better than in the words of the antiquarian William Stukely who praises 'the medium between ignorant superstition and learned free-thinking, between slovenly fanaticism and popish pageantry, between enthusiasm and the rational worship of God, which is nowhere upon earth done in my judgment better than in the Church of England'.[30]

Two years after Hickes's sermon, Thomas Pittis returned to the question of disregard for the Bible, which for Protestants is the standard of 'Faith and Manners', but is 'contradicted both by Papists and Enthusiasts', for 'the former equal their traditions with the Scriptures, and the latter their own Fansies and dreams'.[31] He notices shrewdly that all sects 'pretending to Enthusiasm' tend to be not only contrary to Scripture but also contrary to the tenets of other sects.[32] Hickes underlines both the irrational nature of Enthusiasm and its evil effects when in *Ravillac Redivivus* he speaks of the 'extravagancies of an intemperate, mis-guided and enthusiastic Zeal' and alleges that the 'Re-monstrator Presbyterians were advanced so far towards Enthusiasm, that they despised... men of sense, and began to look upon it as *stinting the spirit* to spend any *study* or *time* in *preparing* themselves to *Preach*'.[33]

In 1700, John Locke added a section to his *Essay concerning Humane Understanding* in which he argued that Enthusiasm is not merely irrational in fact, but not even in theory concerned to be rational. It lays reason by and 'would set up revelation without it. Whereby in effect it takes away both reason and revelation, and substitutes... the ungrounded fancies of a man's own brain, and assumes them for a foundation both of opinion and conduct.'[34] It is founded in neither reason nor revelation, but rises 'from the conceits of a warmed or over-weening brain', and it works 'more powerfully in the persuasions and actions of men then either of these two, or both together'.[35]

It is this last consideration that was to be uppermost when *enthusiasm* works free of the orthodox religious and heretical spheres, so that the word could be used of any emotional driving power, including those geared to good ends.

For a real shower of verbal brickbats that forcibly demonstrates the attitude of the Establishment to En-thusiasts, we cannot improve on a sermon on 'The Perils of False Brethren', delivered by the notorious Dr Henry Sacheverell in 1709. He is castigating

any *Upstart Novelist*, [i.e. innovator] or *Self-conceited Enthusiast* [people activated by pride, perversity or ambition, according to him] to *corrupt* that *Inviolable Fountain* with *Erroneous Conjectures*, and vain *Philosophical Systems*: to *Prophane* and *Degrade* the *Holy Mysteries* of Religion, by Absurd *Interpretations* and Impudent *Reasonings*: Should we stick to call such a Rebel to *God*, and *Traytor* to his *Church*, a FALSE BROTHER?[36]

Even allowing for the typographical exuberance of his time, this rash of italics and capitals suggests unusually excited indignation.

He goes on to couple hypocrites and enthusiasts, applying to them four characteristic and tell-tale adjec-tives – *obstinate, moody, wayward, self-conceited.*[37] It is surprising, after noting so much stress on the ignorance and unreason of the Enthusiast, to find a writer in 1708 saying that none are 'so obnoxious' (i.e. Liable) to Enthusiasm as 'the Learned and Inquisitive'.[38]

The commoner view is expressed some twenty years later by Anthony Collins, when he argues that Enthusiasm, ignorance, error and vice alike spring from an aversion to inquiry.[39] It is no wonder Samuel Clarke felt it necessary for the good name of Christianity to defend its Founder from the 'Imputation of Enthusiasm' – it is a charge of the 'extremest Malice and Obstinacy'.[40]

The eighteenth century continued to argue that the established Church was a bulwark against Enthusiasm (which, for one writer, is one of an unholy trinity together with Popery and Fanaticism).[41] The target of attack changed from the Quakers to the Methodists, but the language is the same. And the Methodists employed the set of words in the derogatory senses that everybody else used, but denied that the application to them was justified.

Whitefield, said his enemies, preached 'Enthusiastical Cant' and encouraged 'Enthusiastical or Whimsical Persons', contrary to the 'Sound Mind' of the Church of England.[42] Thomas Church accuses Methodism of introducing many disorders – his triad comprises Enthusiasm, Antinomianism, and Calvinism. Bishop Lavington, after his extensive onslaught on Methodism, follows with one on the Moravians, seeing both as crypto-catholics. Wesley replies that the Bishop has undertaken to prove Whitefield and himself 'gross Enthusiasts'.[43] He admits that Enthusiasts are vulgarly supposed to be fools, and says simply but sharply that 'if *God* has begun a great work, then the saying He has, is no Enthusiasm'.[44] In a second letter of the following year, he lists Enthusiasts with 'Fools, Madmen, Knaves, Papists or anything' – here he is borrowing his opponents' language, but it could have been his own, for he holds that one 'that believes without or against Reason is half a Papist, or Enthusiast'. We can see why Henry Brooke calls the novel whose hero is an unusually religious gentleman *The Fool of Quality*, and why reviewers thought it 'bewildered' with enthusiasm.[45] Wesley retorts to Church that he accepts his character-study of an Enthusiast, but denies that it fits himself – it is no more like him than he is like a centaur. Indeed, to be charged with Enthusiasm in the religious sphere was to be insulted. Wesley was not offering any compliment when he occasionally described some of his followers as Enthusiasts. A letter he sent to Thomas Maxfield explains the connotations of the word for him and his own attitude:

I dislike something that has the appearance of *enthusiasm*: overvaluing *feelings* and inward impressions: mistaking the mere work of *imagination* for the voice of the spirit: expecting the end without the means, and underrating *reason, knowledge* and *wisdom* in general.[46]

He sees enthusiasm as the first step in a spiritual decline and fall. Certain members of his London society 'first gave way to enthusiasm, then to pride, next to prejudice and offence, and at last separated from their brethren'.[47] He sums up his position after some trouble with George Bell whose excesses were bringing the movement into more than usual disrepute: 'The reproach of Christ I am willing to bear; but not the reproach of Enthusiasm if I can help it.'[48] Yet, as late as 1809, William Magee was talking of 'the pernicious extravagances of this arch-enthusiast' John Wesley.[49]

In America there were similar complaints from the ministers of churches rooted in British non-conformity, but suspicious of those who claimed to be inspired like the ancient prophets. This was 'a strong tincture of Enthusiasm', according to Charles Chauncy's *Seasonable Thoughts on the State of Religion in New England* (1743).[50] *Erroneous* goes with *enthusiastic*[51] and one David Ferris, possessed with Enthusiasm, was 'ignorant', 'superstitious' and 'illiterate', led into 'wild errors' and absurdities. Ferris claimed a higher seat in Heaven than Moses, and believed that nine-tenths of the New Haven Church members were destined to Hell: he condemned all but 'enthusiastic Zealots' like himself.[52]

By the end of the eighteenth century, *enthusiasm* no longer *ipso verbo* signalled a religious context, but as we have seen in secular writers it was used in the old reference well into the nineteenth. Of course it still can be so used, duly hedged, in historical assessments of the past, but its life as a living expression of adverse opinions is surprisingly long.

In 1819, Richard Polwhele published an edition of Lavington's *Enthusiasm* and this was republished in 1833. The introduction contains a coupling of *enthusiastic* and *fanatical* (p. xxix) and gives an account of 'raving Enthusiasts' in the diocese of Lincoln – contemporary Methodists, not eighteenth-century ones – who pretended to 'divine impulses', practised exorcisms (p. lxxxv) and were given to 'many other sorts of impostures and delusions'. For the nineteenth-century editor, Wesley's proceedings were *enthusiastic* (p. cx) in the old sense.[53]

In 1802, George Nott preached a series of eight sermons on the subject. It is noteworthy that he felt it necessary to entitle the series 'Religious Enthusiasm Considered' – in 1702 the adjective would hardly have been needed. But he uses the set of words precisely as his predecessors would have used it in this context. Enthusiasm is a 'restless spirit' whose 'fatal tendency...has always been to unsettle the religious opinions of mankind' (p. ix), and to destroy the peace of the Church. It is the most frequent and prejudicial manifestation of the spirit of delusion (p. 5), it 'uniformly tends to create schism' (p. 7) which the Enthusiast believes does not matter (p. 97), because he confuses 'the visible and invisible church' (p. 119). Nott remarks in a footnote (p. 343) that 'Despair and Madness' have in every age been the common attendants upon the preachings of Enthusiasts, and, occupying the position of earlier apologists, he says that the charge of Enthusiasm once proved against the Apostles (p. 255) 'would justify our rejection of their doctrines'.

In 1806, Dr Edward Ryan still considers Mahomet and his followers enthusiasts in the religious sense,[54] but he has doubts as to the validity of Dr Priestley's fifty-sixth lecture 'on the influence of religions', for Priestley comprehends 'under that term enthusiasm, superstition, and every species of false religion as well as true'.[55] We may append this with the remarks of Trenchard and Gordon a century earlier, that 'neither Ill-Nature nor Enthusiasm, is any wise related to true Religion'.[56]

Of course, divergencies of view make the word unstable. One man's religion is another man's 'enthusiasm'; for some any tincture of religion is 'enthusiastic'. In the mid-eighteenth century John Leland's *A View of the Principal Deistical Writers* points out that they reject all revealed religion as imposture and enthusiasm,[57] and he notes that for Tindal the word contrasts with scepticism.[58]

Robert Burns, who frequently uses the set in its modern eulogistic senses, can nevertheless use it in its old technical meaning or with derogatory overtones. The tenets of the

Buchanites were 'a strange jumble of enthusiastic jargon';[59] in his own youth he was noted for 'an enthusiastic, idiot piety'[60] – and yet he admits that even if Religion exists 'only in the heated imagination of Enthusiasm' he would find the lie more precious than the Truth. But the suggestions of irrationality, the disturbed brain, and lack of foundation are all clear.

As late as the 1840s it was possible to publish 'improving' novelettes whose titles involved *Enthusiasm*. In 1848 came M. A. C.'s *Enthusiasm not Religion: a tale*. Here are the old implications – Enthusiasm produces 'pride, clamour, contempt' for oneself and others, springing from so-called zeal for religion. The heroine, Eleanor Grey, is weak and enthusiastic (p. 20) and cannot believe (p. 23) that one could be 'warm and devoted without enthusiasm'. The attitude is one of injudicious wilfulness (p. 70). Her imprudent conduct leads her husband to consider all religion as enthusiasm or hypocrisy (p. 47); for her, all religion was connected with enthusiasm and entailed noise, bustle, and excitement (p. 67). The marriage is saved from wreck only when she leaves the conventicle for the Church of her fathers, convinced in the end 'that religion is in no way connected with enthusiasm, although it must be an active and living principle' (p. 159).

And that, for the mid-nineteenth century was precisely what enthusiasm normally was, in the secular sphere.

In 1843 had come a tale called *The Enthusiast: or Prejudice and Principle*. It concerns another misguided young woman, Adeline Clarendon, who wishes to desert the Church of England for a perfectionist sect. Dr Sanderson, her parish priest, fears her 'enthusiastic mind', though he recognises that her dissatisfaction springs from the idealism of youth. But he points out to her (p. 21) that 'the authors and supporters of Schism and sectarianism...have very often been high-minded, devout, and honest-hearted enthusiasts who...have become disgusted with their working-day world'. It is the Church of England's duty (how often has it been said !) to 'resist Popery and irregular Enthusiasm'. Adeline thinks she *is* resisting popery when she refuses to go to church merely at the ringing of the bell, or to follow Dr Sanderson's advice instead of doing as she thinks best herself – both ideas which her undisturbed sister smiles at as 'enthusiastic notions'. It would be easy to sum up the teaching of this tale as 'stay put, and don't ask questions' – and nothing could be less enthusiastic, in any sense, than that.

It is a far cry to George Orwell's 'enthusiastic schoolmaster' whom Laurence Brander describes as interested ecclesiastically only in music, vestments and processions.[61]

4

RELIGIOUS AND MORAL ATTITUDES

(i) DISCUSSION

The Letter of Enthusiasm published in the *British Journal* of 13 April 1723 provoked a reply the next year which at once summarises the attack and rallies to the defence. The 'whole Tendency of the Letter...is to enervate and even to ridicule the Doctrine of Grace...and then to establish humane Reason as the only Light and Guide...in spiritual as in natural Things'. This is 'a Notion which strikes at the very Foundation of the Christian Religion and leads directly to Deism'.[1] The author of *The Letter* confounds good and bad Enthusiasm 'all under the worser sort (to which indeed the word is most commonly applied)'.[2] The defender cannot agree that it is the result of 'Distemper of the Body, or the Indispositions of the organs, or that it may be cured by Physick, or a merry Bottle'.[3] He pleads for a recognition that false Enthusiasm should be distinguished from true, and sums up the characteristics of the false under the heads of Affectation, Self-conceit, Pride, Irrationality, pretended Inspiration, extravagancy of Agitations, and sometimes Lightness, Vanity, Immorality and false prophecies.

The Letter had accused the Martyrs of a 'crackt Enthusiasm', but the critic reminds its author, not of their courage or zeal, but of their 'Real Wisdom, Excellent

Learning, and cool and solid Virtue'.[4] One feels that this is a more effective defence than Edward Young's parrying of disbelief in immortality:

> Enthusiastic, this? Then all are weak,
> But rank Enthusiasts. To this godlike Height
> *Some* souls have soar'd: or Martyrs ne'er had bled.[5]

Bishop Warburton admits that there is a 'better sort of Enthusiasts', but fears that however innocent, they usually suffer from 'more than ordinary ignorance .[6] He has met people who argue that a man may become virtuous through a certain fanatic turn of mind and then be 'kept steady' by Enthusiasm.

To the modern it is confusing (not to say somewhat entertaining) to find *enthusiasm* being bandied about between the attackers and defenders of Christianity; both parties define the word in the same way, but while one says the cap fits, the other denies it. A good example of this is to be found in an essay of Dr Richard Graves on the Apostles and Evangelists.[7] In the preface to the first edition[8] he notes that H. Boulanger, an anti-Christian polemicist, had retailed every objection of the English Deists, and stated that amongst them 'that of enthusiasm holds a distinguished place'. According to Boulanger, Christian morality is merely 'that enthusiastic,[9] impracticable, contradictory, uncertain morality, which we see contained in the Gospels, which is only fitted...to degrade the spirit' and produce fanatics. Boulanger declared that the Jews were 'encouraged by enthusiasts or impostors who necessarily sported with credulity': that St Paul was 'ambitious and enthusiastic'[10] (no compliment), that the populace are given to credulity, enthusiasm and ignorance. He links enthusiasm with blindness and obstinacy, and considers it one of the strongest human passions.[11] In the Old Testament, he says, everything breathes it – and fanaticism and madness.

Graves, of course, is ready to disprove these charges, but his own attitude to the nature of enthusiasm is made clear by his language. He couples 'irrational credulity' and 'blind enthusiasm' (p. 10), regards enthusiasm as an emotion sharing the ground with imposture (p. 56) and deceit (p. 59), speaks of enthusiastic caprice (p. 5), inflamed enthusiasm (p. 27) and declares that the characteristics of this failing are precipitation and violence (p. 49).

As late as 1829, Isaac Taylor is in two minds about it. In his *Natural History of Enthusiasm*, he agrees that it may be the fault of an infirm constitution, but says there are exceptional 'high-tempered spirits, distinguished by their indefatigable energy and destined to achieve arduous and hazardous enterprises. That such spirits often exhibit the characters of enthusiasm cannot be denied' (p. 6).

To be a hero, a human being acts in 'the fire and fury of a half-mad enthusiast' (p. 8), but, thinks Taylor, a seraph would act 'in the perfect serenity of reason'. But 'even in a vigorous mind, enthusiasm is still a madness', though it is 'a weakness of the *species*' rather than of the individual. However, he is willing to grant – as early critics were not – that religious enthusiasm 'may sometimes seem a harmless delusion' (p. 11), compatible with amiable feelings and virtuous conduct, but it more often allies itself with the malign passions, and then produces the virulent mischiefs of fanaticism.

Taylor's two books make it clear that *enthusiasm* was

now a kinder term than *fanaticism*, which by this time had taken over the essential religious senses of *enthusiasm*. He also sees superstition as the creature of guilt and fear, but Enthusiasm as 'the child of hope' (p. 14), and therefore in particular concert with Christianity.

In view of his lukewarm approval of religious enthusiasm, and his obvious wish that heroism could be rational enough to do without it, it is surprising to find him declaring (p. 83):

If the reasoning faculty had not its enthusiasm, the sciences would never have moved a step in advance of the mechanic arts, much less would the high theorems of pure mathematics and the abstruse principles of metaphysics, have been known to mankind.

The multifarious nature of Enthusiasm is well put by Abbey and Overton in their discussion of Coleridge,[12] than whom, they write,

few could be better fitted...to deal with those subtle and intricate elements of human nature upon which enthusiasts and mystics have based their speculations, and hopelessly blended together much that is sublime and true with not a little that is groundless and visionary, and often dangerous in its practical or speculative results.

(ii) DIFFERENTIATION

As early as 1737 Melmoth was witnessing to the fact that enthusiasm could be manifest in many spheres and that it was commendable. Enthusiasm has 'been expelled from her religious dominions' but he hopes she will be left 'in the undisturbed enjoyment of her civil profession'.

For him, it is a 'very necessary turn of mind' everywhere but in religion; it is 'a vein which Nature seems to have marked with more or less strength in the Tempers of most men'. To follow 'business, pleasures, or the fine arts' to any purpose one must do so *con amore*:

and inamoratores...of every kind are all enthusiasts. To strike this spirit therefore out of the human constitution, to reduce things to their precise philosophical standard, would be to check some of the main wheels of society and to fix half the world in an useless apathy.[13]

Precisely the same idea was expressed by Vicesimus Knox towards the end of the century. He admits that mistaken or excessive enthusiasms have done so much melancholy damage 'that wise men are justly alarmed at every appearance of it'; but even in religion surely there is a better kind which is regrettably hurt by the 'cold philosophy, which seems to discourage all the warm sentiments of affection and will hardly allow them in anything which concerns religion'. 'Is there not', he asks, 'an ardour of enthusiasm, which admires and produces excellence in the arts of music, painting and poetry?'[14]

This is a point of view with which we should agree, but it seems to have taken some time to be accepted. Wesley's sermon on this subject is of course mainly concerned with explaining the nature of the religious kind,[15] but he states that the term is 'frequently used', indeed 'scarce ever out of some men's mouths; and yet it is exceedingly rarely understood even by those who use it most'.[16] He suggests that modern languages have borrowed the Greek word because its use covered their inability to define the thing, 'it having been always a word of a loose, uncertain sense, to which no definite meaning was affixed',[17] so there is nothing surprising in its various acceptations now. He lays down some definitions of his own, by which *Enthusiast* implies people with a false belief that they are in a

43

state of grace, those who lay claim to false miracles, absurd believers in 'direction', superstitious zealots, nominal or formal Christians (not in the least likely to be called enthusiasts in the twentieth century) and, interestingly, preachers who trust the Spirit for their sermons instead of preparing them properly.[18] Obviously the word should not be bandied about when different persons understand it in different senses 'quite inconsistent with each other'. For some take it in a good sense for 'a divine impulse' which suspends 'for the time, either in whole or in part, both the reason and the outward senses',[19] as with the 'Prophets and Apostles'. Some take it 'in an indifferent sense', with no implication of moral good or evil, to evaluate poets and professionally eminent men. He notes: 'By "enthusiasm" these appear to understand, an uncommon vigour of thought, a peculiar fervour of spirit, a vivacity and strength not to be found in common men; elevating the soul to greater, and higher things than cool reason could have obtained.'[20]

But, he points out, these are not the generally understood senses of the word. All that most people agree on, is that it stands for 'something evil; and this is plainly the sentiment of all those who call the religion of the heart "enthusiasm"...an evil, a misfortune, if not a fault'.[21] Wesley is refusing to apply the word to the religion of the heart. On a less exalted level, we may notice that at present a 'hearty welcome' is less demonstrative than an 'enthusiastic' welcome (which perhaps suggests a crowd on a public occasion rather than a welcome by a friend) and that the tinge of extravagance can be seen in *heartiness* as well as in *enthusiasm*.

Various attempts were made to explain that Enthusiasm differed from various other errors. Enthusiasts deceive themselves, impostors deceive others.[22] Consequently, the former may be innocent of evil intent: Lavington holds they '*set out* with an innocent and well-meaning heart', though 'such a simplicity is of no long continuance'.[23] Thomas Church concedes that an Enthusiast may be sincere even if his actions are abominable: it is his sincerity that distinguishes him from a hypocrite.[24]

In 1795, one of Wesley's followers published a defence of his persuasion in which he comments on the same lines as his leader, though he adds a few points. 'Perhaps', he says, 'there is not another word, which has been received into the English Language that is so frequently used and so little understood as the word *Enthusiasm*.' After a brief note on its etymology, he goes on to point out that many consider it a term of reproach, especially in religion, but that others think it neither morally good nor evil – 'but then they confine it to that vigour, vivacity, fervour and strength, so peculiarly manifest in the works of the Grecian, Roman, and some few of the English poets'.

Then there are those who declare 'that no worship can be acceptable' to God unless it springs from 'Enthusiasm': for them, it is 'another word for that Divine Power' whose '*extraordinary* illumination' enlightened the Prophets and Apostles and whose '*ordinary* influences' enable us to do the will of God.

Finally (and here he strikes his modern note), there are 'some who have extended its directing power to all the concerns of life, and have boldly asserted, that there is no man excellent in his profession, whatsoever it be, who has not in his temper a strong tincture of Enthusiasm',[25] and he concludes: 'But most men fully agree to the proverb that "Enthusiasm is commendable in every thing but religion".'[26]

George Nott notices the misconception of terms[27] which leads to *Enthusiasm* being applied to that zeal and ardour 'without which it has been justly asserted, that nothing great or noble amongst men can ever be produced'.[28] Nor does the word mean 'an holy warmth of devotion, a fervour of sincerity in Religion'. He defines his terms in the historical sense, agreeing with Wesley that 'there is hardly any word which is so vaguely understood, or so incorrectly applied – some esteeming it to be a virtue, and a proof of an exalted mind: others condemning it as a fault, the result of a corrupted judgement, and in some degree at least, of a corrupted heart'.[29]

Despite the confusion between word and concept, this is a fair statement of the troubles of usage in serious writing.

He adds the useful observation that the word is not to be found in Scripture [30] and condemns as fallacious the idea that the thing is 'a distinct principle... existing naturally in the mind' and the contention that 'it is a noble energy of soul peculiar to such as are of a more exalted temper'.[31]

Part of the trouble in conception and definition is that people do not always see the logic of their words and actions. The author of *Impartial Reflections on what are termed Revivals of Religion* (1816) justly notes that Christians will pray daily 'Thy Kingdom come' but any extraordinary signs of its coming are greeted as mere 'Fanaticism or Enthusiasm'. To pray for salvation in the words of the liturgy is all right – otherwise it is 'enthusiastic rant'.[32]

Coleridge, with his flair for subtle distinctions, refuses to accept that Enthusiasts and Fanatics are the same. He quotes Richard Baxter's autobiography, apropos of the numerous seventeenth-century sects. Baxter considers the Behmenists, Fifth Monarchy men, Quakers and some Baptists to be 'proper Fanatics, looking too much to revelations within, instead of the Holy Scriptures'. Coleridge comments that

Baxter makes the usual mistake of writing *Fanatic* when he clearly means Enthusiast. [It is surely a very *unusual* substitution on Baxter's part.] The Field-Methodists are fanatics, i.e. *circa fana densa turba concalefacti*, those who catch heat by crowding together round the same *Fane*. Fanaticism is the fever of *superstition*. Enthusiasm, on the contrary, implies an undue (or when used in a good sense, an unusual) vividness of ideas, as opposed to perceptions, or of the obscure inward feelings.[33]

It is doubtful whether one should tie a word down to its etymology to this extent, and, historically, field-preaching took place well away from any 'fane' – it was precisely this that aroused John Wesley's horrified aversion when Whitefield began it. Coleridge is thinking in terms of quality, not kind, the very thing Isaac Taylor was deploring in 1829.

Coleridge was willing to distinguish between kinds of enthusiasts praiseworthy or regrettable, which implies that the word does not of itself impute blame or ascribe credit. He recognises that for some it is a smear-word, but puts this down to the wrong-headedness of the user. Hume, in Coleridge's view, is wrong in describing 'the founders and martyrs of our Church and constitution, of our civil and religious liberty,...as fanatics and bewildered enthusiasts'. For Hume, the word is alive in the old derogatory sense. Coleridge would withhold it, and insist that

47

enthusiasm, directed to good ends, is a word of commendation – for 'histories incomparably more authentic than Mr. Hume's (nay, spite of himself, even his own history) confirm by irrefragable evidence the aphorism of ancient wisdom, that nothing was ever achieved without enthusiasm'.

He defines the word with an obvious extension from essentially religious to possibly also secular – it is 'the oblivion and swallowing up of self in an object dearer than self, or in an idea more vivid'. When it is genuine, whether in morals, religion or patriotism, it is an 'enlargement of the soul above its mere self', attesting the presence 'of ultimative principles', which 'alone can interest the undegraded human spirit deeply and enduringly, because these alone belong to its essence, and will remain with it permanently'.[34]

Coleridge, of course, uses the words in their historical sense of Familists, of Mystics, of Böhme,[35] and would wish a young theologian's studies to begin with a consideration of 'all the passages scattered throughout the writings of Swift and Burke, that bear on enthusiasm, spiritual operations, and pretences to gifts of the spirit, with the whole train of new lights'.[36]

A modern biographer of Bunyan has noted that the 'sober critics' among his contemporaries 'applied the epithet of enthusiast to mad and sane alike'.[37] He uses the set in the historical sense, sometimes ambiguously or ambivalently: Bunyan's 'enthusiastic evangelism' would make sense either way, but to describe *Grace Abounding* as an 'enthusiastic autobiography' is to make demands on our appreciation of Bunyan's historical circumstance rather than of his personality. On the other hand, when we are told that Bunyan's audiences in London were so great that 'the house could contain neither the multitude nor [their] enthusiasm', the noun is surely being used as we use it now. Since Mr Tindall distinguishes *mechanick* from the modern *mechanic*, it seems a pity that he did not use the equally available *enthusiastick* in the technical sense.[38] It is a distinction not made by Coleridge, who is, however, careful to define his terms by context and exposition, and to show how the overtones of the group vary with the attitudes and sympathies of their users. It is interesting to note that *C.O.D.*'s definition of *fanatic* is '(Person) filled with excessive and mistaken enthusiasm, especially in religion'. Neither adjectives nor restriction would have been necessary in Baxter's time. Dr Johnson equates *Fanaticism* with *Enthusiasm* or *religious frenzy*, and its adjectives with *enthusiastick* and *superstitious*; Ephraim Chambers's *Cyclopaedia* (1779 edn) makes the same equation at greater length, and illustrates the term by using it of the priests who served Isis, the Mother of the Gods, and Bellona, for ancient times, and offering much the same list as Baxter for modern examples.

A change comes over the word in nineteenth-century literary use. W. E. Houghton[39] ascribes to the feeling for which it stands a 'standard of judgement which may be called moral optimism',[40] in contrast to any critical view that leads to satire, pessimism or realism. He notes that *O.E.D.*'s definition (no. 3), 'rapturous intensity of feeling in favour of person, principle, cause', is the normal meaning in Victorian criticism and that 'it is specifically set apart sometimes for the milder mood of kindness and pity'. He would use the word in opposition to Victorian 'earnestness'.

It is not the only Victorian use – Houghton's quotation from George Eliot about Daniel Deronda's 'enthusiasm of self-martyring pity' needs to be set against her other, derogatory uses of the word. There is here a memory of the old religious overtones, awakened by the idea of martyrdom: but Victorian *enthusiasm* may be the signal to feel approving, and be concerned with morality (or sentiment) and not with religion in any cultic sense of that word.

(iii) AMBIGUOUS ATTITUDES

Some references to enthusiastic feelings strike the reader as double-edged. Does the *Critical Review* really approve of the 'violent' agitation the passion causes in love and despair?[41]

There is surely no doubt when this journal comments in 1795 on an author's 'glow of sympathy for the late queen of France' that it 'leaves the extacies of the enthusiastic Burke at a contemptuous distance'.[42] Do not her gallant defenders protest too much?

Rousseau was more likely to appeal to the more progressive *Monthly Review*, which indeed found that his enthusiasm was kindled by 'great objects': liberty, humanity, country, religion (the natural kind, at least).[43]

But how far does the *Gentleman's Magazine* really see sense in 'that enthusiasm in favour of virtue' which led Thomas Day 'to educate two female orphans on the plan of Rousseau'?[44] Or do we approach the statement suspiciously because we know the plan failed? This magazine, however, in the same year was disappointed with Mrs Inchbald's plays because it could find no 'fervent enthusiasm of passion' in them.[45] Such rapture, according to Gerard, is the effect of extreme sensibility,[46] and we may suspect that any approval of sensibility and sentimentality was a passing craze which was against the grain of this period. Poets and novelists might trade in it. Ruffhead has no condemnation for it in Pope's Eloisa – indeed her description of her passion is 'exquisitely affecting, poetical and sublime'.[47] In view of Shaftesbury's assertion that 'all enthusiasm is accompanied by Melancholy, whether in Love or Religion',[48] one can only sympathise with Eloisa, who suffered from this passion really in love and apparently in religion. And opinions, even in popular periodicals, could vary. *The Looker-On* is impressed by the 'disinterested ardour and generous enthusiasm of our gallant forefathers' in love,[49] but *The World* has its doubts. It regards enthusiasm as a form of religion, and declares that love is another form – both break through 'all the restraints of Nature and Custom' and both enable and animate their 'votaries to execute' all the 'extravagant suggestions' of the faith they hold.[50] And the enthusiasm of benevolence is likely to have an adverse effect on 'persons of the finest sensibility', like that of love, for it tends to make people 'of the best dispositions' most liable to deceit and disappointment.[51]

5

ENTHUSIASTS OF BAD
EMINENCE

Seventeenth- and eighteenth-century lists of people then considered enthusiasts in the bad sense provide an enlightening commentary on the views and attitudes of the time when confronted with historical or contemporary figures.

Anabaptists (and everyone responsible for the whole sad story of the Münster excesses), David George (i.e. Joris, of Basel), Mystics, Puritans, Quakers, Methodists and Papists were all enthusiasts in the technical and derogatory sense of the word. The standard of judgement may be Deism or Anglicanism, and there are naturally degrees of disparagement in proportion to the commitment of the critic. Most of the sects that fall short of the Church of England, says Mr Spectator in his two hundred and first paper, 'have in them a strong tincture of Enthusiasm'. But long before the day of the Anglican Establishment, the Friars had set the awful example. Langhorne, in his *Letters on Religious Retirement, Melancholy and Enthusiasm*, exclaims:

Great God! What outrages against reason and thy pure religion did it [Enthusiasm] not commit in the thirteenth century! Where the extravagant *Francis* preached to swallows and fishes, and the diabolic *Dominicus* founded the inquisition – yet these...had more followers than *Whitfield* or *Wesley*.[1]

On the other hand, the non-conformist, Protestant or Catholic, may be blamed for the same sin. The Abbé Milot does not go so far as to put the Act of Uniformity on a level with the Massacre of St Bartholomew, but he does consider that those who suffered from both were invincibly obstinate enthusiasts.[2]

Margery Kempe 'wrote an enthusiastical book', according to the *Monthly Review*.[3] This refers to the brief meditative extracts that were all that was known of her before the publication of the complete autobiography in 1936.[4] If the Reviewer could have read of Margery's wanderings, arguments and unseasonable 'roarings', he would have been thoroughly confirmed in his conclusion that she was an eminent example of an Enthusiast.

Emanuel Swedenborg wrote 'Enthusiastic nonsense':[5] indeed, 'the greater part of [his] theological ideas... appears to be the offspring of a mystic enthusiasm, and calculated more to puzzle whatever is clear and intelligible, and to promote... a fanatic spirit'.[6]

Wyclif was an enthusiast, 'though he never reached that pitch of *madness*, which infected his successors in reformation'.[7]

Nor does Stinstra mean to applaud missionary enterprise when he says it was an enthusiastic spirit that enabled St Francis Xavier to raise 'the power of [the Jesuits] to so high a pitch in the East-Indies'.[8]

Jacob Behmen[9] goes naturally with Swedenborg, but any sign of mysticism was suspect. Fénelon, according to Thomas Green, 'had something of an enthusiastic turn... as appears from his being an admirer of the Mystic Divinity, and being a disciple for some time at least of Madam

Guion...a great enthusiast who pretended to prophecies and revelations'.[10]

Among modern examples, William Law was considered 'strictly and properly an enthusiast'.[11] Warburton says of him that he 'obscured a good understanding by the fumes of the rankest enthusiasm, and depraved a sound judgement still further, by the prejudices he took up against all sobriety in religion'.[12]

Supporters of Law considered this unfair. 'Mr. Payne', says the *Monthly Review*,[13] 'thinks Dr. Warburton has used his friend, Mr. Law, extremely ill, in calling him Enthusiastic, Fanatic', itself a sufficient comment on the tone of the word. Law himself repudiated such views in his *Animadversions upon Trapp's Sermon on the Dangers of Being Righteous Over-much* (1740).

It was noticed, of course, that similar aberrations were to be found amongst Jews, Muslims and Pagans. In 1791, the *Critical Review* declared that 'Superstition and Enthusiasm...are always of the same kind, and scarcely differ with the soil or climate'.[14] Considering that the subject under discussion was the Obeah people of Dominica, contemporary Methodists must have felt even less flattered than usual by this innuendo that their belief was no better than Voodooism.

Beside the great names, the sinister atmosphere implied in *enthusiast* is clear from a scatter of anecdotes about unimportant people who flashed into the news because of some shocking excess to which their self-styled 'revelations' led them. There were, for example, the people in Denmark who believed that the quick way to salvation was to commit murder, repent publicly, and be executed before there was time to blot the clean sheet so bloodily secured.[15]

In 1745, a startling story came from South Carolina. The Dutartres family (parents, four sons, four daughters) lived blamelessly until corrupted by a strolling Moravian who, by his talk and his initiation of them into Böhme's doctrines, 'filled their Heads with many wild and Enthusiastick Notions'.[16] They believed themselves to be the only godly family in the world. Peter Rombert, who married the eldest daughter, 'purposed to destroy Mankind' because the human race was too wicked to live. He divorced his wife and married his youngest sister-in-law. They all refused any civic duties, and fired on the constable sent to arrest them. The local magistrate called out some of the militia; the family shot him dead and wounded several of his men. The house was forced open, one of the family was killed and six were taken prisoner. Five were condemned for murder, but they stuck to their belief that all was done by God's guidance – 'into Adultery, Incest, Rebellion and Murder'. 'And thus ended this Tragical Scene of *Enthusiasm*, in which no less than Seven Persons lost their lives.'[17]

Of course enthusiasts were not always murderers, but they might well be responsible for social upheaval or minor discomfort, results sometimes more dangerous or uncomfortable to the enthusiast than to those who suffered from his peculiar notions.

Looking back at history, the *Critical Review* in 1794 reflects that Enthusiasm

which has in former ages provided the most fatal effects, when victims unnumbered have been sacrificed to the sanguinary idol, is still productive of evils, not indeed to be compared to the massacre of Paris, or the civil commotions by which England was torn during the reign of Charles I, but which call loudly for reformation as the peace of individuals and often of whole parishes has but too frequently felt the baleful influence of the mental disease.[18]

In 1764, the Lord High Chancellor heard 'a very interesting case', wherein a Yorkshire lady was plaintiff, and James Reilly, a reputed Antinomian preacher, and others, were defendants. She obtained cancellation of an annuity deed of £50 for the life of Reilly 'fraudulently obtained by him...from a person labouring under a temporary enthusiastical frenzy'.[19] The interesting thing here is that the enthusiast is the sufferer, and had been taken advantage of by persons in their right mind, though not in their right morals. Spiritual pride was the obvious danger of those who believed that they enjoyed direct personal revelation from God, so it is not surprising to hear from Sylas Neville about two Methodist medical students whose enthusiasm led them to leave their lodgings because a fellow-lodger was such a 'bad' man. Neville thought him truly religious.[20]

John Wesley reports a much worse case, from the theological point of view, if not the social. He mentions six 'wild enthusiasts' who 'had first run into the height of Antinomianism, and then were given up to the spirit of pride and blasphemy'. One believed that there were only two sinners in the world – God, and the Devil!![21]

A different lack of balance is in Addison's mind when he refers to 'those sour Enthusiasts who affect to stigmatise the finest...Authors...as dangerous to Religion'.[22] It is the same attitude that Warton deplores in Puritans averse to plays and dancing – the 'extravagant and absurd spirit of Puritanical enthusiasm'.[23]

Hume (probably not without approval) notices that all enthusiasts have been free from the yoke of ecclesiastics, and have expressed great independence in their devotion, with contempt of forms, ceremonies and traditions.[24] But socially, of course, this sort of thing is subversive. So the Münster Anabaptists had adopted dangerous principles – no magistracy, no distinctions of birth, wealth and rank, along with a community of goods (including wives).[25]

The effect of mob excitement is with us still. Nevertheless, we should not expect the enthusiasm of a political meeting or a football crowd normally to end in disaster, though we know that it could – indeed, some recent enthusiastic after-cup-tie rows go a long way to revive the eighteenth-century tone of the adjective.

In 1737, an Edinburgh mob committed murder, and the city's M.P. was moved to say that

the lowest Class of People in that Country have, generally speaking, a turn to Enthusiasm, and so strong is its Influence, such is the force of delusion, that they can work themselves up to a firm Persuasion and thorough belief that any Mischief they are able to do is not only lawful but laudable.[26]

The moderns who wreck the fitments of special trains, smash shop windows, throw bottles at the opposing side and fight on the terraces, act in the same style, without even so much logical justification.

When Richard Baxter published his book *The Certainty of the Worlds of Spirits* in 1691, he devoted a chapter to 'Melancholy, distracted and Enthusiastick Persons'. Among them are such expected targets as John of Leyden,

Ranters, Quakers, and Fifth Monarchy men: but he adds comments on two of the Millenarians, one of whom, a Dorset man, had submitted some of his writings to Baxter, who reports: 'finding him Ignorant and Enthusiastick, I displeased him by advising him to suppress his Papers; and I after heard that he turned distracted'.[27]

The other was a Scots military engineer who believed that by thunder and lightning he could foretell who would be victorious in a battle. He saw visions, including one of 'a Constellation in the shape of a Lion Rampant against the Moon', one of whose legs broke off and turned into a cock.[28] For this he offered a political interpretation (surely the Scottish coat of arms accounts for the Lion). Baxter sees a two-fold physical explanation of these imaginings – too hot a brain to begin with, and then the fact that it became 'overheated too oft with drinking'.

It is hard to see how Baxter arrived at his judgements, for the alleged angelic and diabolic phenomena described in his book with such confident belief seem to the modern reader as fully 'enthusiastic' as millenarian calculation or visionary cartooning.

Millenarianism, spiritual pride, physical manifestations, distortion of morals, delusion and defiance of reason were all found in mid-eighteenth-century America, according to Dr Chauncy. James Davenport is the personification of these errors, and the immediate target of Chauncy's onslaught.[29] Like a thousand other 'enthusiasts', he believed in the imminence of Judgement Day, and he denigrated his brother ministers whom he considered 'carnal' and 'unconverted'.[30] He took '*mechanical operations of violent voice and action*'[31] for impressions of another, higher mind:

we recall Swift's sardonic comment on the mechanical operations of the spirit. Convulsions, distortions, tremblings, 'freakish and furious' conduct, imagining one was favoured with peculiar intimacy with Heaven, all manifest the fact that enthusiasts disregard the dictates of reason.

Such people 'are certainly in the right, and know themselves to be so', which leads to uncharitable opinions of those not 'in their way of thinking'. They become 'positive and dogmatical, vainly fond of their own imaginings and invincibly set on propagating them'. They can be infallibly distinguished – they disregard the Bible.[32]

Nevertheless, Chauncy recognises that there have been true claimants to the title in a wholly good sense – the Prophets of the Old Testament and the Apostles of the New 'might properly be called Enthusiasts'.[33]

The implication is that they were truly possessed by the true God. Etymologically this was acknowledged to be so: but not all defenders of the Faith were willing to risk using a word of such dubious modern connotations. And so we come on essays which bear titles that strike the present-day world as surprisingly out of focus, for example, *A Discourse Proving that the Apostles were no Enthusiasts*, which Archibald Campbell published in 1730.

Seventeen years later, Dr Doddridge contrasts the *Enthusiastical way* of treating religious topics with the way they should be treated, according to Col. James Gardiner,

in a *Rational*...Manner, with Solidity and Order of Thought, with Perspicuity and Weight of Expression; as well knowing that Religion is a most *reasonable Service*; that *God* has not chosen *Idiots* or *Lunaticks*, as the Instruments, or *Nonsense* as the Means, of building up his Church; and that though the Charge of *Enthusiasm* is often fixed on Christianity and its Ministers in a wild, undeserved, and indeed (on the whole)

Enthusiastical Manner, by some of the loudest or most solemn *Pretenders*
to *Reason*, yet there is really such a Thing as *Enthusiasm* against which it
becomes the true Friends of the Revelation to be diligently on their
Guard; lest Christianity should be greatly corrupted and debased, and
all Manner of Absurdity, both in Doctrine and Practice, introduced by
Methods, which (like *Persecution*), throw Truth and Falsehood together
on a level and render the grossest Errors at once more pleasurable, and
more honourable.[34]

It is noteworthy that the Colonel throws the charge of
enthusiasm back at the accusers, though recognising that
the fault does exist.

The fear of such a charge is all the stronger at this time
because it involves the insinuation that the religious
devotee is ill-bred. This comes out clearly in Richard Hill's
A Lash at Enthusiasm.[35] This is a dialogue between Mrs
Clinker and Miss Martha Steady. Miss Steady regrets that
'all zeal for the glory of God and the good of souls' is
'condemned' as 'frenzy and enthusiasm'. Mrs Clinker
finds it disgusting 'to hear so much about the Spirit and
about inspiration'; she looks on 'every thing of that sort'
as 'little better than cant and enthusiasm'. Miss Steady
points out that the Church of England's liturgy requires
us to pray for inspiration ten times at Morning Prayer!
But Mrs Clinker – how modern she sounds! – thinks that
anyone who keeps talking about religion must either want
'good breeding' or be a 'very great enthusiast'. Which
lady expresses Hill's views? There is a pointer in the fact
that he was one of the dedicatees of J. W. Fletcher's
Logica Genevensis (1772), in which Fletcher notes that
enthusiasm and *mysticism* can both have good or bad
senses: 'I am no more ashamed [he says] of the true
mystics than of the true *enthusiasts*, those who are really

inspired by God.'[36] And Miss Steady's name suggests Hill's approval of her opinions. Mrs Clinker's suggests mere noise. The social stigma had been noticed by John Hildrop of Marlborough in 1722, when he remarked that 'the Wits, the Beaux, the Criticks, and all the Herd of Triflers cavil at this way of talking and call it Cant or *Enthusiasm*'. He adds that they laugh at what they do not understand: religious language is as much an unintelligible jargon to them as an exposition of 'the Doctrine of Colours' would be to the blind or a discourse on optics to devotees of a race-meeting.[37]

As late as 1833 Isaac Taylor was saying that in the eyes of the irreligious 'any degree of feeling in matters of religion is enthusiasm'.[38]

6

COLOUR AND CONTEXT

We have been seeing what constitutes enthusiasm or an enthusiast by having our attention focused on people's activities, but we could deduce the conditions proper for the use of the words from the company they keep. Critics of the emotion provide the colour of the words by their choice of verbal context. They may provide clear-cut adjectives, clear-cut, that is, in that they make the user's attitude plain, however vague or impressionistic the adjectives themselves may be. There may, too, be hints of metaphor or personification not fully worked out.

Writers on religion build up a complete picture of their conception of the evils of Enthusiasm – or, in later times, a quite different picture of its virtues – as much by choice of words as by direct and explicit exposition.

We have been shown examples of the sort of people who practise Enthusiasm in religion. For Jonathan Boucher,[1] in 1769, infidels and enthusiasts err together – both deviate from the true path, though in opposite directions. They are 'oddly blended and united (most of them ignorant and all of them shamefully illiterate)'. No wonder that we read of 'enthusiastic dreams', contrasted with 'mad prophaneness' by Samuel Wesley, who of course disapproves of both 'dangerous extremes'.[2] Green couples 'gross impostors and enthusiasts' given to fanciful impressions that lead to 'errors and indulgences';[3] Waterland speaks of 'indiscreet Zeal or a Spice of

Enthusiasm'.[4] Such enthusiastic minds are 'uninformed' ones.

If infidelity is wrong in being less than belief, one can believe too much also. So, for Shaftesbury,[5] Superstition and Enthusiasm make a pair: so do Visionaries and Enthusiasts. Lavington agrees when he speaks of the wild and pernicious Enthusiasms of some of the most eminent Saints in the Popish Communion. The strength, indeed the virulence, of his condemnation is apparent when he goes on to compare the 'conduct of our modern itinerant Enthusiasts' (i.e. the Methodists) to 'the most wild Fanaticisms of the most abominable Communion in its most corrupt Ages'.[6] Lord Lyttelton is thinking of the same lines when he sandwiches enthusiasm in between superstition and priestcraft.[7] Defoe links the word with bigotry.[8]

No wonder Soame Jenyns was afraid that people would ascribe the authorship of his *A Free Enquiry into the Origin of Evil* (1757) to some 'enthusiast' or 'methodist', some beggar or some madman.[9] He would have been surprised at the generous remark of the *Critical Review* half a dozen years later, which admitted 'There is often in the more illiterate enthusiasm, a dignity that is elevated, touching and astonishing'[10] – though that journal a year before had spoken of the virulence and acrimony of wrong-headed enthusiasts.[11] And even towards the end of the century, the *Gentleman's Magazine* was speaking of the blindness of enthusiasm, and lumping it with superstition and illiberality.[12]

The connection between too little learning and too much enthusiasm can still be found in historical writing and literary criticism. Edwin Honig considers that Bunyan believed the English way to Heaven was being travelled in his day not by knights, as in the *Fairie Queene*, but by 'enthusiastic and semi-literate provincials'.[13] Is Dr Honig using the word in its technical sense, in its wider modern sense, or both?

The lack of mature reason which leads to this frame of mind is vividly implied by Lavington when he says that those who are 'likely to be caught in the trap' of wild, fanatical, and sentimental theological language are 'children, simpletons, the superstitious and Enthusiasts'.[14]

The adjectives that go with Enthusiasm either directly applied or said to be incapable of application add to the picture.

In Dublin, according to John Wesley, there were no Methodists 'headstrong or unadvisable, none that were wiser than their teachers: none who dreamed of being immortal or infallible, incapable of temptation: in short, there were no whimsical or enthusiastic persons. All were calm and sober-minded.'[15]

It is noticeable that 'whimsical or enthusiastic' sums up all the other descriptions, and that 'calm and sober-minded' implies that these adjectives describe qualities that Enthusiasts emphatically do not possess.

If we think *whimsical* not harsh enough in this context – and it is kinder than some adjectives that might have been chosen – we must remember that it seems to have been stronger two hundred years ago. Dr Johnson puts 'freakish' at the head of his definitions,[16] and Dyche and Pardon, who agree, add that it means 'foolish', 'silly'.[17]

Dr Wendeborn, a German pastor long resident in

England, noticed among the English 'rank Enthusiasts', guilty of the most 'glaring Enthusiasm'.[18] We meet *frantic* enthusiasm,[19] and Edmond Fox in a poem on the subject equates 'wild' enthusiasm with fanaticism – they are 'still the same'.[20] Zeal may be at once enthusiastic and 'rancorous'.[21]

Uncomplimentary adjectives may still be found when political enthusiasm is being treated. George Orwell speaks of 'imbecile enthusiasms' existing in persons of 'paralysing stupidity',[22] of 'lunatic' enthusiasm, 'blind' enthusiastic acceptance, and of the 'faint mad gleam of enthusiasm' in O'Brien's eye. He is here applying to politics the words that two hundred years earlier were used of religion; his party-members who must show 'no respite from enthusiasm' are suffering from a disease, and the old equation with madness and its physical manifestations is still there in a different sphere. The whole tenor of *1984* supports Dr Chauncy's phrase 'betrayed into enthusiasm'.[23] The party that governs Oceania certainly approves of this sort of emotion: the author is speaking indirectly for the opposition (which cannot exist openly in that terrible society) through his choice of words.

A favourite adjective at all times, which reinforces Enthusiasm when that implies a bad quality and limits it when it may imply a good, is *extravagant*.

A handful of examples ranging from 1688 to 1955 will bear witness to this fact. It is the nature of this passion 'ever to effect somewhat extravagant and irregular',[24] says Henry Wharton in 1688; 'there is nothing so extravagant or so abominable' that it may not result, says *An Historical*

Account of Montanism[25] and nor were the Apostles governed by 'so wild and extravagant a principle';[26] 'it is an extravagant conceit of being peculiarly bless'd with...supernatural communications',[27] says Archibald Campbell in 1730; John Douglas uses the same word in 1755,[28] and in the same year Ralph Heathcote refers to the 'extravagant flights of crackbrained and enthusiastic men'.[29] And for a twentieth-century example, we may refer to Robert Adams's disapproval of the 'extravagant and unnecessary enthusiasm of the New Criticism for analysis of meaning'.[30]

The modern reader would find the word *melancholy* strange in enthusiastic company. To us the noun *enthusiasm* implies happiness and exuberance whether we like the source or object of these feelings or not. It requires historical knowledge and the remembrance of the old theory of the physical basis of the passion to make sense of Lady Conway's words to Henry More in 1676 when she writes: 'I pray God give us all a clear discerning betweene Melancholy Enthusiasme and true Inspiration'.[31]

The 'good' or 'bad' connotation of *enthusiasm* may be deduced from the other abstract nouns with which it is listed.

For example, Dr Thomas Percival in 1734 joins it and its variants with 'the persecuting zeal of bigotry, the sanguinary honour of duelling, and the toilsome solicitudes of ill-directed ambition'[32] – all of which produce temporary insanity. Henry More speaks of 'vain Fantasy and Enthusiasme';[33] for Robert Burton it goes with devilish illusions, phantasms and apparitions.[34] For Sterne it is the product of ignorance, conceit and melancholy.[35]

Another indication of tone is conveyed by linguistic contrast. There is no overt description of Enthusiasm but the speaker's or writer's attitude which his use of the word suggests is made clear by opposition. Dr Johnson says of the hermit's discourse on *Rasselas* (ch. 22) that it was the 'cheerful without levity, and pious without enthusiasm'. The latter phrase occurs in a letter of advice from a lady to her daughter in 1761 three years later,[36] and again in Bisset's *Sketch of a Democracy*, quoted by the *Critical Review* in 1798.[37] It obviously became a cliché, if it was not one already when Johnson used it in 1759.

In 1775, the *Monthly Review* describes two characters as 'neither gloomy ascetics nor frantic enthusiasts' (which suggests some liveliness in the latter grouping).[38] Fourteen years later, this magazine considered that an 'able Biblical scholar' should not be 'an enthusiast or mystic'.[39] Eight years before this, Dr Nathaniel Forster had preached a sermon at Colchester entitled 'Grace without Enthusiasm',[40] which at that time would have been thought proper by everyone. The *Monthly Review* long before had commented approvingly of a volume of sermons by John Orr in which there appeared 'not the least tincture of bigotry or enthusiasm', but instead 'a manly and rational piety'.[41] This seems to have been the usual approach to sermons the journals wished to commend. The *British Critic* in 1796 approves of Carr's sermons because they are 'Animated without enthusiasm and ingenious without subtlety'.[42] The *Critical Review* opposes error and enthusiasm to 'the sober and rational dictates of the true reformed and protestant church'.[43] That observant German pastor Wendeborn regrets that there are so many enthusiasts

67   3-2

'who prefer the mystical, the marvellous and the incredible, to the plain, sensible and rational'.[44]

Yet it is occasionally plain that an enthusiastic mode of delivery in preaching, if not in subject-matter, might have something to recommend it. Oliver Goldsmith seems to think so when he speaks with tart sarcasm of the 'spruce preacher who reads his lucubrations over without lifting his nose from the Text and never ventures to earn the shame of an enthusiast'.[45]

7

EXTENSION

(i) GENERAL COMMENT

Swift is one of the earliest critics to recognise that Enthusiasm may be found elsewhere than in religion. For him
it is a plant that 'has found a Root in the Fields of *Empire*,
and of *Knowledge*' but that has 'fixt deeper, and spread yet
farther upon *Holy Ground*'.[1] He seems to be historically
wrong in his order of development, but he recognises that
the spirit and its manifestations vary – what passes under
the general name 'hath produced certain Branches of a
very different Nature, however often mistaken for each
other'. He offers a universal definition – 'A lifting up of the
Soul or its Faculties above Matter'. He is treating primarily
of religion, but he notes that various secular projects are
the result of the same driving-force – the search for the
Philosopher's Stone or the Grand Elixir, ideas about
Planetary Worlds, the attempt to find a formula for the
squaring of a circle – and on the ethical and political level,
the pursuit of the *Summum Bonum* and of Utopian
Commonwealths.[2] And it is noticeable that all such
projects were then – and, for the practical purposes of
Everyman, still are – visionary, if not impossible.

Over forty years later, in 1757, John Byrom explains at
length, and amusingly, that we all have our Enthusiasms,[3]
and there is no reason to limit the word to religious
matters, where he feels its use is a regrettable index to the
spiritual state of the time. The word

is grown into a fashionable Term of Reproach that usually comes upper-most, when anything of a deep and serious Nature is mentioned. We apply it, through an indolent Custom, to sober and considerate Assertors of important Truths, as readily as to wild and extravagant Contenders about them. This indiscriminate Use of the Word has evidently a bad Effect; it pushes the general Indifferency of the highest Concern into downright Aversion.[4]

He would like to see the delusive sort called *Endemoniasm*. The trouble with this suggestion is that for the Enthusiast his possession is divine, while for his critic it is demonic – how are we to agree on genuine inspiration? To the modern reader of the old controversies, this seems to be what the whole argument is about. Byrom points out that there is a right Enthusiasm as well as a wrong one – we must have one as surely as we have a head.

> 'What is Enthusiasm?' – What can it be
> But Thought enkindled to a high degree?
> That may, Whatever be its ruling turn,
> Right or not right, with equal ardour burn?
> When to Religion we confine the word,
> What use of Language can be more absurd?

And Byrom lists a number of people whose enthusiasms in quite the modern sense run away with them – the disapproving tone can be clearly heard, and we may not agree in all cases. Byrom refers to the ardent classicist who adores Roman remains, or the Egyptologist with his more recondite interests, Bishop Warburton's enthusiasm for Moses,[5] the clerical historian who neglects his parish. There are enthusiasts in every walk of life,

> Down to lac'd fops and powder-sprinkled *beaux*.[6]

Critics and Poets may be similarly bemused – so are Virtuosos, Connoisseurs and Philosophers

> And Politicians, wiser than events.

Byrom sums up in a comprehensive address to us all:

> Think not that you are no Enthusiast, then:
> All Men are such as sure as they are Men,
> The Thing itself is not at all to blame,
> 'Tis in each State of human Life the same;
> The fiery Bent, the driving of the Will,
> That gives the Prevalence to Good or Ill.
> You need not go to *Cloisters* or to *Cells*,
> *Monks* or *Field-Preachers*, to see where it dwells:
> It dwells alike, in *Balls* and *Masquerades*;
> *Courts*, *Camps* and *'Changes* it alike pervades.[7]

Bishop Warburton, despite Byrom's rather uncomplimentary allusion to his work, agreed with him 'that it is foolish to confine the passion to religion, when it spreads through all human life'.[8] But he makes the useful comment that an '*intense application* of the mind to any object' is not necessarily to be identified with enthusiasm, which is 'such an irregular exercise of it as makes us give a stronger assent to the conclusion than the evidence of the premises will warrant; then reason begins to be betrayed, and then enthusiasm properly commences'. This seems to be a fair statement of what many people think when they use the word today. The bishop goes on to explain that the passion 'is more frequent [or was] in religious matters than in any other...those interests being very momentous, the passions bear the greatest sway, and reason is the least heard'.

James Usher, ten years later, in 1767, is sure that enthusiasm is 'an indispensable appendage of the mind of man' however much we may ridicule its folly: we are only quarrelling with nature.[9] For 'the mind of man is incapable of any exalted pleasure that charms the soul in its hours of reflection, or that brings beauty to the dwelling of thought, unless it be enthusiastic, beyond life'. He is not pleading for the 'manifest abuses' of the passion, but declaring that we 'receive our sublime pleasures by it'.[10] But when Usher proceeds to quote the views of an enthusiastic gentleman given to contemplation of 'the sublime' we begin to feel that element of extravagance that so often intrudes. It is the 'influence of a mighty unknown power...an awful and obscure presence' surrounding us and bestowing on the soul 'an elevation and enthusiasm that do not attend on external ideas'.[11] He argues that if 'the universal spirit had not always dwelt in the soul, enthusiasm would not be infectious, nor could fanatic preachers communicate it all times to their audience'.[12] And he admits that the 'rapture of enthusiasm is as contradictory to all rules of reasoning from the received principles, as its fears'.[13]

It is clear that such comments could be made about literary or political enthusiasm as well as religious. It still seemed necessary as late as the 1760s and 1770s to protest at the restriction of the word to the religious sphere. John Boucher, vicar of Epsom, does not argue very clearly, but he evidently feels he cannot account for the American Revolution by putting it down to 'enthusiasm' *tout court* without risk of misunderstanding or disapproval. He challenges readers of history to deny that nations as well as individuals are liable to paroxysms of insanity and 'phrensy', and that the revolt of America may reasonably be ascribed to a strong spirit of delusion on the subject of politics, as the rebellion of 1641 was to a similar spirit on the subject of religion. Instances of religious infatuation in communities are too notorious not to be acknowledged; but it seems arbitrary to limit enthusiasm to one sentiment of the human mind.[14] But like those who disbelieve in the reality of religious inspiration, Boucher does not believe in the necessary reality of political inspiration. He looks at France (his book was published in 1797) at the success of the Republicans, and declares that he does not think it the result of 'enthusiasm of liberty' – that is the 'groundless conjecture only of enthusiasts'. It is really due to 'the novelty, the irregularity, and the improbability of their attempts'.[15] One suspects that Boucher was no great politician – nor psychologist for that matter.

Burke, on the other hand, argues that people have tried such wild schemes before: fired by the idea of the rights of man, they have believed that what is so seductive must be feasible, and they have failed and run into ruin – 'if any enthusiast was so wild as to wish to engage in a scheme of that nature, it was not easy for him to find followers'. But now, success leads to success, so that 'there is a party almost in all countries, ready made, animated with success, with a sure ally in the very centre of Europe. Ambition, as well as Enthusiasm, may find its account in the party and in the principle.'[16] It is not an enthusiasm of which Burke approves – if he ever approved of such a state of mind. He argues that it is 'no excuse at all to urge in...apology' for Warren Hastings 'that he has had enthusiastical good intentions', and adds 'you know that I am no enthusiast, but according to the powers that God has given me, a sober and reflecting man'.[17]

David Hume would never be suspected of religious

73

enthusiasm. Yet he sees a parallel between exemplars of it and himself. He mentions the French mystics and fanatics in Britain, and notes 'a coldness and Desertion of the Spirit' which afflicts them, sometimes for years, alternating with their exaltations.

As this kind of Devotion depends entirely on the Force of Passion, or consequently on the Animal Spirits, I have often thought that their Case and mine were pretty parralel, and that their rapturous Admirations might discompose the Fabric of the Nerves and Brain, as much as profound Reflections & that warmth or Enthusiasm which is inseperable from them.[18]

A brief list of people to whom the group of words is applied during the eighteenth century will serve to show how the secular intermingles with the religious, and how some are complimented, some blamed. In Jerningham's poem we meet plain religious enthusiasts like Luther, and, to illustrate its non-Christian occurrence, Omar giving orders for the destruction of the library at Alexandria. But Jerningham also illustrates the passion from the burghers of Calais, the barons at Runnymede, and Columbus discovering America.[19]

Charlotte Corday in France[20] and the third Lord Shaftesbury in England[21] may stand as enthusiasts for liberty. Malebranche was an 'Enthusiast in the cause of Truth'.[22]

But what was the discoverer of Mesmerism? The *Monthly Review* in 1785 could not make up its mind whether he was an 'enthusiast or an impostor, or a motley mixture of both these characters'. The magazine grants that 'he is far from being destitute of parts and knowledge', and then spoils the effect by declaring that he is 'certainly what is vulgarly called a clever fellow'.[23] And its contemporary, the *Critical Review*, had no hesitation in calling Martin Madan 'that most absurd of all enthusiasts' because of his book *Thelyphthora*.

This last example should warn us to allow for changing social attitudes. Madan's book, so far from being merely an absurd plea for polygamy, is also a closely reasoned exposition of the financial and social difficulties and dangers of women, and of the nature of marriage. He distinguishes the binding laws of morality from the temporary laws of ceremony, and he supports his doctrines with biblical chapter and verse – as we should expect. And he is fully aware of modern commentary, and of the available findings of anthropology and history. He quotes official documents, but through his scholarly references and statistics shines a deep compassion for deserted women and children. And he has his own targets for the charge of 'enthusiasm', particularly the medieval and early Christian exaltation of virginity: 'If the reader has a mind to see how far folly and enthusiasm can carry people on these subjects, let him read [Tertullian, Chrysostom, Cyprian and others]...then he will begin to find how *Marriage itself* was vilified.'[24] Sex is natural, and the implication is clear when he says that it would be 'the highest presumption, nay even the madness of *enthusiasm*, for any man to pray that the natural appetites of *hunger* and *thirst* might cease'.[25] He has no patience with the monks and priests 'and other *enthusiasts* and *fanatics*' who have involved millions in distress and destruction.[26] Christianity he believes to have been '*disgraced* by the uncommanded austerities of visionaries

75

and enthusiasts'.[27] No doubt, polygamy should not be supported, but Madan hardly deserves his cousin William Cowper's attack in *Anti-Thelyphthora*.

However, even at the end of the eighteenth century, as at the beginning, the element of absurdity is often not far away. We sense it in Dorothea Herbert's description of the French emigrée lady, Madame Bondagée, who 'was an Enthusiast for her Pauvre Roi' and gave 'such an Account of the Attachment of the french for their Sovereign that none could suppose they would Murder him and all his family shortly after'.[28] Enthusiasm out of touch with political reality must be in vain, even if it is sincere – and we may well see it as pathetic. And beside the individuals, there are classes of men. Absurd, in Defoe's eyes, was the 'Enthusiastick Dream' of those idealists who believed people could regain the lost innocence of Eden by turning nudists. In Europe, it would take 'a Sect of Madmen' to attempt it.[29] *Honour*, says Francis Hutcheson, 'has had its foolish Associations, and the true Nature of it has been overlooked, so that the Desire of it has run into Enthusiasm and pernicious Madness'.[30] In the hey-day of duelling this condemnation had added point. And people insatiably pursue wealth with 'Madness and Enthusiasm'[31] – which suggests that the old equation of the passion and the infirmity exists for Hutcheson in the moral and social sphere. Nor does he approve of 'extravagant Admirations, or enthusiastick Desires'.[32]

Smollett, in *Peregrine Pickle*,[33] shows that the connection between enthusiasm and madness was real. His painter, Layman Pallet, professes an 'enthusiastic admiration' for Rubens, though not knowing a Rubens when he sees one.

He feels 'his own pencil adopted the manner of that great man with surprising facility', and that when he has grown whiskers and beard, he is the 'express image' of the Fleming. His wife thinks he looks hideous enough to cause her a miscarriage, and threatens 'to dispute the sanity of his intellects'. The people of Antwerp agree. Smollett calls him both *pseudo-enthusiast* and *enthusiast* and shows us his behaviour in the church where Rubens is buried, worshipping at the tomb to the scandal of the attendant, because he thought 'it was incumbent upon him to manifest some extraordinary inspiration while he resided on the spot where Rubens was born'; and, 'therefore, his whole behaviour was an affectation of rapture, expressed in distracted exclamations, convulsive starts, and uncouth gesticulations'. He regards Antwerp as a 'Musselman' regards Mecca. It may be deduced that he is an enthusiast for Art in his own view, but a pseudo-enthusiast in everybody else's. The religious overtones of the word are fully in evidence and the physical manifestations much the same.

(ii) ENTHUSIASM IN LITERATURE

The idea that poets are divinely inspired goes back to ancient Greece. Professor E. R. Dodds tells us that it belongs with epic tradition, as exemplified in Homer or Hesiod.[1] Poets are the transmitters of tradition, and since there are no written documents they must be inspired or they could not know what happened in the far past beyond living memory. Modern poets – the professor mentions Shelley, Goethe and Lamartine – still claim that their 'creative thinking' is due to some power outside themselves. We may add Claudel from our own century.[2] But epic tradition maintains that knowledge is given by the Muses, not that the poets fall into ecstasy. The idea of the possessed poet in a frenzy is due to Democritus in the fifth century B.C., and Dodds suggests that it is a by-product of the Dionysiac movement. Democritus rather than Plato, despite the *Ion*, deserves the 'doubtful credit' of introducing the conception of poets as different from 'common humanity' and of poetry as 'a revelation apart from reason and above reason'.[3] It is noteworthy that precisely the same sort of conception was held of religious enthusiasts.

Poets and critics in England,[4] even (or, perhaps, especially) minor ones, took up the notion with gusto. Here is James Howell in 1628 writing to Will Austen to thank him for a poem on 'The Passion':

Surely you were possess'd with a very strong spirit when you penn'd it, you were become a true Enthusiast...all the while I was perusing it, it committed holy rapes upon my soul...it were an injury to the public good not to expose to open light such divine raptures, for they have an edifying power in them, and may be term'd the very quintessence of Devotion...[5]

It is noteworthy that here poetry and religion are one.

Dryden's opinion and performance are much more valuable, and he thinks the enthusiastic parts of poetry the 'most noble' variety of it.[6] An older contemporary of Dryden, John Smith, noticed a connection between religious enthusiasm and the literary expression of it. There are four grades of prophecy: the

first and lowest of all is when the *Imaginative* power is most predominant, so the Impressions made upon it are too busie and the Scene becomes too

turbulent for the Rational facultie to discerne the true Mystical and
Anagogical sense of them clearly; and in this case the Enthusiasms spend
themselves extreamly in *Parables*, *Similitudes* and *Allegories*.

Shocked as we may be at finding Imagination at the
bottom of the scale, at least the connection has been
made; and it is refreshing to find that Smith is not willing
to divorce Imagination and Reason – 'Prophetical Enthusiasm lies in the joint-impressions and operations of
both these'. Further, the sort of enthusiasm found in
Plotinus seats itself 'principally in the Higher and Purer
faculties of the soul'.[7]

This might be an adumbration of the considered
argument some hundred years later that Bishop Lowth
propounded in his *Sacred Poetry of the Hebrews*. Poetical
language originates in the 'vehement affections of the
mind' and the 'singular frenzy' denominated *enthusiasm* is
'a style and expression directly prompted by nature itself,
and exhibiting the true and express image of a mind
violently agitated' and opening up the 'interior recesses
of the soul'. True, these inmost conceptions may rush
together in 'one turbid stream',[8] but they can be expressed
with sublimity and energy. Lowth is inclined to hold that
only the sacred poets display true Enthusiasm and he
would distinguish it from what is described as 'true poetic
enthusiasm' by 'a common mode of speaking'.

'True poetic enthusiasm' he defines as the spirit
possessed by a poet who is able, by the force of genius, or
rather of imagination, to conceive any emotion of the
mind so perfectly as to transfer to his own feelings the
instinctive passion of another, and to express it in all its
vigour. He is 'inspired, full of the god', as the ancients

79

said. But this does not imply 'that this ardour of mind was imparted by the gods, but that their ecstatic impulse became the god of the moment'.[9]

Prophetic poetry Lowth thinks best of all, for it possesses all that genuine enthusiasm which is the natural attendant on inspiration; it excels in the brightness of imagination, and in clearness and energy of diction, and consequently rises to an uncommon pitch of sublimity; hence, also, it is often very happy in the expression and delineation of the passions, though more commonly employed in the exciting of them.

In 1701, John Dennis published his essay on the *Advancement and Reformation of Modern Poetry*, declaring that in Poetry there must be an extraordinary Passion: 'I call that ordinary Passion, whose cause is clearly comprehended by him who feels it, whether it be Admiration, Terror, or Joy; and I call the very same Passions Enthusiasms when their Cause is not clearly comprehended by him who feels them.'[10]

He considers that religious subjects 'are capable of supplying us with more frequent and stronger Enthusiasms than the Prophane. Poetical Enthusiasm is a Passion guided by Judgment, whose Cause is not comprehended' (p. 217). For Dennis there are six 'Enthusiastick' Passions: Admiration, Terror, Horror, Joy, Sadness, Desire (p. 338). It is impossible to succeed in Poetry without these passions (p. 386), for Enthusiasm is one of the essential characteristics of a good poet, together with fertility of invention, sallies of imagination, lofty ideas and noble sentiments. The company the word keeps in this sort of context is a world away from that of religious controversy. It is a distinction fully stated in Rees's *Cyclopaedia* in 1819.

In 1759, the author of *The Art of Poetry* defines Poetry as 'that enthusiasm flowing from a fertile imagination, that impetuosity and energy of genius, which raises the thoughts and impressions'.[11] Those who try to explain the nature of Genius as the essence of literary merit, use the word without hesitation, though they set it in the company of complimentary adjectives or solid nouns to guard its brightness. John Baillie, in his *Essay on the Sublime* in 1749, calls such enthusiasm 'noble';[12] Owen Ruffhead, in his *Life of Pope*, tells us that 'it is from imagination that a writer derives the fire and enthusiasm which, with respect to poetry especially constitutes among other qualities, what we call genius'.[13] And Belsham in his analysis of Genius thinks it made up of 'Judgment, memory, understanding, enthusiasm, and sensibility'.[14] He equates enthusiasm with 'ardour of mind',[15] adding surprisingly, in view of current medical and psychological doctrine, 'but this is a quality apparently incompatible with melancholy'.

So Lawson credits Chaucer with 'that Enthusiasm which forms the Essence of Poetry'.[16] But, says Rees's *Cyclopaedia*, it is a 'very different' passion from 'that attributed to the sibyls or priestesses of the oracles and heathen gods, which was little else but fanaticism, and consisted principally in grimace and contortions of the body'.[17] Enthusiasm is an emotion which is proper in 'poetry, oratory, music, painting, sculpture'. Rees's use of the word is as commendatory as ours would be in this context.

It seems that Zackary Mayne was as doubtful about the reality of poetic enthusiasm as others were about religious – his choice of 'looks like' and 'appear like' implies as much. But he is aware of the common opinion about the Poets' special claims to manifest the quality. In his *Essay on Consciousness*,[18] he states his belief that

> They also who act with Enthusiasm, as Poets (and who, 'tis thought, do nothing right or to the purpose without it) are not then as *Conscious* as at other times. For their Imagination, when heated, looks like Inspiration: And their Fictions and Inventions, not proceeding from Premeditation, but coming suddenly upon them, without any deliberate Fore-thought or Consideration, appear like so many Apparitions or Visions, and not as their own proper and natural Productions.

But we wonder whether the *Gentleman's Magazine* reviewer, or indeed Mr Pope himself, really believed the whole of the doctrine that the 'Epic poets not only with a noble Enthusiasm, immediately shew the Effects of the Inspiration they pray for, but as Mr. Pope observes from *Eustathius*, they actually vanish from our view. The Muse herself catches the Narrative and relates to the whole.'[19]

There are complaints when the poetic possession is lacking, as there must be if it is the essence of poetry. In 1781, the *Monthly Review* regrets that the work before it offers 'little of that wild and animating enthusiasm, that ardor animi aethereus, which is the soul and character of the poetry'.[20] Eight years later, it adversely criticised Jerningham's poem, whose subject was Enthusiasm itself, because his treatment was not enthusiastic enough (my adjective, of course). He seemed

> not to have formed in his mind adequate conceptions of the grandeur and dignity of his present subject as a *subject for verse*. The *prose writer* may treat of Enthusiasm with all the apathy of a Stoic, and with langour

creeping through each period; but it is a theme that will be expected to animate, to enflame the poet. It calls for a soul of fire:– for *thoughts that breathe*, and *words that burn*: and if the Muse does not bestow a double portion of her inspiration, so as to make the bard *himself the very theme he draws*, the reader will suffer disappointment.[21]

Walpole's friend West thought that the moral and physical worlds 'all open fairer', to a poet's enthusiastic imagination.[22] Goldsmith considered that 'invention and enthusiasm' constitute genius in poetry,[23] and for Edward Young enthusiasm, thought and picture are 'as the body, soul and robe of poetry'.[24] Exaggeration, so much deplored elsewhere, is accepted as both cause and effect of poetic enthusiasm, towards which it is a favourable propensity, according to Ruffhead.[25] Samuel Parr considers it a licence which has always been granted.[26] In 1819, Rees agrees that *Enthusiast* 'is generally understood in an ill sense...sometimes of like import with fanatic', but that *Enthusiasm* implies a good quality in Poetry, Eloquence and Elocution.[27] There,

it is a species of rapturous elevation and fervour, which transports the critic or speaker beyond the limits of apparent rule, and mere methodical propriety. Like genuine sublimity, to which it is very nearly allied, and with which it occasionally co-operates, in producing the highest impressions that can result from human eloquence, it defies, perhaps, the exactness of logical definition, its very essence consisting in a state of feeling, at once so potent and so evanescent, as to elude the cautious touch of analysis.

Yet the encyclopaedist has some doubts:

It belongs, therefore, only to persons of superior genius, and by such alone must be attempted, since, like all superlative excellencies, it verges for ever on the brink of absurdity.

It must, in his view, be safeguarded by knowledge, judgement and discrimination. It brings success to bigotry and fanaticism. Orators should cherish it (not, we presume, in the furtherance of these two qualities, though doubtless it has often been done), and as for poetry, it is 'admitted to be its very soul and essence'. Rees goes on to observe its physical expression in elocutionary delivery – 'a deep and powerful aspiration', 'an increase of quantity in all the syllables', the more forcible articulation of liquids, 'a restrained vehemence, which spreads the undulations of sound through an extended circle'. The nostrils may dilate, the eye-balls protrude, and the whole muscular system grow tense. If we want a fine description of it, we can find it in Shakespeare 'who felt its influence so frequently' that he could 'describe its operation' in Henry V's speech:

> Now set the teeth and stretch the nostril wide,
> Hold hard the breath and bend up every spirit
> To his full height.[28]

We may compare these remarks with Pater's observation that this emotion, 'dependent as it is to a great degree on bodily temperament, has a power of re-enforcing the purer emotions of the intellect with an almost physical excitement'.[29]

James Usher goes back to the classical conception of poetry when he repeats what appears to have become a cliché, that 'Enthusiasm is the very soul of poetry', for he adds a philological comment – 'there is such an indissoluble connection between them that the same word in the learned languages was indifferently applied to a poet and a prophet'.[30] Eighteenth-century scholars did not normally include Old Icelandic in the circle of the 'learned languages', but the idea of poetic inspiration expressed in

the myth of Odin and the Mead of Poetry bears out the
same idea[31] and the god's name is connected with words
meaning inspiration, fury, madness, and is indeed a
cognate of *vates*.[32]

And of course certain kinds of prose may be all the
better for some enthusiastic elevation. Theophilus Evans
considers it

a common Observation, that nothing remarkable and above the ordinary
Pitch of vulgar Conceptions has been wrote, either in Oratory or Poetry,
but when the Author was actuated by some Enthusiastick Heat, some
Ardor and *Impetus* of the Mind that hath some Affinity to Madness.
Aristides compared it to the Heat by which soldiers at the first joining of
Battle are usually carried and inflamed beyond all sense of Death and
Danger.[33]

So Glover extols the

> Enthusiastic flame, without whose aid
> The soldier, patriot and the bard is faint.[34]

But, as if to make certain that he is commending no
real madness, Evans goes on to point out that Aristotle
maintained that

no Person can excel and shine in any Composition but must feel the
Influence of an Enthusiastic Fire to warm and elevate his soul above low
and ordinary thoughts.[35]

And Aristotle was 'a Man of vast extensive knowledge,
and an Universal Philosopher' – yet these are his views.
As so often in eighteenth-century criticism it is the *yets*
and *buts* that show us what was normally expected.

Meric Casaubon's chapter on Rhetorical Enthusiasm
recalls that 'divers ancient Orators did apprehend themselves, and were so apprehended by divers others, to be
inspired or agitated by some higher power than bare

nature could pretend unto',[36] and that this oratory produced an enthusiastic response in their audiences. He adds that the Greeks did not necessarily mean real supernatural agitation – it could be a mere figure of speech for them: no doubt it was for the dawning Enlightenment. He himself 'allows not any real *inspiration* to any *Poet*' or orator, but he does allow to Poets the purest kind of natural Enthusiasm which 'hath most of heaven in it'.[37] He notes that scholarly opinion in Quintilian's time held 'that Rhetorick and good lines came more by Enthusiasme than otherwise'.[38] The last chapter of Seneca's *de Tranquillitate* is 'perfect *Enthusiasme*'.[39] And Casaubon believes that if *enthusiasm* covers 'all elevation of the mind above ordinary thoughts and conceptions', no great 'fruit of the brain' was ever achieved without it.

But he still has his scholarly reservations, for he quotes Quintilian's objection to those who venture upon extemporary speaking 'as it were by Enthusiasm, that is, without a good foundation laid' – this is 'not speaking but twatling, or prating, or anything else that doth not pretend unto reason'.[40]

This is a tone often heard at present in discussions about enthusiasts whose zeal outruns their scholarship, or, more widely, their common-sense practicality.

Those who felt that the literary effects of Enthusiasm were not always and altogether desirable might disapprove of what the devotees rejoiced in. It could go too far in literature, as in religion or politics.

Thomas Rymer, as we might expect from his severely logical critical approach, has his doubts. He admits that there are those who say:

Poetry is the *Child of Fancy*, and is never to be schooled and *disciplined* by *Reason*; Poetry, say they, is *blind* inspiration, is pure *enthusiasm*, is *rapture* and *rage* all over.

He himself thinks Poetry needs Fancy (which corresponds to Faith in the religious sphere) and Reason – and sums it up neatly when he remarks that

Those who object against reason, are the Fanaticks in Poetry, and are never to be sav'd by their good works.[41]

The implication may be that they never perform any, since it was a common charge that to follow the inward light is to follow a false guide, all too likely to end in a ditch.

Vicesimus Knox has no objection to 'animated oratory and enthusiastic poetry',[42] if they are written in English which is strong, nervous, and flowery – the last adjective seems to us out of step with its companions. He is assessing the language, not anyone's particular use of it. He dislikes a writer whose 'literary enthusiasm had certainly transported him...beyond the limits of his own reason'.[43] Like others, he felt that oriental poetry was the product of 'the wild enthusiasm of an irregular imagination'.[44] The same sort of comment was made by the *Critical Review*, according to which eastern literature is a recondite store 'where the human mind unfettered by system has wandered with wild enthusiasm'.[45] And yet it fulfils William Duff's requirements for original genius in poetry – Irregularity, Vehemence, Enthusiasm.[46]

Richard Graves thinks that religious enthusiasts write badly. Their

imagination is heated, a confusion of ideas ensues, the style becomes forced and obscure, full of mysterious and metaphorical dark and distorted allusions. With this obscurity is most frequently combined an exaggerated and extravagant strain of thought and expression.[47]

Here surely the style is the man, muddled and irrational. To a satirist, poetic enthusiasm in a bad poet, i.e. fake inspiration, coupled with exaggerated style, was a standing temptation to parody and mock-heroic. An amusing example of it is the skit on Sir Richard Blackmore ('Maurus') entitled *The Flight of the Pretender* (1708).[48] The author explains his position, beginning with a comment on Blackmore's language:

When his *Sun* rises, distance must be kept, least it *Amaze, Consternate, Astonish* and *Confound* the inferior Rank of Mortals...till his *Enthusiastick* spirit walks amongst *Revolving Moons* and *wandring worlds.*

The parodist will use him as a model:

His design being Romantick, it was fitting the Poem should be Epical, at least, if not Heroical; and no Persons Enthusiastick Genius and Blustring Expressions coming up to such a high Understanding, except those of Maurus, it was thought fit to make use of his noble Flights and Expressions.[49]

How to characterise Poets?

Calm they must be, and yet with equal Grace,
Enthusiastick in a proper Place.
Always the same, when merry, very glad,
And when at weeping cross, extremely sad.[50]

Exhausted after his effort, the parodist seeks new inspiration – in brandy. It is a neat skit on Poetic 'fire'.

'Tis done, I've compas'd my ambitious Aim,
And Brandy burnt, restores the Poet's Flame.
The Bellows blow, now, now, my Bosom glows,
I strive with strong Enthusiastic Throws.
Put in more Brandy – more, till all on Fire
I sing young Perkin's praises to my Lyre.[51]

Considering that Dryden appears to be the first on record to use *Enthusiasm* of poetic fervour, in the Preface to his translation of *Juvenal*, in 1693, the irreverent seem to have started early.

The fullest modern comment on *Enthusiasm* in early eighteenth-century poetry is to be found in Sister M. K. Whelan's analysis of the two kinds of poetry as she defines them, the classical and anti-classical.[52] Her thesis is that just as Anglicanism and rationalism were opposed by the 'enthusiastic' sects, so intellectual and formal poetry was opposed by the poetry of imagination and emotion. She sees the 'enthusiastic' poet as a believer in inspiration, emotion, freedom from artificial restraint, a lover of melancholy engendered by the solitude of nature,[53] a prophet of happier days to come or one who looks back with longing to a past innocent Golden Age. The Enthusiast whether religious or poetic stands for freedom, individual personality, non-conformity, imagination – in a phrase, for the heart rather than the head. It is clear that all these qualities and attitudes are descriptions of the Romantics well before the age to which that term is normally applied, and for Sister Whelan Shaftesbury in theory and Joseph Warton in practice are its prophets. It is also clear, from early reviews of Keats and Wordsworth, that critics might think of poetry in much the same terms as of religion. If persons 'of a lively fancy, weak judgement and heated passions' are likely to engraft into religion 'visions, dreams, extasies, and other whims that are the fruit of a distempered imagination',[54] are not persons of such a turn of mind likely to do the same in poetry?

If poets are inspired by enthusiasm, they also inspire it in their readers. Obviously, here the words do not mean the same thing, for one use implies cause, the other response. We hear often of Shakespearean enthusiasm, for 'no Englishman' can speak of him without it.[55] This is justifiable enough, for, as the *Critical Review* says: 'The nation that can boast of a Shakespeare may be allowed to be enthusiastic in their admiration of his genius.'[56]

Vicesimus Knox holds that 'in reading Homer, every sensible mind finds itself animated with a warmth approaching to enthusiasm'.[57] (The metaphor hints that *sensible* here means 'sensitive'.) It is characteristic of eighteenth-century caution that he seems to doubt whether it would be complimentary to suggest that readers should go all the way. And yet, in 1775, the *Critical Review* had said that Aeschylus 'read Homer with the warmest enthusiasm',[58] surely casting no slur on the dramatist's judgement. The critics appear to have disagreed in their thermometric readings. Pope, according to Ruffhead,[59] always spoke of Homer 'with a kind of grateful enthusiasm' – again we sense a little hedging, though Ruffhead records that Pope applied himself to the poets 'with great eagerness and enthusiasm'.[60] This was entirely proper, for 'There is not...a stronger indication of true genius, than the enthusiastic veneration with which an early candidate for literary fame looks up towards' the great.[61] Pope himself agrees that he had a very great eagerness and enthusiasm for reading poetry[62] and commends his *Eloisa to Abelard* to Dr Cowper because of its 'Enthusiastic spirit', which is the character of the Ancient Poets.[63]

Of course response to particular poems varies and when critics use the same terms they prove that their words are ambiguous. The *Critical Review*, for example, declared in 1775 that Gray's *Bard* 'is animated with an uncommon spirit of lyric enthusiasm'[64] – surely intended as a favourable judgement. This represents an interesting change in critical attitude, for in 1757 this same periodical had described the poem as 'all enthusiasm, extasy and prophetic fury',[65] which does not mean that the editorial board liked it.

George F. Nott considers that *enthusiasm* used of poets, and artists, bears a secondary sense. It used to be distinguished as 'Natural' and was 'attributed indiscriminately to poets, orators and men of genius' – and 'genius' implies 'that extraordinary fervour which in particular moments hurried them on to great exertions, with an impetuosity hardly referrible to any human cause'.[66]

He mentions Tasso's belief that he conversed with a celestial being, Cellini's belief that God assisted him with one of his statues, adding that if the artist had turned his thoughts to religion 'he would have become almost unavoidably an Enthusiast'.[67] We inevitably think of William Blake. And we may reasonably suspect that some people in the eighteenth century would have used the word 'enthusiasm' with some doubt of Romantic writers in general. Angus Fletcher in 1964 points out that we must remember that the term is religious and suggests 'certain consequences of ritual behaviour' (irrational, extravagant behaviour, the earlier critics would have said). The modern critic is discussing the 'enthusiasm' of Burke, Kant and Schiller, and claims that 'we need to give a fresh estimate of its nature': it 'is not simply excitement bordering on hysteria'. These authors 'were concerned with an "enthusiastic" experience based on an oceanic involvement of the self with the Universe'.[68] It is doubtful whether there was ever any approach to hysteria among English men of letters at the period under review: hysteria then belonged in the religious and revolutionary spheres. It seems to have been left to our day to observe in the fans of the exponents of 'pop' music those physical hysterical manifestations that used to be found at the more extreme revivalist meetings and among those 'Mahometan Fanatics' for whom 'violent agitation of the body' is both cause and effect of Enthusiasm.[69]

We may let a poet and a critic add their comments.

Shelley tells us of 'the pleasure and the enthusiasm arising out of these images and feelings in the vivid presence of which within his own mind consists at once the poet's imagination and his reward'.[70] And Hazlitt concludes that wherever 'any object takes such a hold of the mind as to make us dwell upon it, and brood over it, melting the heart in tenderness, or kindling it to a sentiment of enthusiasm...this is poetry'.[71]

A Note on Enthusiasm for Shakespeare

Although *Shakespearolatry* is recorded from 1864, and Bernard Shaw simplified it to *Bardolatry* in 1901, the attitude behind these words was fully formed at the time of the Stratford Jubilee, when it was taken more seriously than now. The ode recited by Garrick contains the phrase 'The God of our Idolatry' and though he delivered it with a 'noble enthusiasm', according to Dapperwit in George Colman's *Man and Wife*, there were critics who regarded this kind of language as superstition and blasphemy, which tends towards another, older, use of *enthusiasm*.[72] The date 1864 tells its own story.

Perhaps even with Shakespeare it is as well to remember that the 'enthusiastical admirers of a favourite author, like ardent lovers, view those objects with rapture which cause in others indifference or disgust'.[73] We may note that Boswell believed Mrs Gastrell had shared her husband's guilt in cutting down Shakespeare's mulberry tree, which 'the enthusiasts for our immortal bard deem almost a species of sacrilege'.[74]

It is almost as if we are dealing with the relics of a saint.

(iii) FROM RELIGION TO POLITICS

As long as it is the common belief that Church and State are co-terminous, any disruption of the one will necessarily be seen as a cause of disruption in the other. The Civil War had shown how far such disturbances could go, so it is not surprising to find at the end of the seventeenth century and in the earlier decades of the eighteenth that there were controversialists who blamed the political upheavals of the recent past on the 'Sects', and uttered dire forebodings as to the dangers likely to arise from them in the future.[1] The Fifth-Monarchy men were 'Phanaticall *Enthusiasts*',[2] according to Evelyn; a marginal note in *Ravillac Redivivus* remarks that the 'Whigs [i.e. the fanatics in question] are arrived to the highest pitch of Enthusiasm, and are as ready to do as much for the *Spiritual*, as the Fifth-Monarchy-Men are for the Temporal Kingdom of Jesus'.[3] It is hard to believe that these parties were mutually exclusive. Were the 'Enthusiastical Cut-throats' who murdered Archbishop

Sharp moved by religion or politics or both?[4] Not surprisingly, Henry Sacheverell looked back fifty or sixty years when, in 1702, he had preached his *Discourse on the Dependence of Government on Religion*, a sermon against occasional conformity. He thunders his rhetorical questions against the Sects:

And is *This* then the Religion, *This* the People that We must *Complement* into Our *Church* and *Government*, to Both which They are Sworn Enemies, and That too at no Less an Expence, than the Hazarding Our Eternal Safety and Preservation, the Giving up Our Ancient Faith, Constitution, and Form of Worship and the Razing those Venerable Boundaries of Law and Discipline, that have so long Secur'd Us from Their Malice, Purg'd Us from their Enthusiasm, and Supported Us Against all their Conspiracies and Designs.[5]

Seven years later, Thomas D'Urfey's satirical play *The Modern Prophets* presents Lord Noble expressing the hope that 'the Law Civil or Military will rid us ere long of all the Enthusiasts of that kind'.[6] For him, their 'pernicious designs' include Jesuitism and Treason. The two inevitably went together in the English mind and had done so since the reign of Elizabeth I, when it was governmental dogma that no Papist was ever executed for his faith, but rather because his faith entailed the belief that the Pope had more claim to his allegiance than the Queen.

Even in 1802 the same sort of danger was apprehended from Protestant non-conformists. The end at which enthusiasts aim, said T. E. Owen, 'is the total subversion of the hierarchy, and as an inevitable consequence the ultimate destruction of our civil establishment'. The implication of 'No Bishop, No King' died hard. Presumably a better civil establishment need not be inconceivable, or a purer religion, but for Owen there is no doubt about the 'easy and quick transition from Enthusiasm to Anarchy and Infidelity'.[7]

John Hildrop in 1729 linked together Jack Cade, Wat Tyler and Oliver Cromwell, who, 'at the Head of an Army of Vagabonds and Enthusiasts, attempted to reform the Abuses of Government, which they intended to subvert and destroy'.[8] The interest here seems to be purely political, though Cromwell is *the* great example for the eighteenth century of the religio-political Enthusiast, a true successor of Mahomet.[9]

'What advantage did not Cromwell draw from enthusiasm', asks Green, 'with respect to the part he chose to act?'[10] And he goes on to state that

it has been found true by experience, that enthusiasm does not only corrupt religion, but when it has attained sufficient strength, and over-turned *Civil* government, and when the public peace is disturbed, or in danger at any time by the practices of *enthusiasts*, or any opinions entertained by them, they can lay no claim to toleration, or an exemption from punishment.[11]

One who believes himself under the direct impulse of God may do anything: to him, 'every crime becomes Lawful, and every Design, that turns up in his Head, is a divine Impulse'. So 'the blackest Crimes are Glorious' to him. 'The Prejudice, that blinds him, is gross Ignorance of the Nature of God, and an unmeasured Opinion of his own Excellency. He thinks God capable of commanding anything and himself of performing anything. He knows nothing of the Immutable Reason of Things.'[12] And if Superstition and Enthusiasm meet, men are likely to be 'stirred up to Butcher one another for Religion'.[13] Arab imperialism was an obvious example of the effect of misguided religion as a driving political force in the eyes of historically minded observers, whose point of view Sir William Temple states. The Muslim power was 'built upon Foundations Wholly Enthusiastick' and was therefore 'unaccountable to common Reason, and in many points contrary even to Human Nature'.[14]

Dr Johnson noted and deplored the militant tendencies of religious enthusiasm when he commented that the change of religion in Scotland 'raised an epidemical enthusiasm compounded of sullen scrupulousness and warlike ferocity'.[15] Theophilus Evans couples the Scottish zealots with the Spaniards – surely a comparison that would have horrified both parties: 'the *Scotch-Covenant* and the *Spanish Inquisition* are Correlatives and Cousin-germans...the Zeal and Fury of a *Northern* Enthusiasm is altogether as keen and vindictive as that of a mere grave Don that basks in a warm sun!'[16] His book demonstrates as vividly as anything could the horror that went with the word when it was applied to English history. A few references will suffice. Enthusiasm inspired by Rome was the *deluding* Spirit (p. xi) that actuated the Regicides: Felton, the murderer of Buckingham, was a 'bloody Enthusiast' (p. 39), and so were those who 'brought the good and pious King, by their pretended Inspiration to the fatal Block' (p. 40); so too were the Fifth-Monarchy men (p. 26). 'The Rabble Multitudes, instigated by their *enthusiastical Teachers* committed all Manner of Rapine, and Sacrilege, and Prophanation' (p. 43); 'the principal objects of their fury...were monarchy and episcopacy', and hence this 'Spirit of Enthusiasm imports no less

Danger and Disturbance to the *State* than to the Church.'

Pittis, much nearer to the Civil War, had written in 1682 that unlawful claims to God's patronage had 'raised Rebellion, Murdered Princes, in design and act...At this rate', he continues, 'we shall cheat our neighbours by a secret impulse, and murder God's Anointed by a special command, and no man can be safe in his Life and Fortune, if a praying *Hector*, or a dreaming Enthusiast has a mind, and power, to take them away.'[17]

For Bishop Warburton, knavery always gets mixed up with Enthusiasm: 'when once the Fanatic becomes engaged in Politics'. Extreme emphasis on the doctrine of Sola Fide leads to acting by so-called divine impulse, without regard to morality, and so produces the dire progression from Antinomianism to Immorality to Rebellion.[18]

As the French Revolution intensified in violence, it seemed as if history was repeating itself. But *Enthusiasm* was now being used with no religious overtones, and the separation of the two spheres was plain. 'Junius' had already accepted it as a fact that 'there is a holy mistaken zeal in politics as well as religion'.[19] And Burke, suggesting that there is a danger of Christianity being abolished by doctrinaire reformers, shows how wide the cleavage had gone: 'They who will not believe, that the philosophical fanatics who guide in these matters, have long entertained such a design, are utterly ignorant of their character and proceedings. These enthusiasts do not scruple to avow their opinion that a state can subsist without any religion better than with one.'[20]

The *Anti-Jacobin* remarks that people had believed that 'a disbelief in Revealed Religion arose from a refinement and corruption of manners' which led to 'a state of total indifference'. But, it continued, 'the French Revolution has proved that Enthusiasm does not belong only to Religion; that there may exist as much zeal in blaspheming *God* as in praising him; as much spirit and perseverance in demolishing his Altars as in defending them'.[21]

The same general combination of ideas, though less shocked in tone, is to be seen when the Rev. W. Bagshaw Stevens writes in his journal in 1792 that Francis Mundy was 'an ingenious Enthusiast – full of fancies, rich in Animal Spirits; and happy in expression, a Democrat and a Free-Thinker'.[22]

Nowadays we could all be enthusiastic politicians; it would not imply that we had 'radical tendencies', like Akenside,[23] or that we imitated Blake, who in his enthusiasm for the French Revolution wandered about London 'wearing the bonnet rouge'.[24] We could equally well be enthusiastic Tories,[25] monarchists, imperialists, or 'reactionaries'. We need not subscribe to Hume's opposition between the political effects of superstition and enthusiasm – the former 'is an enemy to civil liberty', the latter 'a friend to it'. For 'enthusiasm, being the infirmity of bold and ambitious tempers, is naturally accompanied with a spirit of liberty'.[26] He might have agreed, historically, with the first proposition in Brown's *Estimate of the Manners and Principles of the Times* where there is a neat triplet:

Enthusiastic Religion leads to *Conquest*; rational Religion leads to rational *Defence*; but the modern Spirit of *Irreligion* leads to *rascally* and abandoned *Cowardice*.[27]

But as Burke and the *Anti-Jacobin* writers were to say, in the terror of the French cataclysm, the last part of this statement need not be true.

In 1709, John Trenchard had painted a startling picture of the holy Enthusiastic zealot who

longs to feast and rest upon human sacrifices, turn Cities and Nations into Shambles, and destroy with Fire and Sword such as dare thwart his Frenzy, and all the while like another Nero, plays upon his Harp and sings *Te Deum* at the conflagration.[28]

Substitute the purely political zealot and the Parisian mobs dancing round their Goddess of Reason, and we can see only another manifestation of what happens when any over-riding belief, divorced from humane control, looses 'the wild enthusiast to destroy'.[29]

No wonder Burke looked back to the excesses of heathenism.

Is this a triumph [he asks] to be consecrated at altars?...to be offered to the divine humanity with fervent prayer and enthusiastic ejaculation? – These Theban and Thracian orgies, acted in France, and applauded only in Old Jewry...kindle prophetic enthusiasm in the minds of very few people in this Kingdom.[30]

He is still using the tangled religio-political language when he contends that the fanatics of the past upheld the divine right of kings and those of his own day supported democracy:

The old fanatics of single arbitrary power dogmatised as if hereditary royalty was the only lawful government in the world, just as our new fanatics of popular arbitrary power maintain that a popular election is the sole lawful source of authority. The old prerogative enthusiasts, it is true, did speculate foolishly, and perhaps impiously too, as if monarchy had more of a divine sanction than any other mode of government[31]

– to Burke an absurd opinion.

Approval of political enthusiasm at this time came from those who sympathised with the French Revolution – probably not so few as Burke liked to think. Thomas Paine, fearing that the movement was in danger of falling short of its original high ideals, reminds the Convention of 'that enthusiasm and energy which have hitherto been the life and soul of the Revolution'.[32] He opposes it to 'cold indifference and self-interest', speaking for all those who (so wrongly, in Burke's opinion) regarded the British Constitution and Government in Church and State 'as illegitimate and usurped or at best as a vain mockery', so that they look abroad with 'eager and passionate enthusiasm'.[33]

When *enthusiasm* is used of political interest at a time when the close ties between church and state have been loosened or broken, the religious overtones of the word may still be strong at the early stages of the transfer: the political devotee is worshipping his ideological god – all too often, it is implied, a false one.

When Mr Wodhull wrote a poem called 'The Equality of Mankind', the critic of the *Monthly Review*, Dr Langhorne, remarked that the author 'seems strongly to have imbibed the spirit of that *Platonic* and *Roussovian Enthusiasm* which, worshipping at the feet of *Freedom*, looks up to the goddess and sees nothing beside'.[34]

Similarly, doubts of Rousseau, but without any religious reference, were felt by the *Critical Review*, when a book of *Travels through the Interior Parts of America* was submitted to its judgement. 'The author's declamation in praise of a savage, in comparison of a civilised life', says the reviewer, 'is too much in the manner of Rousseau to please a less enthusiastic enquirer.'[35] However, in the second half of the eighteenth century, enthusiasm for liberty, especially the kind guaranteed by the English Constitution, is often hailed as wholly proper. Voltaire, so Boswell writes to his friend Temple in 1764, talked of our Constitution with 'a noble enthusiasm'.[36] By 1798, the *British Critic* is writing of the 'glowing enthusiasm of liberty'.[37]

The *Critical Review* comments on 'the degree of enthusiasm in favour of the universal liberty of mankind' apparent in Major Peter Labillière's *Letters to the Majesty of the People*[38] – though there were also those who felt that to ascribe majesty to the people was treason. But sympathy could be found for France and America – 'warm, eager, enthusiastic Frenchmen! you deserve liberty for you know how to value it!' exclaims this same journal in 1790.[39] For Edward Jerningham, in 1789, America is 'a neglected child nursed by Enthusiasm'.[40] By now, the fact that *enthusiasm* of itself could not be depended on as a signal to put oneself into a condemnatory attitude is clear from two contrasted comments. A political pamphlet, in the opinion of the *Literary Magazine* of 1791, is a 'sally of a silly and uninformed enthusiasm',[41] which could imply (though it may not) that enthusiasm might be informed and not silly; and Vicesimus Knox at about the same time considers that the 'passion which every independent Englishman feels for liberty' is 'a rational, as well as an enthusiastic passion'.[42] Negative or positive, they witness to the possible upgrading of the word, but the combination of the adjectives in Knox's remark demonstrates that it has now some need of qualification, for the same passionate feeling can spring from sense or nonsense equally. Pastor Wendeborn, too, considers that 'a sensible Englishman speaks of himself. . . with modesty, but he talks of his country with pride and a kind of enthusiasm'.[43]

Nevertheless, doubts remain. The *Anti-Jacobin* approves of 'the enthusiastic attachment of the Peasantry'[44] of Switzerland and yet considers that when this sort of zeal is displayed by the Cantons of Lucerne and Zürich it 'amounts to infatuation' – yet it is 'an honest enthusiasm in favour of *ancient manners and customs* to repel the infection of the diabolical and destructive fanaticism of the Rights of Man'.[45] Here enthusiasm plays white to fanaticism's black.

Even honest enthusiasm is not enough. Soame Jenyns holds that ancient moral systems are built on 'the innate beauty of virtue, or enthusiastic patriotism', both of which he fears to be sandy foundations.[46] Reason too is needed – yet is that enough either? Shebbeare sees that by itself it is not, for it cannot be guaranteed to provide the necessary driving power. He says: 'There has never yet been a nation, who has greatly exalted itself by what is called superior reason; some kind of enthusiasm has been the source of all great actions.'[47] It is this fiery force that makes republicans invincible,[48] this eagerness that enabled the French nation to restore public credit – and yet not enough account was taken of 'the probable effects of giving enthusiasts uncontrolled power'.[49] The 'Bastille was attacked with an enthusiasm of heroism, such only as the highest animation of Liberty could inspire'[50] – and the *Literary Magazine*, quoting this passage, declared *The Rights of Man* to be an admirable work.[51]

Patriotic enthusiasm was commendable in ancient Rome – Gibbon goes so far as to call it 'generous' when shown by the military order after Aurelian's death,[52] and the *Looker-On*, soberly examining the ancient republics, perceives 'that their prosperity and even existence depended upon the operation of a national spirit and patriotic enthusiasm in the mass of the people'.[53] Still, the eighteenth-century patriot was capable of drawing the line at 'my country, right or wrong': 'I am not such an enthusiastic Englishman as to be blind to the modern defects of my country-men', admits a writer in the *Gentleman's Magazine* of 1786.[54]

Just how far can political reform go? Sylas Neville, who is inclined to give the word its older derogatory – or, at best, dubious – colouring, records Timothy Hollis's admission that members of the Calf's Head Club were supposed to be Republicans, but that he imagined 'they were of the enthusiastic sort'.[55] And Neville himself, trying to be kindly in his judgement after meeting one who 'took great pains in the cause of liberty', confides that he is 'desirous to conclude that what seemed madness in him was only a high degree of enthusiasm'.[56]

One suspects that a not very remote earlier generation would have seen the reformer's passion as a symptom of madness to come, and that one soon to follow would have seen it as altogether praiseworthy. If patriotism is inspired by love of liberty and made manifest in military expeditions, it is natural that one of the spheres in which the groups of words soonest comes to suggest a desirable feeling should be that of military ardour. Nevertheless, such love of glory may lead to irresponsible behaviour, regarded as in need of excuse by the more sober-minded. Certainly neither Lord Lyttelton nor Horace Walpole approve of the military 'enthusiasm' of Norborne Berkeley, whom they think Quixotic: it is an excuse offered by friends who want to put the best construction on an act in which rashness is more noticeable than thoughtful preparedness.

Lyttelton speaks of Berkeley's 'knight-errantry' in joining young fellows at his age – it would have been all very well twenty years ago, but not now (1758), when he is responsible for his family. He has been blamed by friends and outside critics, and it is indeed 'so very improper that one can only account for it by supposing that the Military Enthusiasm like the Religious is catching in Men of warm blood when they come within the sphere of its Activity'.[57]

Walpole tells Conway that Berkeley 'has converted a party of pleasure into a campaign' and is gone with the expedition, without a shirt but what 'he had on, and what is lent him'.[58] The expedition was to St Malo, supported by aristocratic volunteers, but unsuccessful.

But there is no doubt in the mind of the *Anti-Jacobin* writer who records the military appearance and enthusiasm of the Bernese troops in 1798,[59] or when that publication concludes that, linked with vigour, this passion could supply, at least for a while, 'the place of experience and military practice'.[60]

Probably that was true of Joan of Arc, 'who by her bravery and enthusiasm' had once 'so much contributed to revive the courage of the French'.[61] There is no hint that the writer was bearing St Joan's Voices in mind, but she also qualifies under the older acceptations of *enthusiast*.

A clear-sighted cynic – or a detached observer – might have doubts about some kinds of military enthusiasm, especially when combined with the religious variety. Bernard de Mandeville has no love of either, and states their effects bluntly. Let a military chaplain preach patriotically on Victory, so as to rouse a 'catching' enthusiasm, and 'a Fellow who lay with a Whore over Night, and was drunk the Day before, if he saw his Comrades moved, might be stupid enough to think, that he had a Share in God's Favour'.[62]

John Dennis regards the love of glory as an 'enthusiastick' motive early in the eighteenth century,[63] and Clara Reeve towards the end of the century considers that it may inspire people 'to actions honourable to themselves and advantageous to their country'.[64] These writers are primarily literary critics, and remind us that in their field *enthusiasm* and its relatives have normally stood for ideas regarded as praiseworthy.

It is interesting to find at the present day that the translator of Heer's *Intellectual History of Europe* into English uses the group of words of the Nazis and Hitler, where the author is arguing that these German Enthusiasts descended from those of 1770–1830,[65] and suggesting that Hitler's Nuremberg pageants were in line of succession to the festivals of the French Revolution.[66] Presumably this is what Diana Spearman has in mind when she says that 'the experience of the twentieth century has amply justified the eighteenth-century distrust of enthusiasm',[67] though it is to be noted that she gives no warning that the word was so often used as a technical term.

And yet, when we have allowed for all the aberrations and excesses, we must in fairness agree with Hume – whom no one could call less than hard-headed – that 'whatever disadvantageous sentiment we may entertain of Mankind, they are always found to be prodigal both of Blood and Treasure in the Maintenance of public Right'. And that, says Hume, 'may be denominated Enthusiasm'.[68]

(iv) FROM RELIGION TO AFFECTION

Henry Coventry's *Philemon to Hydaspes*[1] offers us a dialogue on False Religion, but it begins with a discussion of Pope's poetry and demonstrates how religious and poetic fervour could be thought of together. Hortensius says[2] that the 'Enchantment' cast by Pope's poetry on his reader's mind is like 'that *mysterious* change which is wrought upon the Poet's *own* in his inspired Moments, when under the *Propitious influence* of his invoked Muse and in the full *Ecstasy* of her *divine Communications*!' He speaks of the heat and glow of Fancy, and the discussion goes on to contrast the 'irregular Ferments of Imagination' with the 'soberer Exercises of Reasoning and Philosophy'.

This discussion leads to a character-sketch of Sebastius,[3] 'a Man of Great Parts and Genius' who has become a recluse, so that 'his natural *good Sense* by having been unhappily misapplied, does but add new Fuel to his Distemper, and establish him in a more confirm'd state of *Enthusiasm*'.[4]

And all because he has been crossed in Love! But surely there is no 'Alliance between the Passions of *Love* and *religious Enthusiasm*'?[5] Granted, that there is 'generally an *Enthusiasm* in Love; but sure 'tis of a very different kind from what is called such in Religion'.

The argument develops: it is 'only the same Passion... *differently* applied and exercised'. Indeed,

Enthusiasm has been more indebted for Converts to the Quarter of *disappointed Love*, than to any other whatsoever. *Affectionate* Tempers must *settle* somewhere, if they find not the expected *Returns* of their Passion upon *Earth*, nothing more common than for them to take Refuge in *Heaven*. And if the Expression might not be censured as too bold, I would add, to sollicite the *Deity* with as much warmth, and in a great degree of the same *Kind*, as they did before a Mistress.[6]

St Augustine is quoted as an example of this transference, but this is surely an ill-chosen instance, since the Saint was crossed in earthly love not by his mistress, but by his ambition (and his mother) rather than by his faith, though no doubt his conversion sublimated *eros* into *agape* or *caritas*.[7]

This discussion naturally leads on to some comment on the erotic and 'luscious' imagery of certain kinds of religious lyric. The awful examples for the eighteenth century were the Moravian songs (and to a less degree the Methodist hymns, though these were less obnoxious, since John Wesley took a similar view and indeed did some censoring of Charles's writings).

For Coventry's interlocutors, such writers, instead

of speaking the Language of a serious, rational, unaffected Piety, abound wholly with rapturous Flights of *unhallow'd Love,* and strains of *mystical Dissolutions.* They *pollute* the Soul with *luscious* Images, warm it with irregular Ferments, and fire it with false Passion; dissipating all due Composure, and Recollection of the Mind, and laying open the Heart to the *wild extravagances* of frantic Enthusiasm.[8]

Mysticism is a system

of the most *luscious* and *unintelligible* Jargon that even the *Wildness* of *Enthusiasm* itself could ever devise. The true spirit of acceptable Religion, which is in its own nature a *liberal* and *reasonable Service*, is here made wholly to *evaporate* in *unnatural Heats*, and *extatic* terrors.[9]

And yet this sort of warm temperament, Coventry considers, is part of friendship, of Genius, and as we have seen, essential to the poets:

Men of *superior Parts*, and *livelier Imagination*, and more *refined Genius*, seem of all others to be most in danger of it for *they*, 'tis well known, are generally observed to be of that sort of *temperament* which is the most *natural* Soil for *Enthusiasm* to spring up in.[10]

Nevertheless, the enthusiasm of friendship quite late in the eighteenth century is viewed with some reservation. Beside the *Critical Review*'s approving remark that a certain 'eloge' is written with 'the same eager zeal, the same warm enthusiasm of friendship which usually appear in the biographical sketches of the French memoirs',[11] we must set the comment of the *Gentleman's Magazine* of three years earlier on the partisanship of Mr Hayley, who, it thinks, has 'written in the ardour of enthusiastic friendship, which occasionally hurries him to give ample scope to express the feelings of a mind incapable of holding friendship with Dr. Johnson'.[12] The hint of unbalance is duly given.

The intriguing title of *The Amicable Quixote, or the Enthusiasm of Friendship* (1788) will lead us to expect some extravagance in the story, and we are not disappointed. George Bruce, the hero, is thus described:

One favourite propensity, the effect of a noble disposition, had often led him into ridiculous situations, by which he was exposed to the laughter of his acquaintance; this was the *enthusiasm of friendship* which glowed in his heart with such uncommon rapture and such invariable philanthropy, that his whole study was to admire every one he knew of both sexes, and to bind himself to them by the strongest ties of inviolable attachment. Bruce had engraved upon his mind all those sublime and glittering precepts of poets and philosophers, which generally aggrandize sentimental effusion, and consecrate disinterested regard, without ensuring or cementing any solid friendship.[13]

Indeed, he found on the slightest acquaintance some virtue or some recommendation, carrying his reverence for their qualities 'to a ludicrous height', though on everything else 'he conversed rationally, and sometimes elegantly'. But 'the enthusiasm of friendship', once roused, 'overwhelmed his discretion, and clouded his perspicacity'.[14]

The book is fundamentally serious, but there is an element of comic satire in the fact that he is said to have 153 friends – and nineteen intimates in Russia whom he has never seen! No wonder this is called an 'amicable phrenzy'.[15] The sensible Miss Bryant is entertained by all this, but sees in it affected raptures and empty sentiments – reasonably enough, since Bruce can see no wrong in his friends even when they are bores, hypochondriacs or slanderers. He cannot even rebuke the brutal Sir Harry Hyndley for drunkenness: 'He was rational or absurd as his companions excited his good sense or enthusiasm.'[16]

Experience leads him to renounce his 'little madness' in the end. His

romantic enthusiasm...was, after his marriage, entirely rectified: he had seen enough to convince him, how despicably fallacious is that credulity which implicitly relies upon the ardour and the duration of any friendship.[17]

(v) VARIOUS SECULAR INTERESTS:
PHILOLOGY, SCIENCE, ART

When *enthusiasm* broke free from religious contexts and came to stand for the sort of feeling one could have in any secular sphere and for any secular subject, people who did not share the enthusiast's attitude might use the words with a disapproval that can be deduced from the tone of the whole context, or signalled by the accompanying adjective or that tell-tale piece of syntactic machinery, the contrast-clause introduced with *but* or one of its equivalents.

There may well be some hesitation in the *Critical Review*'s reference to Gilbert Wakefield's observations on Pope: they show 'an enthusiasm proverbially attached to commentators'.[1] The *Monthly Review*'s remark that 'Mr. Cornish admires with a degree of enthusiastic fondness, the genius and learning of Erasmus'[2] sounds simply subdued – until we find that the reviewer thinks Erasmus wrote 'mere rant'. And there is no doubt about the *Gentleman's Magazine* when it writes of 'the undiscerning enthusiasm of Chatterton's admirers',[3] a judgement with which we agree. A different kind of philological ineptitude is noticed by the *Monthly Review* in its account of Bishop Newton's *Dissertation on the Confusion of Languages* (1782), in which 'he combats...the hypothesis of those enthusiastic admirers of the "primitive and sacred tongue", as they call Hebrew, who would deduce every other tongue from it'.[4]

Laelius and Hortensia mentions another sort of philological crank (one who may 'be deemed an enthusiast') –

the person who argues that 'because there are seven original tones in music, therefore seven is the properest number for vocal sounds in language'.[5] The *Critical Review* had justification for such adjectives as *gaping*[6] and *wrong-headed*[7] as companions for *enthusiasm*.

Lack of discernment is implied in Hogarth's comment that there has been no lack 'of artful people, who have good profit of those whose unbounded admiration' for Antiquity 'hath run them into enthusiasm': art dealers ought to have had a fair amount of faking on their conscience.[8] This was financial fraud taking advantage of innocent but undiscriminating interest. And of course not all the specialists with a new field of research were able to convince their readers that their excitement was justified. The *Critical Review* thought that Miss Brooke had carried too far her enthusiasm for ancient Irish poetry: they were far from condemning her, but hoped she would excuse their smiling at it.[9] Did the magazine share the feelings of a writer on the Chinese and their agriculture? He 'dwells upon both with such raptures as plainly shows his enthusiasm for that favourite art'.[10] It seems a more sensible one than that felt for the usual sort of Chinoiserie.

We would agree with this review's warning about new medical ideas: 'it is...necessary to guard against the warmth, the enthusiasm, of an inventor or improver'[11] – and we might add, of the general public. Thalidomide babies are the sad witness to the need for caution as well as keenness. Shebbeare puts belief in one universal remedy on a level with belief in the power of saints, asking, 'is it not equally the effect of enthusiasm or superstition?'[12] The *Review* is perhaps unfair to the devisers of scientific nomenclature, which makes for precision and saves time, but it has a point when it declares that 'the botanical descriptions of the cincona have not increased its febrifuge virtues, and an enthusiast only would neglect objects of importance, to waste his life like Plumier, in verbal disquisitions'.[13]

Plumier stands for the new science, according to which phenomena are neatly classified and labelled. A representative of the older approach was that 'most enthusiastic chemist' whom Sylas Neville encountered in 1772, obviously thinking him a little mad, for 'he actually acknowledges having tried to discover the Philosopher's stone'.[14]

It was observed that Science as well as Love or Religion could lead its enthusiasts into unsociable behaviour: it 'inspires people with so fond a passion for particular studies that by degrees they acquire a dislike and frequently a contempt for all objects which do not coincide with their own pursuits'.[15]

It is to be expected in the classically minded eighteenth century that enthusiasm for Greece and Rome and such relics of their world as had survived would be regarded as praiseworthy. Alison is concerned with people of good taste who remember 'descriptions given by ancient authors' that revive all those enthusiastic ideas of ancient genius and glory, which the study of so many years of youth so naturally leads them to form.[16]

Nor does Melmoth disapprove of the enthusiastic admirers of Homer.[17] But in 1793 Dr Gregory contributed a paper to the Philosophical Society of Manchester on the uses of classical learning, in which he admitted that an unreasonable and enthusiastic regard has sometimes been paid to the writings of the ancients.[18] It sounds defensive and self-depreciatory. On the other hand, there is no doubt about the approval of the *Gentleman's Magazine* for Mr Samuel Lysons's undertaking to rescue the Roman remains at Woodchester – 'these noble relicks' – from oblivion: it is 'a laudable enthusiasm'.[19]

Art enthusiasts were early on the scene, and the attitude of observers runs through the whole gamut from reprimand to recommendation. The *Grub Street Journal*, quoted in the *Gentleman's Magazine* for 1733,[20] thought it inspiration or enthusiasm if one imparted a 'judgment of Art without Education and Study', but Sir Joshua Reynolds put it on record that in his opinion a painter should 'work himself to as high an Enthusiasm as he please in order to form his mental picture as lively and as noble as possible'.[21]

There were enthusiastic admirers and collectors of Claude and Poussin in the 1790s[22] and for the new art of landscape painting.[23] But Sir Uvedale Price, who notes them, cannot be trusted to use the word in the complimentary sense. Hogarth, he says, 'had a most enthusiastic admiration of what he called the line of beauty, and enthusiasm always leads to the verge of ridicule and seldom keeps totally within it'.[24] Which suggests that he thought Hogarth a crank so far as his favourite theory was concerned.

There are similar reservations over architecture and sculpture. Alison recognises that writers on architecture speak with enthusiasm of the beauty of proportion, but seems to suggest that the layman might not;[25] whereas the author of *Laelius and Hortensia* considers that when we contemplate both architecture and poetry, 'the mind is wholly passive, and the imagination feels a temporary and enthusiastic pleasure'[26] – surely an agreeable criticism. Price argues, however, that this passion, if not properly controlled, can work in detrimental ways as well as in encouraging ones. 'The enthusiasm of Michael Angelo, which produced the grandest and most striking attitudes, at other times led him to twist the human figure into such singular and capricious forms, as borders on caricatura.'[27]

Enthusiasm under control can astonish the critics. In 1758, the *Critical Review* read William Hanbury's *Essay on Tree Planting*, and commented:

> Our author is an enthusiast on this subject; but his enthusiasm is un-attended with folly or extravagance. It is the ebullition of a mind over-flowing with gratitude to God, and benevolence towards his fellow creatures: it is the enthusiasm of a warm, sensible, honest English heart.[28]

The attitude is religious, the subject secular, and the use of *sensible* and *honest* as well as *warm* is noteworthy.

Much later than this unusual bit of modernism it is normally the enthusiast's lack of sense that is assumed or emphasised. Lyttelton makes Messala say to Cato: 'The Enthusiasm you are possessed with is a noble one, but it disturbs your judgment.'[29] Lyttelton reflects that if 'the great Mr. Hampden had conversed with our modern race of wits, he would have been told that it was a ridiculous enthusiasm to trouble himself about a trifling sum of money'.[30] The common derogatory associations of the word are clear, even if Lyttelton himself is thinking of Hampden's stand against Ship Money with the en-thusiasm of a modern patriot.

Women 'are prompt to receive and seize novelty, and become its enthusiasts':[31] running after novelty by the fair but less instructed sex is not likely to help the word to the status of serious compliment.

Nor did the eighteenth-century writer have any idea of the modern compliment that 'enthusiastic fox-hunter' would probably be now meant to convey. You cannot 'relish a fox-chase' without enthusiasm – by which is meant that no rational man would find anything to say for it nor anything to persuade him to indulge in it.[32]

(vi) RESPONSE TO SCENERY

Alison acknowledges 'that deep and enthusiastic delight which the perception of Beauty or Sublimity bestows',[1] and the loveliness and impressiveness of Nature were regarded by many people of the eighteenth century as inspirers of enthusiasm. Alison praises Thomson for 'the singular felicity' of the descriptions in *The Seasons* and the 'fine Enthusiasm which the poem displays and which it is so fitted to excite with the works of Nature',[2] and the poet himself wrote in the early preface to *Winter* in 1726:

I know no subject more elevating, more amusing [i.e. offering more pleasurable interest], more ready to wake the poetical enthusiasm, the philosophical reflection, and the moral sentiment, than the works of Nature. Where can we meet with such variety, such beauty, such magnificence? All that enlarges and transports the soul!

So Gray's friend Nicholls finds that he has a 'partiality' to Bonstetten, his Swiss admirer, because he was born among mountains and talked of them with enthusiasm.[3]

Boswell, who is much given to the approving use of the word, writes to John Johnston: 'I feel an enthusiasm beyond expression. Good heavens! Am I so elevated? Where is gloom?'[4] All this rapture is due to the fact that he is in a 'beautiful wild valley surrounded by immense mountains'. He feels as free and vigorous as a lion in the desert. And yet, is there not a slight hesitation in him when he admits to 'an almost enthusiastic notion of the felicity of London'?[5]

Gilpin, that traveller in quest of romantic scenery, found Matlock 'a romantic and most delightful scene'. There one can be 'carried at once into the fields of fiction and romance. Enthusiastic ideas take possession of us; and we suppose ourselves among the inhabitants of fabled times.'[6] Scenic grandeur produces 'an enthusiastic sensation of pleasure' which makes us 'feel' rather than 'survey the scene'.[7]

The collocation of enthusiasm, fiction and romance emphasises the out-of-this-world aura of the terms, and we may be reminded of Scott of Amwell's contrast between the conditions in which

> the enthusiast Fancy's reign
> Indulg'd the wild romantic thought

and those of soberer life, where

> Observation's calmer view
> Remarked the real state of things.

Scott pictures Collins

> On Havant's banks, in groves that breathe
> Enthusiasm sublime...[8]

but how far is this poet, doomed to madness, a good recommendation? According to Young

> Seas, Rivers, Mountains, Forests, Deserts, Rocks,
> The Promontory's Height, the Depth profound[9]

infuse 'enthusiastic heights of solemn Thought'; but if you retreat among them, and fancy yourself a hermit or a philosopher, it is to be feared that 'your vulgar neighbours (will) look upon you as an enthusiast at least, if not a madman'[10] – which suggests that the words have a dignified and a popular sense.

In the second half of the eighteenth century, people were growing enthusiastic about much more exotic scenery and conditions. The Hon. Edward Montagu, according to Samuel Sharp,[11] was 'in the most enthusiastic raptures with Arabia and the Arabs'. The use of the superlative and the coupling with *rapture* shows how the force of the word can weaken. Montagu's subsequent career must have reinforced all the old overtones of extravagance and madness in the minds of sober Englishmen.

The *Critical Review* in 1790[12] claimed that 'it is impossible to survey Sicily without an admiration rising to enthusiasm',[12] which suggests that for careful writers the word is superlative enough of itself. And in 1798 this review was taking to task a descriptive writer for not being as enthusiastic as his subject deserved. When he gave his account of Mount Edgcumbe after a 'not incorrect account of Plymouth' he seemed not to have felt sufficient enthusiasm for the delightful scenery of the park.[13]

The offending author was William George Maton, who the previous year had published *Observations relative*

*chiefly to the Natural History, Picturesque Scenery and Anti-
quities of the Western Counties of England made in the years
1794 and 1796.* He says that Mount Edgcumbe 'in the
situation, disposition of the grounds and natural embellishments has recommendations superior to those of
most spots in our island. From the Sound...its effect is
singularly striking in point both of grandeur and decora-
tion, and the house appears to great advantage', commanding 'a view almost unparalleled for variety and
magnificence of objects'. He calls it a 'princely seat'. No
doubt real enthusiasm would have omitted the reservations implied in 'superior to...*most* spots', '*almost* unparalleled'; and he might have called it *royal* instead of
princely. But would the result have been a truer
account?[14]

No such fault could be found with Mrs Radcliffe's
characters, who respond with enthusiasm to natural
scenery. The green pastures, woods, wild mountain walks,
the river, the distant plains of Saxony are remembered by
St Aubert 'with enthusiasm and regret'. He and his wife
would 'saunter among cliffs that seemed scarcely accessible
but to the steps of the enthusiast' (evidently thought of as
a pleasing eccentric). His daughter Emily responds to 'the
gloom of the woods, the trembling of their leaves, at
intervals in the breeze', to the flittering bat and the cottage
lights which lead her mind to 'enthusiasm and poetry'.
She gazes with enthusiasm on the vastness of the sea and
indulges in 'enthusiastic admiration' for the 'towering
precipices of the Pyrenees'.[15] Over seventy years later,
Trollope uses *enthusiasm* in an anti-romantic and satirical
way of Lizzie Eustace's shallow but gushing response to

the Clyde shore: 'She had stood on it before, and had stretched her arms with enthusiasm towards the just visible mountains of Arran.'[16] And her appreciation of the river is no deeper than her appreciation of Shelley. The two heroines contrast at every point.

And in our own century Thomas Hardy recognises the enthusiasm that scenery can inspire, by coining a word for it, though only to admit that the colour and warmth he once experienced are gone:

> I looked and thought, 'All is too gray and cold
> To wake my place – enthusiasms of old'.[17]

8

TRANSITION AND
UNCERTAINTY

Both noun and adjective can suggest mixed emotions and reactions, of approval mixed with surprise, horror, or doubts as to the validity of the feeling. In Glover's *Athenaid* (1787), the patriotism of the Athenian women before the battle of Salamis makes them emulate their men, and so

> enthusiastic ardour seems to change their sex.[1]

To his contemporaries, this might be impossible or shocking – certainly astonishing. But Glover makes the tone of the word clear on a later occasion. Lycides proposes a pact with the Persians, and the Greek women, in their horror at such an unnatural alliance, propose the killing of his wife and family –

> His counsel rous'd enthusiastic rage

– and Glover describes it as an 'enormous thought', which implies Dr Johnson's third definition of the adjective *enormous*: 'wicked beyond the common measure'.[2]

Lighter indeed, but still flawed, is the sense of the noun when Thomas Day writes (1773) to Edgeworth about the 'fantastic emotions' of his heart, a young man's 'schemes of happiness' which are conceived with enthusiasm, pursued with ardour and then 'dissipated for ever, as he advances' in life.[3] There is usually a transience about the emotion indicated by *enthusiasm* once it has ceased to be a technical religious word. So, in a modern example, we are told that early Italian re-formers could raise enthusiasms by their preaching and example, but that 'these subsided all too easily after they had died'.[4]

It is easy to find the group used sarcastically, super-ficially in the modern approving sense, but applied to people, institutions or proceedings of which the user strongly disapproves. The *Anti-Jacobin* imagines a para-graph in some future *Morning Chronicle* recording that the celebration of this great Epoch of the French Revolu-tion has excited a 'general enthusiasm' – in the *Anti-Jacobin*'s opinion, of course, it ought not to have, and had not, in England.[5]

These writers printed a story about a lecturer who went about 'kindling a holy enthusiasm of Freedom', but by his own doctrine and practice gravely disrupted what had been a happy, law-abiding home.[6] Equally disapproving is the description that appeared of a priest 'lavishing the most enthusiastic encomiums on the lawless and blood-stained tribunals of France'.[7]

And there is no doubt as to the tone of Burke's con-cluding reservation, when he remarks that

the circumstance of the Io Paean of triumph, the animating cry which called 'for *all Bishops* to be hanged on the lamp-posts', might well have brought forth a burst of enthusiasm on the foreseen consequences of this happy day. I allow to so much enthusiasm some little deviation from prudence.[8]

Ferguson's comment on the effect of Greek legends on modern political thought must be interpreted in the light of the goodness or badness of the policies involved. The legends 'served to inflame that ardent enthusiasm with which so many different republics afterwards proceeded in the pursuit of every national object'.[9] The *Critical Review* in 1792 seems to have no doubt as to the evil of one line of political theory: it writes approvingly of the author of *Thoughts on the Origin and Excellence of Regal Government* (1790):

The design of this author is to invalidate the principles of those political enthusiasts who have lately contended with much vehemence for the unalienable rights of man, and who labour to expel subordination from civil society.[10]

It is a palpable hit at Tom Paine and Mary Wollstonecraft.

Doubts on the enthusiasm appear even where the writer admires the exponent of it. Hayley, in his *Life of Milton*, comments that

Enthusiasm was 'the characteristic' of his mind: in politics it made him sometimes too generously credulous, and sometimes too rigorously decisive.[11]

And Fielding, who surely loved his creature Parson Adams, admits that 'if this good man had an enthusiasm, or what the vulgar call a blind side, it was this: he thought a schoolmaster the greatest character in the world, and himself the greatest of all schoolmasters'.[12]

There will obviously be doubtful cases where the words may carry the old technical meaning with, perhaps, the modern general one superimposed, and where it is far from easy to see whether the author is offering an outright compliment, a guarded one, or none at all.

For example, the *Annual Register* for 1766 quotes a military commander's description of an Austrian army composed mainly of labourers: 'though their religion does not rise to any degree of enthusiasm, probably for want of being excited by an able leader: yet it keeps them sober and free from vice'.[13] Is the general deploring the lack of religious enthusiasm or being thankful for it?

In 1781, the *Critical Review* noticed *A serious and affectionate Address to all orders of Men, adapted to this awful Crisis*.[14] The author was Thomas Mills, a Bristol bookseller, who was 'an enthusiastic admirer of the late William Law's works' – indeed, he thought them 'divine'. The tone of the context suggests that the *Review* considered Mills both fanatical in his ideas and keen on his philosophical and religious master. Five years later the *Review* is quoting a statement not whole-heartedly complimentary to our ancestors, from *Strictures on Female Education*:

In the ages immediately succeeding those of chivalry, it was fashionable to speak of women as of prodigies in science [i.e. knowledge]...Interest, policy, or fashion, has continued what enthusiasm then began.[15]

Women, in fact, are being given an exaggerated and unwarranted importance: the enthusiast cannot be trusted to be accurate in his evaluation. Similarly, Boswell palliates Dr Johnson's roughness to Mr McQueen, a fervent supporter of 'Ossian'; Johnson, says Boswell, was not making 'severe imputations against him' but putting his position down to 'inaccuracy and enthusiasm'.[16] Boswell admits that the value which he himself sets on his pedigree will be regarded 'in a commercial age' as the glow of 'genealogical enthusiasm'.

The Rev. William Bagshaw Stevens remarks that 'Enthusiasm of every sort is at once enviable and contemptible – enviable in its effects and contemptible in its cause. It is weakness generating Energy.'[17] This neat aphorism would sum up the attitude of many users of the word, old and new. Just how much energy does it generate, however? Sir Joshua Reynolds had his doubts. He told his students in 1769 that mere enthusiasm would carry them 'but a little way';[18] and in the following year that 'enthusiastic admiration seldom promotes knowledge'.[19] Hard work first, flights of imagination later, is his doctrine. When the student has

well established his judgement, and stored his memory, he may now without fear try the power of his imagination. The mind that has been thus disciplined, may be indulged in the warmth of enthusiasm and venture to play on the borders of the wildest extravagance.[20]

But there is no advice to go across the border. Sir Joshua is aware that not everyone shares his austere view:

To speak of genius and taste, as in any way connected with reason or common sense, would be, in the opinion of some towering talkers, to speak like a man who possessed neither, who had never felt enthusiasm.[21]

– his irony is obvious.

A modern historian, Professor Sidney Painter, who uses the group frequently, illustrates the doubtful nature of its tone.[22] Benedict Biscop was 'more than a religious enthusiast' (p. 87), for he was a scholar and teacher. Isidore of Seville was 'enthusiastic' as a scholar but rather confused (p. 126). Pope Urban was unlucky in his emissaries who preached the Crusade: they responded to his enthusiasm but not to his good sense (p. 201). The 'enthusiasm and energy' of the Italian cities brought party strife as well as progress (p. 233). Enthusiasts have not convinced us of the overall plan of the symbolism of the Gothic cathedral (p. 431). Richard Coeur de Lion was a poet whose enthusiasm outran his skill (p. 451). Professor Painter mentions enthusiasts whose heresies brought them to death (p. 363), others whose devotion to poverty embarrassed the secular clergy (p. 304), and princesses whose enthusiasm was for illicit love (p. 453).

All these cases imply zeal not according to knowledge, sense or prudence, though we may commend the courage of the heretics and Observants. It is noteworthy that Painter describes certain chronicles as 'overenthusiastic' (p. 471) – a compound that would have been impossible in the earliest period of the use of the adjective.[23] Indeed, O.E.D. appears to have no example of it.

Enthusiasm may be imprudent and excessive, and yet have something to recommend it, or at least to render it innocuous. It seems that Jane Austen, disapproving as she is of literary enthusiasm, could find some good in such sentimentality, though not much. In 1801 she comments that a lady of her acquaintance 'is very unreserved & very fond of talking of her deceased brother and sister, whose memory she cherishes with an enthusiasm which tho perhaps a little affected, is not unpleasing'.[24]

Nowadays, is not enthusiasm a joyous emotion?

Burke's tone is regretful rather than disapproving when he notes that 'Criticism is almost baffled in discovering the defects of what has not existed; and eager enthusiasm and cheating hope have all the wide field of imagination, in which they may expatiate with little or no opposition'.[25]

Against the modern rationalistic outlook, both in religion and economics, he puts in a good word for the monasteries, whose revenues were directed to the public benefit, whose inhabitants were 'dedicated to public purposes' and 'denied to self-interest'. The institutions were the products of enthusiasm: 'they are the instruments of wisdom'.[26] It is clear from his comment a little later that he is using *enthusiasm* in the technical and disapproving sense, so that the last two statements form a contrast. He goes on to refer to 'the ancient founders of monkish superstition',[27] whom he contrasts with the equally superstitious modern pseudo-philosophers. If man must choose between 'what errors and excesses of enthusiasm he would condemn or fear, perhaps he would think the superstition which builds to be more tolerable than that which demolishes...'.[28]

But superstition is superstition wherever and however it is displayed.

The lack of sound judgement in the enthusiast struck Jane Austen: from her earliest satirical sketches onwards she views enthusiasm on any subject 'with a certain amount of ironical detachment', as Dr F. W. Bradbrook remarks.[29] Her early Catherine's 'judgement...was not always infallible', but that did not prevent her from defending it with 'a Spirit & Enthusiasm which marked her own reliance on it'.[30] Mr Parker was 'a complete Enthusiast' on the subject of Sanditon[31] – and Jane Austen does not really see the development of that village into a seaside resort as necessarily a move for the better. More than anything else, she distrusts literary enthusiasm born of sentimentality. The Father, in her Plan of a Novel, is to be an Enthusiast in Literature and to expire 'in a fine burst of literary Enthusiasm'.[32] And is there not a partial echo of the same distrust in Harry Levin's *Christopher Marlowe* when he notices that the dramatist's nineteenth-century

reputation 'came from professional enthusiasts like Lamb
and Swinburne'?[33] He is supported by Moody E. Prior's
comment that the nineteenth-century enthusiasts in their
excitement glossed over a good deal of ineptitude in
Elizabethan drama.[34]

A similar dichotomy between feeling and solidity is
suggested when another modern scholar tells us that
'subjective scholarship' gets 'enthusiastic support' from
a public which pays only lip-service to research.[35] Indeed
we often do contrast enthusiastic appreciation with the
lack of scholarly evidence which alone would justify our
conclusions. Characteristically, a good statement of the
difference of attitude involved comes from Joseph
Priestley, who writes to Faujas de St Fond that the 'de-
composition of water is of so much importance in Natural
Philosophy...that, so far from admitting the fact upon
slight evidence, and as it were from enthusiasm, it were
rather to be wished that all objections that may be made...
were completely rejected'.[36]

The same danger exists still, and so we find a modern
scholar deploring the imaginative biographers whose
enthusiastic admiration for their subjects leads them to
make up for historical evidence by 'venturesome hypo-
theses and romantic embellishments'.[37] Less factually, but
in the same spirit, modern critics have 'required a poet to
say no more than he means', because 'shapeless enthusiasm
and uncontrollable exuberance' are suspect.[38] Bishop
Butler two centuries ago had argued that enthusiasm
'greatly weakens the evidence of testimony, even for facts,
in matters relating to religion'.[39]

It would seem that this drawback is not restricted to

religion. A neat example of the bad and good effects of enthusiasm is offered by a modern archaeologist, who points out how some enthusiasts can hurt this discipline. There are the lunatic ones who locate sites by 'drawing straight lines on maps' and 'extract fantastic prophecies from measurements of the pyramids'.[40] But he admits that there are 'investigators blind or enthusiastic or both' who do not bother about the expenses their researches will incur, and who are therefore admirable from the point of view of study.[41]

The idea of misguided zeal and harmful excess is frequent in present-day scholarly writing. To W. J. Harvey,[42] the late Victorians who put George Eliot on a level with Shakespeare were wrong in their enthusiasm and have done no good to her reputation. George Eliot herself would have agreed, since for her 'enthusiasm is a fine thing under guidance', as Mr Brooke says of Ladislaw,[43] which suggests that otherwise it is not.

So M. C. Battestin, editing *Joseph Andrews* and *Shamela*, describes as victims of 'gross enthusiasm' people like W. Slocock who saw pure morality in *Pamela* instead of stigmatising it as 'silly and immoral'.[44]

Those who would identify Milton with Satan or Samson are to Robert Adams 'fervent romantic enthusiasts';[45] W. A. Craik thinks it is only enthusiasts who never tire of such Dickensian characters as Mr Skimpole, Mr Dick, and Mrs Nickleby.[46]

The Renaissance had an uncritical enthusiasm for antiquity, says Daniel Waley,[47] and Tillyard describes G. G. Coulton as a 'most enthusiastic medievalist', learned, but with more enthusiasm than judgement.[48]

The 'more enthusiastic than...' formula with its variants pinpoints what is lacking, and what no amount of enthusiasm can compensate for. So Sir Herbert Read comments rather wryly that he once in his youth published an essay 'with more enthusiasm than discretion'.[49] Earlier, one of Mrs Sherwood's heroes writes a letter to 'a young lady of more enthusiasm than experience'.[50] And Evelyn Underhill writes of those with 'more enthusiasm than commonsense'.[51]

Nor has enthusiasm by itself any power to alter facts: a church newspaper discussing 'foolish chatter' about imminent ecumenical progress, speaks of 'those who close their eyes, in enthusiastic optimism, to the problems that schemes of union must raise'.[52]

Coleridge, in his youth, indulged uncritically in philosophical enthusiasms, says Father Appleyard.[53] The plural of the abstraction, reducing its wide sweep to concrete instances, the coupling with *uncritically*, and the choice of *indulge* constitute a triple derogation of a zeal and interest that Coleridge surely thought good.

It is, in fact, somewhat surprising, in view of popular colloquial usage, to find so many moderns using the group in completely derogatory senses. For is not W. E. Houghton exaggerating cynically when he claims that 'today...enthusiasm is entirely out of fashion – indeed, suspect'? He backs up this conclusion by drawing a contrast between the English undergraduates who cheered Charles Kingsley's pep talks (I use this expression because it sums up the tone of the passage) with the American ones who cheered C. B. Tinker in 1923 when he advised them to 'Greet the unseen with a leer'.[54] Some half-century later, undergraduates are more likely to be accused of over-enthusiastic support of causes.

In a turning of the tables that would have astonished the philosophic sceptics, G. R. Cragg tells us that the Deists claimed Locke as the source of their principles 'with vociferous and embarrassing enthusiasm',[55] and in the literary field equally uncomfortable adjectives are used by Hart Crane when he criticises Walt Whitman for his 'clumsy and indiscriminate enthusiasm'.[56]

The implication of empty-headedness, however, reached its climax long ago in some lines about a raft from France in the *Anti-Jacobin*'s take-off, 'The Loves of the Triangles', and the appended note.[57] 'Imps of Murder' are besought to

> Shield from contusive rocks her tender limbs
> And guide the sweet *Enthusiast* as she swims!

Obviously a raft has no soul to be inspired well or ill – but the footnote is a hit at humans. It is quoted from *Chambers's Dictionary* and defines 'sweet Enthusiast' as

A term usually applied in Allegoric or Technical Poetry to any person or object to which no other qualifications can be assigned.

9

PROTESTS AT
EXTENDED USE

Despite the clear acceptance of *Enthusiasm* as a word properly applied to a quality (often desirable) in the secular world, there are belated protests at such straying from the religious sphere.

In 1802, George Nott attempts a differentiation, recognises two levels of usage, and finds the linguistic situation regrettable:

What we admire in the soldier, or the scholar...as Enthusiasm, is something quite distinct from [the religious variety of which he is treating]. The enthusiastic scholar does not pretend that he obtained his knowledge by illumination; nor the enthusiastic soldier that he performed any great achievement by divine inspiration. Did they make these assertions, they would be treated as objects of ridicule rather than of honour. This enthusiasm consequently means no more than a laudable warmth of zeal in their several pursuits; in this case the use of the word is improper and may be dangerous. At all events, if it be tolerated in this sense in familiar conversation, it ought never to be so employed in writing.[1]

Unfortunately for the purist, it had been so employed for several decades, even if we disregard the vexed question of whether poets thought themselves really inspired by a divine afflatus.

Isaac Taylor in 1829 was still trying to stem the tide. If one writes a book on the *Natural History of Enthusiasm*, one must define the key word, in the third decade of the nineteenth century, at least. Taylor calls it 'fictitious piety' (which might not strike us as enthusiastic for it could be dull, quiet and self-absorbed) and states that he 'has endeavoured so to fix the sense of the term... as to wrest it from those who misuse it to their infinite damage'.[2] We might suppose that the misapplication of a word would do damage to the language rather than to the speaker, but Taylor goes on to explain:

> To apply an epithet which carries with it an idea of folly, of weakness and of extravagance, to a vigorous mind, efficiently as well as ardently engaged in the pursuit of any substantial and worthy object, is not merely to misuse a word, but to introduce confusion among our notions, and to put contempt upon what is deserving of respect.
>
> Where there is no error of imagination – no misjudging of realities – no calculations which reason condemns, there is no enthusiasm, even though the soul may be on fire with the velocity of its movement in pursuit of its chosen object. If once we abandon this distinction, language will want a term for a well-known and very common vice of the mind; and, from a wasteful perversion of phrases, we must be reduced to speak of qualities most noble and most base by the very same designation. If the objects which excite the ardour of the mind are substantial, and if the mode of the pursuit be truly conducive to their attainment – if, in a word, all be real and genuine, then it is not one degree more, or even many degrees more, of intensity of feeling that can alter the character of the emotion.

Enthusiasm is not a term of *measurement*, but of *quality*.[3]

He goes on to observe that 'enthusiasm is not now justly chargeable upon any body of Christians' – a statement that may still be made, but in blame, not commendation or relief. Nevertheless, the reference ought still to be fixed, in this field, because it 'is the word vaguely and con-tumeliously applied by many to every degree of fervour in religion which seems to condemn their own indif-ference'. This implies that for a considerable number of people, any degree of religious fervour is undesirable, so that enthusiasm instead of being essentially wrong, is 'a mere fault of excess', 'an error of degree'. But how do we distinguish 'between the *maximum* and *minimum* of emotion which sobriety approves'? It is a 'hopeless and fruitless' task, 'because we should need a scale adapted to every man's constitution'.[4]

Taylor's concern for precision is laudable, and his assessment of the dangers of its lack valid and fair. And yet the danger of misunderstanding exists only when a word is working clear of its old connotations – in common speech we have no difficulty, for our ears are alert to older meanings only when the context gives us a warning hint. Taylor, like Nott, is struggling against the tide. And what he deplored and feared has happened: to us, enthusiasm *is* a matter of degree; nor do we insist that the word must be used only of zeal directed to obviously serious and grave ends.

Do we really find it difficult to supply the loss of *enthusiasm* in the older, disapproving, religious sense? We can explain circuitously – after all, Dr Johnson's definition is clear, if we want a straight statement. If we want a slanted one, several words spring to mind – *Fanatic, Impostor, Zealot, Devotee, Crank*. True, they are inexact, but so was the original word all too frequently. If anyone, religiously, politically or poetically, does believe himself to be divinely inspired – and it is a big *if* – the phenomenon would be singular enough to warrant the use of an explicitly descriptive sentence. The development of the word's application surely demonstrates that older senses die with the death of what they refer to, but new ones may well come into being and live on to describe different but similar types of experience.

10

MAINLY MODERN

We have seen that the seventeenth century was mainly a period of restriction: the eighteenth was a period of transference. What is the later status of the group? What particularly is its status now in the last third of the twentieth century? Are the words eulogistic in everyday conversation, but vibrant with some of the older overtones in serious writing?

There is clearly a feeling among serious writers that *enthusiastic* is not necessarily a complimentary adjective. Feelings so described are no substitute for common sense, worldly wisdom, facts (and the ability to deal with them) whether in life or literature. If a writer does not give his readers proper explanations, no enthusiasm 'can replace their loss or make them unnecessary'.[1]

William Morris told his readers that the enthusiast of the Renaissance looks towards his 'idealised ancient society as the type and example of all really intelligent human life'.[2] Was there not a hint that if one were less carried away, one would change one's ideas of that society? Morris was anticipating a modern historian's reference to the Renaissance 'with its uncritical enthusiasm for antiquity'.[3] Modern literary critics may find in their authors 'a venturesome enthusiasm' springing 'from the sincere belief that one's own ideals of life are the only true ones'[4] – an exact parallel to one of the senses of the word in its religious context.

The same sort of transference is clear in Wellek's remark that Hamann 'acquired a group of enthusiastic followers who studied his works as if they were the Bible'.[5] As Wellek describes Hamann's ideas as a 'weird mixture' we may assume he is not applying his adjective in any complimentary sense, though he willingly recognises the zeal of Hamann's group.

A similar implication that enthusiastic writing lacks solid and desirable qualities appears in Wellek's comments on Herder's style. He characterises it as marked by 'a fervid, shrill, enthusiastic tone' which is the result of heightened emotion, and is expressed by rhetorical questions, exclamations, dashes, and an overdose of figurative writing, lacking in reasoned argument.[6]

And even when enthusiasm is merely keen insistence, it need not be desirable. The Deists' stress on the Lockean origin of their principles was, as we have noted, 'vociferous and embarrassing' in the view of the modern historian of *Reason and Authority in the Eighteenth Century*.[7] When he comes to discuss the climate of opinion at the end of the century, he notes Burke's indignation with the 'doctrinaire enthusiasts',[8] and his recognition that they were given to shameless oversimplification of complex issues.[9] Further, just as the atheist can be enthusiastic for his disbelief, so one can be an enthusiast now for reason – even though our ancestors would have thought this a contradiction in terms as in a sense it is – for Cragg considers that William Godwin paid such 'unquestioning reverence' to the power of reason that 'he recapitulated earlier trends, and, in an excess of enthusiasm destroyed their results'.[10]

Yet it is the rational or informed approach which is felt usually to be lacking in modern enthusiasts in literary writing, though popularly enthusiasts are normally those who know most about their pet subject. The Gothic Revival was more enthusiastic than intelligent,[11] and we can probably all remember discussions where there were enthusiasts not conscious of the weakness of their 'proofs'.[12] So Sir Herbert Read sums up Fontanelle's calm intelligence as equally devoid of enthusiasms and prejudices.[13] This derogatory twist is not always present; it is perhaps less frequent in the United States than in Britain. It is possible to read a history by an American which uses the group on every other page, and one on the same period by an Englishman which uses it hardly at all – though certainly this could be a difference of personal temperament.[14] It is surely unusual, in British usage, to describe one's selection of a particular subject of research as one's 'enthusiastic choice of this field'.[15] And one feels that Gibbon, who disliked 'the wind-filled Enthusiast', might need to make some linguistic readjustment if he could read that he himself in the view of the modern 'was unstinting in his enthusiasm for Greek Tragedy'.[16]

In the less formal language of speakers in broadcast comment or discussion, the group lives a double life. The Member of Parliament who described the social situation in Vietnam as one where enthusiasm was being generated for self-help, improvement and redevelopment, clearly felt it a good thing, directed to good ends.[17] But one doubts the complimentary tone of the interviewer who wondered whether enthusiastic amateurs might not do more harm than good in the Voluntary Community

Service.[18] No doubt at all can arise when a speaker comments that there is nothing more boring than the enthusiasm of a teacher who cannot get a class to share it.[19]

We can still find the abstract noun accompanied by derogatory adjectives. Boswell, says the historian of Dr Johnson's politics, wrote addresses to the king in a spirit of 'fatuous enthusiasm'.[20] We must, indeed, judge the import of the abstract noun to be mere description – it is the adjective which carries the weight of approval or disapproval, not the noun.

In May 1968, a speaker in the B.B.C.'s 'Today in the West' programme commented on a 'quiet enthusiasm for transplant surgery', and when we find 'wise enthusiasm' rubbing shoulders with 'mellow learning' and 'refined taste' our word takes its place in the laudatory triad.[21] Henry James is not blaming his heroine when he says that enthusiasm made Isabel Archer 'almost happy' when it came to her; it had been her old habit to live by it – 'to fall in love with suddenly perceived possibilities, with the idea of some new adventure'.[22] Nor was the sixteenth-century 'educational enthusiasm' wrong-headed, when 'advanced minds like Erasmus, Roger Ascham, John Colet...William Camden...and Sir Thomas Elyot' were dreaming of finding in the past 'a living source of instruction' for the present.[23]

Enthusiasm occurs at times with unexpected adjectives. Sir Robert Peel, writing to Sir Walter Scott (3 April 1829), wishes he could have seen and described the Clare election adding that no pen but Scott's 'could have done justice to that fearful exhibition of sobered and desperate enthusiasm'.[24] The separation between the intensity of inward feeling and the calmness of the outward manifestation is here complete. And so Lord Cockburn speaks of Professor Murray's 'long and silent enthusiasm' for Oriental studies.[25]

The modern everyday use of the group stands in sharp contrast to both historical and (often) literary use.

Enthusiasm, said the third Lord Shaftesbury, 'is in itself, a very natural honest Passion'[26] – he was one of the first to say so. He is more in line with modern popular feeling and usage than William Falconer, who appears to be the first on record to use *enthusiast* for one too easily duped into accepting false values for true, in a secular sense.[27] It occurs in his poem 'The Demagogue', which is a satire on William Pitt, Earl of Chatham.

> A fond enthusiast, kindling at thy name;
> I glow'd in secret with congenial flame:
> While my young bosom, to deceit unknown,
> Believ'd all real virtue thine alone.

But the poet was disappointed and disillusioned.[28]

We should probably be willing to extend to things in general the charity expressed by Hester Chapone, who thought that any 'absurdities' arising 'from the fancied ardors of enthusiasm...are much less pernicious to the mind than the contrary extreme of coldness and indifference in religion'.[29] It depends on how much the ardour gets out of hand. We might well agree with Horace Walpole's comment about the Gordon Riots: he reports (8 June 1780) that 'both women and men are lying dead drunk about the streets: brandy is preferable to enthusiasm'. Of course here the religious overtones are still audible since the Gordon Riots were an anti-Romanist outbreak, though their connection with religion as distinct from sectarian fury is no more patent than it would be if the word were used (as it well might be) of manifestations similar in kind, if not in degree, in Northern Ireland today.

On the whole, we are inclined to think that enthusiasm is better than apathy, even if it sometimes shows itself in regrettably ebullient ways. We should agree with Shaftesbury that it takes 'a noble Enthusiasm'[30] to perform greatly in the roles of heroes, statesmen, orators, poets, musicians and philosophers, and indeed anywhere else, though *noble* might sometimes be too strong a word. Yet despite this widening reference, it is possible to find comments that take *enthusiasm* in its old religious sense, but which imply approval of the state of mind involved. Emerson's essay on the Oversoul claims that it is a necessity of the human constitution that 'a certain enthusiasm' should attend our consciousness of the divine presence.[31] Its character and duration may vary from 'an ecstasy and trance and prophetic inspiration. . . to the faintest glow of virtuous emotion, in which form it warms, like our household fires, all the families and associations of men, and makes society possible'. Some tendency to insanity is inseparable from the religious sense where men are 'blasted with excess of light'. Emerson mentions Plotinus, St Paul, Porphyry, Behmen, the Quakers, Swedenborg, the Methodists – all the old examples – and considers their experiences to be 'varying forms of that shudder of awe and delight with which the individual soul always mingles with the universal soul. The nature of these revelations is the same; they are perceptions of the absolute law. They are solutions of the soul's own questions. They do not answer the questions which the understanding asks.'

In contrast, at a less rarefied level, today any great keenness will be called by the term, which neither dignifies nor vilifies – it merely intensifies. So we hear of (female) enthusiasts for parachuting,[32] for clocks,[33] for attending an amateur hovercraft rally,[34] and of 'gossip enthusiasts' in the Programme Notes of B.B.C. 4.[35]

Likewise we have heard of the 'drive and enthusiasm' of the people of Australia for a proposed atomic power scheme,[36] or of public enthusiasm for a new type of aeroplane,[37] and of the need to make an attempt to recover some of the enthusiasm for a football club.[38] Obviously, here the word simply implies depth of interest, with no touch of disapproval.

Railway enthusiasts seem to be amongst the most note-worthy of the recognised groups. They had a magazine of their own by 1933 and are catered for by various publications.[39] But it is a comment on the enduring ambiguity of the word that a radio interviewer could report that many of them dislike the term, though the speaker being interviewed welcomed it.[40]

Many people could be described as theatre or cinema enthusiasts, though the word *fan* might come more naturally to some of them. They have royal support, for George III in 1785 declared himself an enthusiast for Mrs Siddons.[41]

The modern tendency of the group to be available in any field is well exemplified by the translator of Heer's book on European intellectual history, who uses *en-*

thusiasm of the religious variety (Methodism), of the kind
that is felt for Nature (Macpherson, Rousseau), of the
Romantic kind in Germany, and all three of them combined to make the amalgam that was James Hervey.[42]
Any reader of Hervey, troubled by his over-poetic style
of prose, might well wonder whether the word is used of
him historically or as part of a loaded statement. And are
English people to feel complimented when told that one
of their four national characteristics is enthusiasm? For
the other three are eccentricity, neuroticism and sexu-
ality.[43]

Definitely derogatory examples are easy to find. The
Friedmans, in their demolition of the methods of those
who find in Shakespeare a magnified cipher, quote and
apply a remark from E. R. Vincent's book on Gabriele
Rossetti in England, in which Rossetti is accused of mis-
representing medieval literature by 'unsystematic research in which we see an enthusiasm plunging farther
and farther from the logic of facts and good sense until
truth is lost in the dreadful nightmare of an *idée fixe*'.[44]
Likewise, David Daiches speaks of the Burns cult and the
'steady level of irrational enthusiasm' at which it has been
maintained since the poet's death.[45]

On the other hand, there is nothing derogatory in a
reference to Bacon's 'enthusiastic' proposals for his
scientific Academy in *New Atlantis*,[46] when Robert
Hooke is described as an enthusiastic experimental
scientist,[47] or when Ricardo Quintana couples *enthusiasm*
and *newly-released energy* in an essay on Swift.[48]

A modern critic considers that Mackenzie's Harley was
endowed by his creator with 'the enthusiasm and strength

necessary for life in a world of struggle', because Mackenzie himself was 'vigorous and cheerful'.[49] If this were true, we should scarcely have expected Harley to die of joy, but the facts of the novel do not invalidate the linguistic evidence for the tone of the word.

It is clear that a good deal of explanation and hedging is frequently needed nowadays – the group of words does not come announced by a clear muffin-bell of its own, as Galsworthy claimed for good slang, and as philosophers and purists wish all words to do. We cannot finally tie down words to meanings, as Dr Johnson pointed out, because human nature is capricious.[50] So warnings and apologies occur, sometimes in the guise of inverted commas. Professional and business men, says an expert on memory, and various sorts of 'enthusiasts' could do as well in their own fields as a professional memory-man.[51] Are the inverted commas really needed? Every man in a free country is at liberty to choose his own interests, and if they seem odd to those who happen not to share them, 'De Gustibus' is a tag that still covers the situation. People whose interest in a given subject enables them to remember detailed information about it beyond the capacity of the uninitiated are surely enthusiasts in an acceptable and approving modern sense, but if our ancestors might have accused them of making their subject the god of their idolatry, we hardly shall. Whether we regard their feelings as *unguarded*[52] enthusiasm or *naive*[53] or *judicious*,[54] we can choose our type of adjective: and this our ancestors usually could not do. But the popular un-discriminating use of *enthusiasm* and its adjectives tends to make it suspect. One sympathises with I. A. Richards's comment on *A Manual of Rhetoric*[55] which spoke of Bacon's 'enthusiastic appreciation': in the critic's view, it was 'a poor phrase to smudge over him'.[56]

We still consider that enthusiasm leads to extravagance and to statements that we should deplore in our more sober moments. Sir Walter Scott writes to Shelley, 1 May 1811, to caution him 'against an enthusiasm which while it argues an excellent disposition and a feeling heart, requires to be watched and restrained, tho' not repressed'.[57] A century and a half later we find a critic taking T. S. Eliot to task for an 'extravagant' remark uttered in 'a mood of enthusiasm'. What else would induce the poet to wish for a completely illiterate audience?[58]

11

METAPHORS

The metaphors we choose mirror our attitudes and our mental furniture: those that have been used – and some of them that are still in use – in reference to Enthusiasm are no exception to the rule. From them we can build up a composite picture of how the thing struck contemporaries.

The figure that is commonest and most long-lived is that of heat, with every variety of cause and manifestation from spark to molten lava. But it is far from being the only one. Disease, madness, drunkenness, natural forces like water or rocks, the enchanter and the invader, a vegetable growth or a landscape, even such unlikely metaphoric vehicles as clouds, clogs, veils, and wheels are found to carry the tenor of the word.

When Enthusiasm is spoken of as a disease or form of madness, the metaphorical use of these words may be late in developing, for the rational explanation of the state of mind concerned was that it resulted from physiological conditions or neuroses that actually were diseases or lunacy. If the blood was overheated and the sufferer thrown into a fever, it follows that some early references to heat are also to be taken literally. And as the effects of feverishness and of intoxication may be much the same, literal meaning may be intended where we see figurative when the victim is said to be drunk.

It is highly unlikely that the 'heat' ascribed to religious Enthusiasm by rational eighteenth-century critics has anything to do with the *calor* which, with *canor* and *dulcor*, makes up the technical triad of the medieval mystics (whom the eighteenth century tended to denigrate as 'enthusiasts').[1] The combination of *heat* with *vapour* and *blown up* suggests on the one hand Swift's *Discourse concerning the Mechanical Operation of the Spirit*, which, as Lord Orrery said,[2] 'is a satyr against enthusiasm and those affected inspirations, which constantly begin in folly, and very often end in vice'. On the other hand, we are bound to be reminded of the modern expressions 'hot air' and 'gas' in their transferred, slangy and pejorative senses. Both come from the United States, the former recorded from 1899, the latter from 1847, though it had its predecessors more vividly in eighteenth-century references to inflated (and deflated) balloons. So a modern critic sums up Swift's Aeolists as 'the emblems of gassy dissent' and compares the fate of 'early Christian enthusiasts' at the hands of Gibbon, whose 'Latinate imagery' transforms them into 'mere bags of wind'.[3]

Disease

When the *Critical Review*[4] of 1791 ascribes John Wesley's Enthusiasm (which Wesley himself denied possessing) to 'hereditary disease' in the family, there is no doubt that a scientific explanation is being offered for 'that disease of the mind'. The same is true when Lavington considers that the sufferer's brain is intoxicated 'with the heated Fumes of Spirituous Particles',[5] and Warburton has this in mind when he speaks of 'the fumes of the rankest enthusiasm'.[6] Some forty years earlier than Lavington, John Trenchard had asked, 'Why may not...the poisonous and melancholy Vapours streaming from an Enthusiast cause distraction and Raving as well as the bite of a Mad Dog?'[7] For Thomas Green, 'natural fervours' may be mistaken for divine inspiration and 'ardency of temper' for religious zeal, so that Enthusiasm, 'due to heated Melancholy', is merely 'the natural effect of a heated imagination'.[8]

The natural causes had natural results, and so we are told not to be surprised that 'Enthusiasm should warm it's Votaries to a Holy Madness, and excite the Wildest Transports and Agitations throughout their Whole Frame.'[9] The author of this comment instances the wife of a Welch Fusilier at Ghent in 1744 who was 'an enthusiastic Devotée' and was so affected by psalm-singing that she 'was heated to a frenzy', trembled with agony, foamed at the mouth and uttered hideous cries, so that she had to be gagged and carried out. He recognises the psychosomatic problem in his remarks on the St Medard manifestations, where the devotees claimed to have been miraculously cured by a pseudo-saint:

> Their Minds being thus heated and inflamed, and every Faculty of their Souls burning with the raptures of devout joy and enthusiastic Confidence, must it not appear far from being impossible after the instances we have assigned above that in some cases a Change might be wrought in the Habit of the Body?

As a disease, Enthusiasm is catching: Green is being figurative when he says that the Enthusiasm of the Flagellants spread like an 'epidemical distemper',[10] and so is the author of *Reflections upon a Letter Concerning Enthusiasm*, in 1709, when he admits that 'when infected we have all Enthusiasm of our own', and perhaps also when he mentions an 'infected Person' who is a 'tainted Airy Enthusiast'.[11] But the 'fact' that the 'Effluviums which stream from the body of an Enthusiast' might 'infect others with the same Distemper' is literal. Late in the eighteenth century Vicesimus Knox was saying that

Enthusiasm has exhibited in some tempers all the symptoms of a malignant disease and terminated, at last, in real and most deplorable insanity.[12]

He holds to the same opinion as Lavington, who says that

Enthusiasm and Madness are but the same thing in different words for the former is due to Melancholy, Hysterias, Hypochondriacks [which] have in themselves a certain Degree of Madness.[13]

We wonder whether Dr Moss was being literal or figurative, when he spoke of Enthusiasm as

a religious Distemper...always attended with dangerous, and for the most part, incurable symptoms, heated with ignorant zeal and blown up by arrogant Conceit, but it ends in fatal Delusion and oft downright Frenzy.[14]

The *Oxford English Dictionary* quotes only one example of 'infectious' in a good sense before the nineteenth century: it is Dryden's 'infectious virtue'. It seems unlikely that the eighteenth century would have described Joseph Priestley's scientific enthusiasm as 'infectious', and resulting in a 'rapid extension of natural knowledge', as his modern biographer has done.[15] For Dr Johnson, *infection* is 'mischief by communication': all his illustrative quotations refer to pestilence, literal or figurative. But 'infectious' is now a common part of complimentary phrases: laughter, smiles, gaiety, courage – and enthusiasm itself – are things we want to catch.

For Joseph Trapp,[16] Enthusiasm is a 'baneful Plague',

'a Pest', and is exemplified in the Quakers, who in his view are 'one of the most pestilent sects that ever infected the Christian Church'; Isaac Taylor sees it as 'a sickening infection',[17] especially as manifested by the early Christian ascetics, and to Charles Chauncy it seemed 'in one word' a pest to the Church in all ages.[18] That this was a common choice of words is clear from the ironical lines in John Byrom's poem on the subject, where he imagines the critic's injunctions:

> Fly from Enthusiasm. It is the pest,
> Bane, poison, frensy, fury, and the rest.[19]

Taylor also describes it as *vertigo* and *venom*.[20] A belated nineteenth-century ascription of political enthusiasm to sickness is quoted in Professor Asa Briggs's *Victorian People*:[21] Bagehot, though he stood (unsuccessfully) as a Liberal candidate for Parliament, told a friend that he lacked sympathy with the party: 'I hate the Liberal enthusiasts. I feel inclined to say, "Go home, Sir, and take a dose of Salts, and see if it won't clean it all out of you".'

Poison, drunkenness, madness

Indeed, from infectious disease to drunkenness and poison are easy steps. Evans speaks of the 'poison' of Mme Bourignon's 'Enthusiastic Rants'[22] and some seventy years earlier, in 1680, George Hickes was lamenting 'the Poison of Enthusiasm', which is 'the Spiritual drunkenness' which 'so distempers the minds of men of the other Communions with extravagant phancies as to make them more or less affect the extraordinary Gifts of the Spirit and then conceit, like Poets in Religion, that they have them, and are inspired'.[23]

Green is another who believes in the connection between Enthusiasm and Melancholy; he mentions 'an enthusiastic sect among the Turks' who are sufferers from what we should call Melancholia, which 'may be looked upon as a kind of natural inebriation' and that is a spiritual fever.[24] The same idea is implied in Thomas Adams's adjective *sottish* which he applies to Enthusiasts who condemn all learning. Such people are 'drunk, but not with wine'.[25]

William Blake, despite his use of *really*, is combining the figures of madness and inebriation when he writes to Hayley:

Excuse my enthusiasm, or rather madness, for I am really drunk with intellectual vision whenever I take a pencil or graver into my hand, even as I used to be in my youth.[26]

It will be observed that Blake is discussing Art, not Religion. A modern scholar, writing on eighteenth-century pulpit-oratory, tells us that preachers tried to prohibit 'the heady wine' of 'enthusiasm'.[27]

Heat and light

Accounts of Enthusiasm, religious or poetic, may be found given in terms of heat and light even in academic lectures and encyclopaedias. Morhof renders it as:

calor, ignis, ardor, ardor animi, ardor mentis[28]

and Diderot describes it as

la fureur poétique établie dans le monde comme un rayon de lumière transcendente[29]

which sounds very much like Edward Jerningham's

Bright emanation of th'eternal beam.[30]

It is, Diderot continues,

une flamme vive qui gagne de proche en proche, qui se nourrit de son propre feu et qui loin de s'affoibler en s'étendant, prend de nouvelles forces à mésure qu'elle se répand et se communique.[31]

The loftiest metaphor for enthusiasm – and it is noticeable that it is used of the poetic kind – is Young's. He contrasts the

well-accomplished scholar and the divinely-inspired enthusiast; the first is as the bright morning-star; the *second* as the rising sun.[32]

The least effective of the English words are such generalising ones as *warm(th)*, *fervour*, *ardour*, which are to be found at all times. Probably *fervour* and *ardour* were livelier metaphors in the eighteenth century than now. Gerard in 1758 terms the enthusiasm of the genius 'an elevation and warmth of sentiment'.[33] Wesley speaks in his Sermon on Enthusiasm of 'the fervour' of poets.[34] The *Critical Review* of 1792 mentions the 'warm gestures and language'[35] of enthusiasm and its 'warmest glow'.[36] The author of *Die and be Damned* in 1758 coupled 'powerful vociferation' with 'enthusiastic warmth';[37] and we have recently been told that William Gifford altered Charles Lamb's enthusiastic review of *The Excursion* 'into something rather less warm'.[38]

Of course verbs like *quench, cool, chill, dampen* imply the same picture: Johannes Stinstra in 1774 may well be right when he says that the enthusiasm of sectaries 'cools by degrees when they are left to enjoy their full liberty';[39] Asa Briggs tells us that Lytton 'chilled'[40] the enthusiasm of the people and, thinks his biographer, Joseph Priestley's ill-success with his trial-sermon 'must surely have dampened his enthusiasm'.[41] By contrast, John Trenchard offers a much livelier picture in his remark about the sectarian individualist who has 'no church-buckets to quench his fiery Religion'.[42]

Glow, with its suggestion of steady controlled heat, is a more comfortable word than *flame*, with its overtone of fierceness and intermittence. So Burke uses it, coupling 'the fervid glow of enthusiasm' with 'the sanguine credulity of youth' in his admiring picture of a lad in 1704 looking forward to the immensely developed America of 1775.[43] And his words of commendation for what he admires in Rousseau's style are *glowing, animated* and *enthusiastic*.[44] A reviewer of *Peter Bell* declared that Wordsworth writes 'under the impulse of a glowing and real enthusiasm'.[45]

But fire may suggest warmth raised to fever-pitch, and destructiveness. It is not always the 'nourisher of life', as the Eddic poet's word implies – and he uses it ironically for the fires of the Doom of the Gods.[46] Because *inflame* is a medical term for an undesirable condition of body, the verb tends to be used of undesirable enthusiasms, with 'to fire' for the better ones, though this is not always so – Briggs says that Robert Lowe 'fired the working classes to a feverish enthusiasm for reform',[47] which suggests some doubt as to the propriety of the method though not of the aim. Certainly one would be 'inflamed' with lust rather than with love. There is a hint of the bad sense of *inflame* in the *Spectator* (no. 201):

When the Mind finds herself very much inflamed with her Devotions, she is too much inclined to think they are not of her own kindling; but blown up by something divine within her.

Richard Graves speaks of rousing and inflaming the smaller sparks of enthusiasm into extravagance and rage.[48] Contrast Miss Sweeting's description of English scholars in fifteenth-century Italy who were 'fired by the enthusiasm of Italian collectors and patrons of letters'.[49]

A curious reversal of usage occurs in the remark by a modern historian who says that the belief in Prester John 'had repeatedly fired Western enthusiasm',[50] or in the modern philosopher who describes the enthusiasm of the Humanist ideals as 'kindled in the lived life'.[51] Earlier, Enthusiasm was itself the fiery particle in need of no heat from outside – as it still is for Miss Sweeting when she states that enthusiasm for language provided the spark of energy which fired men in the Tudor period.[52]

John Douglas contrasts the 'pure flame' of religion with the 'false glare' of Enthusiasm.[53] It had been contrasted by Gilbert Burnet with Superstition, which 'extinguishes the light of Reason; Enthusiasm dazles the Mind with a false Glare'.[54] For the author of *An Answer to the Letter of Enthusiasm*, Enthusiasm is by implication an Ignis Fatuus.[55] So it is for Dr Trapp, who also calls it a 'glaring Meteor'.[56] Trenchard equates the Inward Light claimed by visionaries of all ages with an Ignis Fatuus of the mind.[57]

Lightning, fire and inflammation appear all together in Warburton's summary of Dr Middleton's views on the subject:

a sudden flash of lighting, under the fancied figure of *cloven tongues*, kindles the fiery imaginations of a number of enthusiastic men, met together in tumultuous assembly and inflaming one another's fanaticism by mutual collision.[58]

Enthusiasm is a wild-fire (a figure that effectively combines getting out of control with destructiveness): it 'runs like wild-fire from breast to breast', according to Green,[59] and Wesley admits that all revivals of religion suffer from some admixture of Enthusiasm – 'some wild-fire...mixed with the sacred flame'.[60]

More imaginative and careful writers may present a fully worked-out metaphorical sequence. Burke, for instance, discussing, though not approving, the animating effect of the French Revolution on Dr Richard Price, says that it

inspires a juvenile warmth through his whole frame. His enthusiasm kindles as he advances and when he arrives at his peroration it is in full blaze.[61]

So a modern historian regrets that Pope Innocent III with all his good qualities 'lacked the spark that might have kindled sympathy and enthusiasm' – here again the source of heat is not *in* enthusiasm.[62]

A stranger series of pictures is given by Pittis in 1682 when he describes how Enthusiasts

fetch candles from Rome's Altars, that they may set them up in their own Breasts. As if there were no difference betwixt *the Holy Spirit guiding men into truth*, and walking by the light of their own fires.[63]

For Law, secular enthusiasms are 'heats arising from flame kindled by straw'; atheistic enthusiasm is 'a *dull burning* fire', and that of infidels 'a *bold* fire' needing to be constantly blown up.[64]

More violent metaphors occur in the *Letter of Enthusiasm*, which compares 'Flaming Enthusiasm' to 'Gunpowder in a Granado or Mine', or to a subterranean fire.[65]

The figure of fire in various forms persists in modern use both colloquially and in literature. Sometimes it is incidental, as when Sidney Painter speaks of St Joan's 'fiery enthusiasm',[66] or implied, as when he comments that the enthusiasm of the German princes 'cooled'.[67] It may be vivid, as when Pater remarks that Winckelmann in his youth had no 'vague romantic longing; he knows what he longs for, what he wills. Within its severe limits his enthusiasm burns like lava.'[68] It may be worked out in detail, as when Oswald Doughty refers to the poetic 'flame so carefully fanned by the Millers at Bath' which was not extinguished 'before the enthusiasm of a fresh literary coterie had been lighted at its fire'.[69] Early last century, Lord Cockburn tells us that his friend Mrs Grant

was always under the influence of an affectionate and delightful enthusiasm, which, unquenched by time or sorrow, survived the wreck of many domestic attachments, and shed a glow over the close of a very protracted life.[70]

The unquenched enthusiasm surviving the wreck of domestic attachments suggests a flame on the hearth; but the glow at the close, the light of the sinking sun: if this is a wavering metaphor, it is a beautiful one.

A very different kind of enthusiasm is described in Cockburn's account of Thomas Chalmers; when he got his congregation

within the flames of his enthusiasm [Cockburn remarks] Jeffrey's description, that he 'buried his adversaries under the fragments of burning mountains' is the only image that suggests an idea of his eloquent imagination and terrible energy.[71]

Here is a vivid and powerful metaphor for Chalmers's volcanic style. We may compare a metaphor from an article by Bronson Alcott, published in 1840 in *The Dial*:

Let the flame of enthusiasm always fire your bosom. Enthusiasm is the glory and hope for the world. It is the life of sanctity and genius, it has wrought all miracles since the beginning of time.

The eighteenth century would have agreed as to the genius but not the sanctity. And yet, at the same period, Daniel Webster could call a determined support for Abolitionism a 'strange enthusiasm'.[72]

On the other hand, modern usage is sometimes rather muddled. When we are told that English enthusiasm for William III, 'kindled' by his Irish victories, *waned* later on, the fire has become light rather than the heat we should have expected.[73] A modern choice of adjectives produces that curious collocation 'lukewarm enthusiasm'. Bosola in the play shows no more than a 'lukewarm enthusiasm'[74] and we read of an American scholar who could raise at best only a lukewarm enthusiasm for fish.[75] It would have struck our ancestors as a strange description of an emotion *per se* hot: they would have felt more at home with Samuel Beckett's Malone, who says he will be 'neither hot nor cold any more' but tepid –

I shall die tepid, without enthusiasm[76]

– which implies that enthusiasm is *not* lukewarm.

Metaphors from Landscape and Gardening

For the anti-enthusiast in the religious context, to become an enthusiast is to deviate from the straight and narrow way marked out in England by the national Church. You would be in danger of running into the very wilds of

Enthusiasm,[77] or following its gloomy paths, leading to an equally gloomy wilderness,[78] where your reason and common sense might be lost.[79] For Richard Graves, the plants in the wilderness (a jungle rather than a desert) are of the Enthusiast's own sowing. Many who have set out, he says, as 'avowed scoffers at Religion, have in the End, run so far into the other Extreme' as to be lost 'in all the wilds of Enthusiasm, the Seeds of which have been in their Minds from the beginning'.[80] For Theophilus Evans, the Enthusiastick spirit can hurry 'melancholy Tempers' into 'inextricable Mazes and Labyrinths'[81] – and since these devices are products of human ingenuity (a perverse ingenuity to the victim, though of his own misapplication), Evans is implying that Enthusiasm is not of divine origin.

At best a weed, at worst a jungle. Goldsmith thinks of Superstition and Enthusiasm as both growing out of Religion – they 'are, if you will, the bastard sprouts of this heavenly plant'.[82] For Dr Chauncy, the 'enthusiastical Spirit' is the true Spirit of Quakerism and the Seed Plot of Delusion.[83] As it is also 'naturally a spreading, growing evil',[84] 'care must be taken to check its growth and progress; for there is no knowing how high it may rise, or what it may end in'.[85]

An interesting variant of this – especially as it is both modern and disapproving – is the description of Coleridge's genius 'running to seed in a succession of enthusiasms',[86] with its suggestion of a fine plant growing rank, its flowers never plucked when they had reached perfection of form.

Approving and rare are Miss Mitford's metaphor and

adjective when she speaks of that 'virtuous enthusiasm which is the loveliest rose in the chaplet of youth'.[87]

Water

Despite the incongruity with enthusiasm as a fire that can be damped by water, water in its overwhelming power is a natural figure for anything as uncontrollable as Enthusiasm. George Nott holds that the Church of England's claims are 'founded in a Rock which can never be moved, even though the waves of Enthusiasm should rage horribly'.[88] This is a landsman's figure: the seaman will understand why the author of *Methodism Vindicated* thought of Enthusiasm rather as a rock – 'that most dangerous rock...on which myriads have been wrecked'.[89]

G. H. W. Parker speaks of 'tides of enthusiasm, popular and ascetic'[90] when he is discussing the Observant Franciscans, and in a secular field we have been told that Cambridge finally approved the establishment of an English School because Congregation was swayed by a 'torrent of enthusiasm'.[91]

One would suppose that no enthusiasm could be calm, so it is not surprising to find 'stormy' applied to it,[92] nor to read of 'the tempest of enthusiasm'.[93]

Swift has an extended water-metaphor when he writes that

whosoever pleases to look into the Fountains of *Enthusiasm*, from whence, in all Ages have eternally proceeded such fatning Streams, will find the Spring Head to have been as *troubled* and *muddy* as the Current.[94]

Swift is concerned here with politico-religious deviations from reason. The danger of similar aberrations in the philosophical sphere is suggested some eighty years later by Thomas Taylor, the Platonist, in a sustained metaphor which combines the ideas of phantom, shadow and water – all three transient, all three unstable, and the third ruinously powerful. In the preface to his translation of Plotinus (*An Essay on the Beautiful: From the Greek of Plotinus*)[95] he thinks it necessary to caution his readers to distinguish the doctrine of this discourse from 'modern enthusiastic opinions', for

> there is not a greater difference between substance and shade than between ancient and modern enthusiasm. The object of the former was the highest good and the supreme beauty; but that of the latter is nothing more than a phantom raised by bewildered imaginations, floating on the unstable ocean of opinion, the sport of the factious party. Like substance and shade, indeed, they possess a similitude in outward appearance, but in reality they are perfect contraries, for the one fills the mind with solid and durable good; but the other with empty delusions; which, like the ever-running waters of the Danaides, glide away as fast as they enter, and leave nothing behind but the ruinous passages through which they flowed.[96]

One of Swift's editors goes further, when he says that the Drapier's *Letters* 'launched [the Irish] on a maelstrom of enthusiasm'.[97]

Figures from the Supernatural

In his *History of the Royal Society*, Sprat sees the new scientists as 'a race of young men...who were invincibly armed against the enchantments of enthusiasm'.[98] One has a fleeting picture of Arthurian or Spenserian heroes setting out on a quest. Shaftesbury calls it 'a kind of Enchantment'[99] and Melmoth sees virtue in certain kinds of enthusiasm, and calls it 'a beneficent enchantress'.[100]

The false variety, to the *Critical Review*, is a 'sanguinary idol',[101] and it is, as we have seen, 'a phantom' to Thomas Taylor. In all these expressions lies the idea of unreality, though the bloody excesses of the worshippers of the false god have been often all too real. Some people are immune to the enchantment the enthusiast feels, as R. W. Chapman implies when he admits that you have to be an enthusiast to be enchanted by Jane Austen's letters.[102]

Military

Exaggeration and enthusiasm are 'invaders of mirth and harmony' for the *Looker-on*[103] – we should hardly blame enthusiasm in such a connection today. More seriously, the author of *Methodism Vindicated* holds that Enthusiasm (in the technical sense) 'saps the foundation of all true piety',[104] and Owen, in *Methodism Unmasked*, accuses it of infidelity, of making 'destructive inroads into true religion'.[105] These all seem rather faded metaphors.

Minor figures

Clara Reeve describes enthusiasm as a veil that casts a shade upon every object[106] – which fits in with the idea that it is a deceiver: we cannot see things in their proper light. Wesley, by collocation of words, implies that it is dross – 'We have lost only the dross, the enthusiasm, the prejudice and offence. The pure gold remains.'[107] This is a parallel to the false glare and true light figure: Enthusiasm may look like the real thing, but it is a false Florimell. Thomas Sheridan speaks of religion being 'stripped of the frightful mask with which her face had been covered by bigotry and enthusiasm'.[108] Landor speaks of the 'hot and uncontrolled harlotry of a flaunting and dishevelled enthusiasm'.[109]

Warburton considers that among the ancient philosophers the dogmatists 'grew *enthusiastic*' and the sceptics *immoral*, thus falling into the 'two worst dangers that can befall a searcher after truth; for her abode is neither in the clouds nor on the dunghill'.[110] If enthusiasm dwells in the clouds, this too suggests that she is unreal or irrational. But until we recall that Mme Guyon, the Quietist, was reckoned among the Enthusiasts, we may be surprised to find Gilbert Burnet the younger calling 'the supineness of Contemplative Enthusiasm' a 'Clog upon Society'.[111]

On the other hand, Melmoth, who thinks secular enthusiasm all to the good, speaks of its forces as 'some of the main wheels of society'[112] – and indeed we should agree that it usually is what makes things go.

Biblical

Chauncy considers that Enthusiasm has been 'a stone of stumbling to multitudes in the world':[113] the phrase sounds like an echo of Romans 9: 33. Either Chauncy was treating it like any accepted phrase or being ironical – for the stone was originally a symbol of the heavenly kingdom, precisely what Enthusiasm does not lead to, in the eyes of its critics.

More vividly, Leslie considers in his vigorous but rude historical narrative of the times, that the Devil

entered into the Herd of our Swine, the Beasts of the People; and drove them over Precipices of Enthusiasm to perish in the Ocean of Heresie and Error.[114]

But the most striking figure of all is that in which John Scott sums up the predicament of Christianity and the Church of England in his time: they are

in danger of being crucified, like their blessed Author, between those two thieves (and both alas, impenitent ones) Superstition and Enthusiasm.[115]

Little allegories of the origins of Enthusiasm in the religious sense show their inventors' attitudes. For John Douglas, Enthusiasts are the 'spurious children of the reformation'.[116] George Campbell in a sermon provides a more complicated birth certificate.[117] Superstition and Enthusiasm are both 'false religion' arising from ignorance of God and of ourselves. In the apprehensive and timorous, the effect is *Superstition*; in the arrogant and daring, it is *Enthusiasm*. *Ignorance* is the mother of both by different fathers. The second she had by *Presumption*, the first by *Fear*. Hence that wonderful mixture of contrariety and resemblance in the characters of the children, which is no doubt why Superstition and Enthusiasm may 'pass alternately into each other at intervals', as David Hartley observes.[118]

A modern example occurs in the Modern Judgments volume on Swift where J. J. Hogan points out that Swift applied the word to the 'offspring of passion and disordered intellect'.[119]

12

POSTSCRIPT

How can the semantic development of such variable and ambiguous words as *enthusiasm* and its relations be summed up?

We can try to trace the broad changes and put them in their chronological frame, though this is necessarily an uncertain procedure because not every use of the words is recorded in writing or print. Written examples usually come after the colloquial, unless we are dealing with the technical terms of specialised sciences or occupations. True, *Enthusiasm* and the rest were technical at first in the religious sphere, but more people in seventeenth-century England were caught up in religious controversy than in twentieth-century England. Still, the broad sweep of the reigning primary sense of *Enthusiasm* can be mapped, as long as we remember that nobody wakes up on one New Year's Day partly forgetting sense A and prepared to use a word only in sense AB, and then at a later date forgetting this modification of the older sense and using only sense B. There must be some overlap, especially among the middle-aged who are in the best position to bear the older sense in mind and to notice (perhaps to resent and resist) new ones.

We can tentatively say, therefore, that *Enthusiasm* for most of the seventeenth century meant 'celestial inspiration', whether the source of it were Bacchus, Apollo, the Muses, or Jehovah. The sense of 'poetical fervour' with no ascription to God or Muse appears to result from Dryden's application of the word.

Since there are always both hypocrites and sceptics among us, and we are dealing with an abstract noun which sums up and reflects people's interpretation of the same emotional or intellectual phenomenon, we should not be surprised to find that for some two hundred years following 1660, the word implied 'fancied inspiration' or some vaguer 'ill-regulated' religious feeling.

By the first quarter of the eighteenth century the word need refer to neither religion nor poetry. The first example in *O.E.D.* dates from 1716 and concerns Gustavus Adolphus's enthusiasm for one of his projects. We cannot suppose that Bishop White Kennett, who uses the word of him, thought the warrior-king of Sweden inspired by God.

Enthusiast for the person who erroneously believes himself inspired dates from 1609 (earlier than in the sense of 'one who really is inspired'). It is not considered obsolete by *O.E.D.*, whose last quotation is dated 1856 and we saw how it was implied by Disraeli in 1868. I suspect that only historians would so use it now. The non-committal historical sense of 'one who is or thinks he is divinely inspired' dates, says *O.E.D.*, from 1641, often with reference to Pagan religious manifestations – the fury of Sybils, Pythian prophetesses and the like. Oliver Goldsmith is credited by the Dictionary with the first use of *enthusiast* to mean 'one entering with enthusiasm on a cause or pursuit', but this needs to be ante-dated. William Melmoth was using it of a wide range of people and absorbing interests by 1737. So was John Byrom fifteen years later. Johnson in his Dictionary quotes it of poetic and musical enthusiasts.

Enthusiastic is found earlier by six years than *Enthusiast*. We might suppose the noun would have come first, but Philemon Holland (see above, p. 2) could have taken it straight from Greek. Crashaw uses it of poetry. The extended sense to 'Ardent in support of things in general' is first illustrated by *O.E.D.* from Burke in 1786, but Johnson had defined it in 1755 as 'vehemently hot in any cause'.

The sense 'irrational, quixotic' began with Dryden, and lasted till the end of the eighteenth century, says *O.E.D.*, overlapping with both the 'deluded in religion' and the 'ardent in a cause' senses.

The modern use of *enthusiasm, enthusiast* and *enthusiastic* is very much dependent on our point of view. In a play broadcast in November 1970,[1] a schoolmaster who is an ardent believer in the value of the ancient classics, talks of his work and is told he is an enthusiast. He interprets this as a polite way of telling him that he is a bore. If we are interested, we call it 'enthusiasm', if not, we call it 'misplaced enthusiasm' – something perhaps irrational and quixotic, despite the Dictionary's belief that this sense is no longer found.

On the other hand, when the Prince of Wales spoke about the same time on the anniversary of the foundation of the United Nations Organisation, he said it wanted 'enthusiasm and hope' – a contrast to the eighteenth-century association of enthusiasm with melancholy.

With this category of 'point-of-view' words, their use frequently tells us more about the user than the referent –

they carry his attitudes, tastes, prejudices and beliefs, and it illustrates vividly that one man's meat is another man's poison.

Nevertheless, I think we can conclude that *Enthusiasm* and its congeners are a prime example of the ups and downs of evaluative words: this study of semantic shift could almost equally well be subtitled 'semantic see-saw'.

'ENTHUSE'

The verb, transitive and intransitive, is a nineteenth-century back-formation first found in the United States and dubbed colloquial by the *Dictionary of American English*. This dictionary's first example comes from the *Congressional Globe* dated 16 February 1859, and concerns people who were 'what they call in the country "Enthused", run mad on the subject' – a most interesting quotation in more ways than one. The word has the apologetic inverted commas, it is merely what the folk in the country say, it is equated with madness though not with the seventeenth-century medical implication, and the subject with which they were enthused was Cuba, which some Americans favoured wresting from Spain. *Enthused* would not have been used for the Cuban crisis of 1962. By 1891, the word has spread to England but is again provided with inverted commas, because it is what 'the Americans' say. This was the *Newcastle-upon-Tyne Daily Journal*, wondering whether a speaker 'enthused' his audience. The Dictionary's twentieth-century quotations have no inverted commas. *O.E.D.* is less kind than its American complement, calling the verb not only 'colloquial' or 'humorous', but by derivation an 'ignorant back-formation from ENTHUSIASM'. It offers examples from 1869 to 1887, none with inverted commas. The Supplement (1933) adds the 1859 quotation. It is still labelled colloquial in the *Penguin English Dictionary* of 1965.

Yet it seems to be on the upgrade, for it appears in serious writing of various sorts. The intransitive verb seems to be often derogatory, implying to 'gush', to be sentimentally approving. The transitive verb, used passively, seems to hold far more strongly the idea of inspiration, not of course necessarily in any religious sense. But the intransitive verb in current usage seems to be growing less derogatory in tone, though of course it still can be.

Brian Vickers, writing on *The World of Jonathan Swift*, suggests ironically that a modern Gulliver confronted with the King of Brobdingnag would *enthuse* about the advantages of our civilisation as demonstrated by the use of napalm.[1] Moira Dearnley records that Goldsmith enthused about Christopher Smart's poetry, in contrast to Dr Johnson who thought it contemptible.[2] She notes also that Tutin enthused about it, finding the *Song to David* 'highly imaginative, passionate and vigorous'[3] – and so do we. But we may wonder whether George Watson intends a compliment to the sixteen-year-old Coleridge when he records how he enthused over Bowles[4] – at that age, one's critical powers are immature. But when we read of a man being enthused by the genius of his country,[5] the inspiration is surely real. The speaker in 'Wild Life Review'[6] who hoped that visitors to Africa would be enthused by the sight of the wild life there was wholly approving. So is Hugh Montefiore when he states that faith to be alive must enthuse and inspire at all levels[7] – surely an approving use of the apparently intransitive verb, although an odd one, since an object is implied but not stated.

In her *Anatomy of Inspiration*, Rosamund Harding quotes from Evan Charteris's book on John Sargent the words of a sitter who found the artist painting 'at fever heat' and generating an almost unbearable sense of strain, which made him fear that he would 'spoil the pose' that enthused him (i.e. Sargent).[8] A colloquial comment leaves some doubt as to what precisely the speaker meant: he had, he said, been 'dragged along' to a Promenade Concert by some 'Enthusiasts', and he 'enthused'. Whether his feeling was genuine or merely polite cannot be deduced from cold print, but he sounded as if he had enjoyed his experience.[9]

APPENDIX 2

'ENTHUSIASM' AND 'SCHWÄRMEREI'

Enthusiasm has meant many things during its comparatively short career in English. Most people have accepted it as a word, whatever they have thought of the manifold concepts for which it stands. There have been the playful, like Lord Byron, who transmogrified it into *Entusymusy*,[1] but it was Carlyle, with his habit of basing theories on etymologies as likely to be wrong as right, who felt it to be unsuitable.

Discussing the fruits of democracy, he remarks that 'there soon comes that singular phenomenon, which the Germans call *Schwärmerei* ("enthusiasm" is our poor Greek equivalent) which means simply "*Swarmery*" or the Gathering of Men in Swarms'.[2]

Philological opinion is against Carlyle, and the subsequent career of *Schwärmerei* in English and in German is much less dignified than that of the 'poor' Greek word. The *Stanford Dictionary of Foreign Words in English* (1886), it is true, defines it as 'extravagant enthusiasm': the word appears in the *O.E.D. Supplement* more unkindly defined as one especially used of 'a schoolgirl attachment to another female' and all the illustrations present this idea of a 'crush'. Though basically related to *swarm*, the word goes back to a root that implies agitated, confused, deflected movement; giddiness, raving, rioting. There is never any idea of divine or demonic inspiration, though in German *Schwärmerei* has been historically used where our ancestors used *Enthusiasm* – e.g. of the Anabaptists. By the end of the eighteenth century, like its English counterpart, its sphere of reference was widened and it could be used of any 'muddle-headed, gushing, emotional type of enthusiasm',[3] and this is its modern use. 'It would be quite wrong to equate it with our modern use of enthusiasm, as it is definitely pejorative, and indicates that the craze will not last.'

NOTES TO THE TEXT

1 H. James Jensen, *A Glossary of John Dryden's Critical Terms* (1969).
2 Richard Greaves, *John Bunyan*, Courtenay Studies in Reformation Theology (1969).

CHAPTER I, pp. 1–13

1 E.g. Erwin Rohde, *Psyche* (1925); H. P. Nilsson, *A History of Greek Religion* (1925); A. Delatte, *Les Conceptions de l'Enthousiasme chez les Philosophes Pre-Socratiques* (1934); W. K. C. Guthrie, *The Greeks and their Gods* (1950).
2 Our phrase would be different in implication from one apparently similar used by N. Spinckes in 1709. In his book *The New Pretenders* (pp. 303–4), he concludes that with all his research he cannot decide whether the founder of the Manicheans 'were really an Enthusiast or an Atheist' or both by fits and starts: but the 'Enthusiastick Atheism' resulting he considers 'an Apology for all the Religions in the World, and for all the extravagant Madnesses that could ever come into the Brain of any under the pretext of the Inward Light and Spirit'. Spinckes is using his term with technical care, whereas we are noting a degree of involvement.

   On the theory that atheism and Enthusiasm spring from the same attitude of mind, see Philip Harth, *Swift and Anglican Rationalism* (1961).
3 [Edward Fowler] *Reflections upon a Letter concerning Enthusiasm* (1709), p. 54.
4 O.E.D.'s first example from Pyper's translation of Urfé (*History of Astraea*) concerns the Bacchanals.
5 Not all do. Professor G. A. Starr uses *enthusiasm, enthusiast* and *enthusiastic* throughout his book *Defoe and Spiritual Autobiography* (1965) in their technical senses without warning – a compliment to the reader, though it may be that not all readers of Defoe come to his critic with the proper background of religious controversial writings in their minds.
6 Our *good* normally refers to academic standards, theirs to morals.
7 Ronald A. Knox, *Enthusiasm* (1950). Some of the earlier writings include Meric Casaubon, *A Treatise Concerning Enthusiasme* (1655);

Henry More, *Enthusiasmus Triumphatus* (1662); Theophilus Evans, *The History of Modern Enthusiasm from the Reformation to the Present Times* (1752); and Isaac Taylor, *The Natural History of Enthusiasm* (1829).

8 M. K. Whelan, *Enthusiasm in English Poetry of the Eighteenth Century* (1935).

9 See Casaubon, *op. cit.*, and More, *op. cit.*; also Richard Burton's *Anatomy of Melancholy* (1621).

10 T. G. Steffen, *The Social Argument against Enthusiasm* (1941); E. C. Walker, *The History of 'Enthusiasm' as a Factor in the Religious and Social Problems of the Eighteenth Century* (1932).

11 A. P. Persky, 'The Changing Concepts of Enthusiasm in the Seventeenth and Eighteenth Centuries', Unpublished doctoral diss. (Stanford, 1959).

12 Frank E. Manuel, *The Eighteenth Century Confronts the Gods* (1959).

13 See *Gentleman's Magazine*, VIII (1738), 139, quoting the *Old Whig* for a comparative table of the effects of Superstition and Enthusiasm.

14 See James Buller, *Reply to the Rev. Mr. Wesley's Address to the Clergy* (1756), p. 24.

15 Knox, *Enthusiasm*, p. 356. He describes the word in its historical sense as a 'cant term', 'pejorative', 'commonly misapplied' (p. 1).

16 P. G. Rogers, *The Fifth Monarchy Men* (1966). Quotations seriatim from the preface and pp. 28, 36, 95.

17 Michael Walter, *The Revolution of the Saints* (1966), pp. 12, 306, 320.

18 Norman Cohn's *The Pursuit of the Millennium* (1957) uses the set, but nowhere clearly in the technical sense, as might be expected from the subject-matter.

19 Warren Derry, *Dr. Parr: the Whig Dr. Johnson* (1966), p. xiii, inverted commas adjusted.

20 *ibid.* p. 166.

21 C. M. Webster, 'Swift and some Earlier Satirists of Puritan Enthusiasm', *P.M.L.A.*, XLVIII (1933), 177.

22 Webster, 'Swift's *Tale of a Tub* compared with Earlier Satires on the Puritans', *P.M.L.A.*, XLVII (1932), 177.

23 *ibid.* p. 177.

24 A. Calder-Marshall, *The Enthusiast* (1962), p. 291.

25 *ibid.* p. 174.

26 Laurence Sterne, Sermon XXXVIII, in *Letters and Sermons*, ed. D. Herbert (1872).

27 Robert Blake, *Disraeli* (1966), p. 510, quoting from *Letters of Queen Victoria*, 2nd Series, ed. G. E. Buckle, 1 (1926), 550.
28 Blake, *Disraeli*, p. 745.
29 *ibid.* p. 503.
30 Benjamin Disraeli, *Sybil* (1845), World's Classics edn, p. 255.
31 *ibid.* p. 344.
32 Disraeli, *Coningsby* (1844), Chiltern Library edn, p. 109.
33 *ibid.* p. 256.
34 *Sybil*, p. 45.
35 *ibid.* p. 178.
36 William Cobbett, *Rural Rides* (1830), Everyman edn, I, 42.
37 *ibid.* pp. 130–1.
38 M. A. Hopkins, *Hannah More and her Circle* (1947), ch. xx.
39 In chapter v.
40 A. Fleishman, *A Reading of 'Mansfield Park'* (1967).
41 End of chapter xi.

CHAPTER 2, pp. 14–25

1 *Gent. Mag.*, LXIV (1794), 20.
2 Anthony Ashley Cooper, Third Earl of Shaftesbury, *Characteristicks of Men, Manners, Opinions, Times* (2nd edn, 1714), I, 52.
3 John Wesley, *Sermon on Enthusiasm* (1750), Sermon XXXII in *Standard Sermons*, ed. E. H. Sugden (1921), II, 33–4.
4 Daniel Defoe, *The Review*, VIII, 94. In its Greek form it was applied to the Anabaptists by Erasmus in 1535 (see P. S. and H. M. Allen, *Opus Epistolarum Des. Erasmi Roterodami*, 1936 (vol. XI, 1534–6)).
5 James Usher, *Clio* (1767), 1778 edn, p. 243.
6 Thomas Blount, *Glossographia* (1656), s.v. *O.E.D.* doubts whether any such sect was so called, but most people thought it the right word for those holding such ideas.
7 Edward Coles, *English Dictionary* (1696), s.v. *Enthusion* appears to be an error for *Enthusian* (*O.E.D.*).
8 The Cocker Dictionary was a bookseller's compilation.
9 Nathaniel Bailey, *Universal Etymological Dictionary* (1721). His indebtedness to Blount and Phillips is obvious.
10 Thomas Dyche and William Pardon, *A New General English Dictionary* (2nd edn, 1744). The syntax seems confused.
11 Benjamin Martin, *Lingua Britannica Reformata, or A New English Dictionary* (1749).

12 [John Wesley] *The Complete English Dictionary* (1764). The work was originally anonymous, but see G. H. Vallins, *The Wesleys and the English Language* (1957), ch. 2, for the authorship.

13 Samuel Johnson, *Dictionary of the English Language* (1755). William Kenrick's Dictionary (1773) lifts Johnson word for word. Sheridan in 1780 is equally indebted. In 1775, John Ash's Dictionary defines *Enthusiast* in Johnson's last sense, putting his first as an alternative, which suggests a change of emphasis.

14 Quoted in *Gent. Mag.*, v (1735), 203.

15 Johannes Stinstra, *An Essay on Fanaticism*, tr. from the French version of the Dutch by Isaac Subremont (1744).

16 James Lackington, *Memoirs* (1791), 13th edn, 1810, p. 138.

17 Thomas Ludlam, *Four Essays* (1797), essay IV, p. 68.

18 Samuel Taylor Coleridge, *Philosophical Lectures* (1819), ed. E. J. K. Coburn (1949), lecture XI, p. 327. Jakob Böeme (1575–1624) was earlier known in English as Behmen.

19 Coleridge, *The Friend*, ed. Barbara Rooks (1969), I, 432. The periodical was launched in 1809, rewritten and published in book form in 1818.

20 *Critical Review*, 28 (1769), 243.

21 Joseph Entwistle, *Letter to the Author of an Anonymous Treatise on Inspiration* (1799), inverted commas adjusted.

22 Quoted in James Beattie, *London Diary* (1773), 24 Aug. 1773.

23 William Duff, *Essay on Original Genius* (1767), pp. 169–70.

24 Shaftesbury, *Characteristicks*, 'Letter Concerning Enthusiasm', sect. VII.

25 Defoe, *The Review*, VIII, 94.

26 Isaac Taylor, *The Natural History of Fanaticism* (1833), p. 27.

27 Charles Chauncy, *A Caveat against Enthusiasm: Enthusiasm described and caution'd against* (1742), p. 3.

28 Clarendon's *History of the Rebellion* (1702–4), 1888 edn, book XVI, sect. 88.

29 [William Tong] *The Nature and Consequences of Enthusiasm Consider'd* (2nd edn, 1720), pp. 8–9.

30 *ibid.* p. 10.

31 R. G. Robinson, *Definition* (Oxford, 1950).

32 C. L. Stevenson, *Language and Ethics* (Yale, 1944).

CHAPTER 3, pp. 26–38

1 Milton's *Works* (Columbia edn, 1932), VII, 186. He also calls the 'millenarian sectaries' *Fanaticos* in this work (it was rendered 'Fantastic Enthusiasts' by John Lilburne), *ibid*. I, 332.

2 *ibid*. VIII, 80.

3 Richard Montagu, *Acts and Monuments of the Church* (1642).

4 Daniel Featley, *The Dippers Dipt: or the Anabaptists Duck'd and Plung'd* (1645), 5th edn, 1647, p. 3.

5 *ibid*. p. 105.

6 Casaubon, *A Treatise*.

7 *ibid*. p. 6.

8 *ibid*. p. 10.

9 Henry Hammond, *A Paraphrase and Annotations upon all the Books of the New Testament* (1653), 1657 edn, p. viii.

10 *ibid*. p. xi.

11 M[artin] M[adan], *A Full and Compleat Answer to the Capital Errors, Contained in the writings of the late Rev. William Law* (1763), A4, vi.

12 Samuel Parker, *A Discourse of Ecclesiastical Politics* (1670), p 58.

13 *ibid*. p. 74.

14 John Owen, Πνευματολογία: *or, a discourse concerning the Holy Spirit* (1674), p. 157.

15 *ibid*. p. 270.

16 William Hubbard, *The Present State of New England*, pt. II (1677), p. 61. Hubbard has more respect for etymology than Casaubon (see above, p. 26).

17 William Darrel, *A Vindication of Saint Ignatius*... (1688), pp. 2–3.

18 Henry Wharton, *The Enthusiasm of the Church of Rome* (1688), p. 9. Cp. Addison's disappointed English Merchant who was resolved 'to turn Quaker or Capuchin' (*Remarks on Several Parts of Italy, etc.* (1741 edn), p. 293).

19 Wharton, *op. cit.* p. 15.

20 *ibid*. p. 16.

21 *ibid*. p. 17.

22 *ibid*. p. 20. A favourite example. John Wesley disagreed, and was taken to task by Warburton (Warburton, *Works* (1788), IV, 661).

23 Thomas D'Urfey, *The Modern Prophets* (1709), fol. A2 *verso*.

24 *ibid*. p. 43.

25 Wharton, *op. cit.* p. 43.
26 George Lavington, *Enthusiasm of Methodists and Papists Compar'd*, I (1749), 8.
27 *ibid.* pref. A1.
28 George Hickes, *The Spirit of Enthusiasm Exorcised* (1680), p. 44.
29 *ibid.* p. 72.
30 William Stukeley, *Stonehenge* (1740), pref. section VII.
31 Thomas Pittis, *A Discourse Concerning the Trial of Spirits* (1682), p. 16.
32 *ibid.* p. 345.
33 Hickes, *Ravillac Redivivus* (1678), 2nd edn, 1682, p. 2.
34 John Locke, *Essay concerning Humane Understanding* (1690). Part IV, 19 added in 1700.
35 *ibid.* p. 7.
36 Henry Sacheverell, *Perils of False Brethren* (1709), p. 12.
37 *ibid.* p. 30.
38 *A Dissuasive against Enthusiasm* (1708), p. 84.
39 Anthony Collins, *Scheme of Literal Prophesy Considered* (1727), p. 111.
40 Samuel Clarke, *A Discourse concerning the Being and Attributes of God* (1705–6), 5th edn corrected, 1719, II, 294.
41 *Extracts of Letters relating to Methodists and Moravians* (1745).
42 *Letter to the Rev. Mr. Whitefield* (1739). Cp. Thomas Sheridan, 'the spleen, hypocrisy and enthusiasm of Calvinism' (1754), quoted in *Swift, The Critical Heritage*, ed. Kathleen Williams (1970), p. 228.
43 Wesley, *Letter to the Author of Methodists and Papists Compar'd* (1749), I, ii, 49–50.
44 Warburton applies the terms freely to Wesley and his followers in *The Doctrine of Grace* (1762).
45 Henry Brooke, *The Fool of Quality* (1766). See the review in *Monthly Review*, XLII (1770), 330.
46 T. Coke and H. Moore, *The Life of the Rev. John Wesley, A.M.* (1792), p. 337.
47 *ibid.* p. 347.
48 *ibid.* p. 341. Cp. Lady Hesketh, writing to John Johnson about William Cowper: 'It is my wish that...nothing should be brought forward that should cause him to be considered as a Visionary! an Enthusiast! or a Calvinist! for I am very sure he was neither' (Catherine B. Johnson, *Letters of Lady Hesketh to John Johnson* (1901), p. 114). Wesley warned: 'If you preach doctrine only, the

people will be antinomians: if you preach experience only, they will become enthusiasts' (quoted in Franz Hildebrandt, *Christianity according to the Wesleys* (1956), p. 12).

49 William Magee, *Discourses* (1809), I, 155n.

50 Chauncy, *Seasonable Thoughts on the State of Religion in New England* (1743), p. 189.

51 *ibid.* p. iii.

52 *ibid.* p. 209.

53 Cp. Thomas Clerk's edn of Hogarth's *Works* (1810), which comments on the plate 'Credulity, Superstition and Fanaticism' that 'the annals of our time have furnished melancholy proof of credulity and enthusiasm' (I, 192). It is interesting that Clerk uses the word that Hogarth might have used, but did not.

54 Edward Ryan, *The History of the Effects of Religion on Mankind* (3rd edn 'enlarged', 1806), pp. 346, 360, 364.

55 *ibid.* p. 448.

56 J. Trenchard and T. Gordon, *The Independent Whig* (1720-1), collected edn, 1732, p. 283.

57 John Leland, *A View of the Principal Deistical Writers* (1754), p. 2.

58 *ibid.* p. 129.

59 Robert Burns, *Letters*, ed. J. de L. Ferguson (1931), p. 18.

60 *ibid.* p. 106.

61 Laurence Brander, *George Orwell* (1954), p. 95.

CHAPTER 4, pp. 39-51

1 *British Journal* (1724), 'Advertisement' (i.e. preface).

2 *ibid.* p. 17.

3 *ibid.* p. 15.

4 *ibid.* p. 6.

5 Edward Young, 'Night Six', in *Night Thoughts* (1742), 1758 edn, p. 128.

6 Warburton, *Doctrine of Grace, Collected Works*, ed. R. Hurd (1811), VIII, 306.

7 Richard Graves [of Ardagh], *Essay on the Apostles and Evangelists*, in *The Whole Works*, ed. R. H. Graves (1840). The *Essay* was first published in 1798.

8 Graves, *ibid.* p. ccxxv.

9   Warburton (*op. cit.* p. 307) says we can find 'none of that *shining light* ordained and employed to gild the *good works* of Grace, in the morals of innocent Enthusiasts'.

10 Graves, *op. cit.* p. ccxxviii. Thomas Hardy imagines that a modern crowd listening to St Paul would proclaim him 'An epilept enthusiast' ('In St Paul's a while ago', in *Collected Poems* (1965), p. 679). A compliment or not?

11 Graves, *op. cit.* p. ccxxix.

12 C. J. Abbey and J. H. Overton, *The English Church in the Eighteenth Century* (1878), p. 616.

13 William Melmoth, *Letters of Sir Thomas Fitzosborne on Several Subjects* (1737), letter I, 'Concerning Enthusiasm'.

14 Vicesimus Knox, *Christian Philosophy: Cautions Concerning Enthusiasm* (1795).

15 Wesley, *Sermon on Enthusiasm, passim.*

16 *ibid.* sect. 5.

17 *ibid.* sect. 7.

18 *ibid.* sect. 12. Cp. Hammond, *A Paraphrase*, p. 27 above.

19 Wesley, *op. cit.* sect. 8.

20 *ibid.* sect. 9.

21 *ibid.* sect. 10.

22 [John Douglas] *The Criterion: or, Miracles Examined* (1754), p. 8.

23 Lavington, *Enthusiasm*, II, 49.

24 Thomas Church, *Remarks on the Revd. Mr. Wesley's Last Journal* (1745), p. 60.

25 *Methodism Vindicated from the Charge of Ignorance and Enthusiasm* (1795), pp. 41–2.

26 Was it really a proverb? The *Oxford Book of English Proverbs* does not include it, and as the approving attitude to enthusiasm anywhere can have had only a century to grow, *epigram* might be a better word.

27 George F. Nott, *Religious Enthusiasm Considered* (1803). For his protest at linguistic misuse, see below, p. 131.

28 Nott, *op. cit.* p. 5.

29 *ibid.* p. 9.

30 *ibid.* p. 10.

31 *ibid.* p. 36.

32 *Impartial Reflections on what are termed Revivals of Religion* (1816), by 'a member of the Church of England', pp. 5, 15.

33 *Coleridge's Notes on English Divines*, ed. Derwent Coleridge (1853), II, 39–40. See also Coleridge, *Aids to Reflection* (1825), I, 353: '*fanaticism*, or as the Germans say Schwärmery, that is Swarm-making'. This is echoed by Carlyle, for whom see Appendix 2, pp. 167–8.

34 Coleridge, *The Statesman's Manual* (1816), I, 432.

35 *Aids to Reflection*, pp. 128, 353, 355 (*seriatim*).

36 *ibid.* p. 156.

37 W. Y. Tindall, *John Bunyan, Mechanick Preacher* (1934), 1964 edn, pp. 17, 43, 23, 210 (*seriatim*).

38 Or, like the translator of Friedrich Heer, *The Intellectual History of Europe*, use *Enthusiast* in the narrower sense, *enthusiast* in the wider. See below, p. 141.

39 W. E. Houghton, *The Victorian Frame of Mind 1830–1870* (1957).

40 *ibid.* p. 297, ch. 11 *passim*.

41 *Crit. Rev.*, 35 (1773), 232.

42 *op. cit.* n. arr. XIV (1795), 293.

43 *Month. Rev.*, XLVIII (1793), 515.

44 *Gent. Mag.*, LXI (1791), 938.

45 *ibid.* p. 255.

46 Alexander Gerard, *An Essay on Taste* (1759), p. 96.

47 Owen Ruffhead, *The Life of Alexander Pope, Esq.* (1769), p. 150.

48 Shaftesbury, *Characteristicks*, I, 13.

49 *Looker-On*, II (1793), 320.

50 *The World*, no. 79 (1754).

51 *Crit. Rev.*, 50 (1780), 302, quoting David Williams, *Lectures on the Universal Principles and Duties of Religion and Morality* (1779).

CHAPTER 5, pp. 52–61

1 John Langhorne, *Letters on Religious Retirement, Melancholy and Enthusiasm* (1762), letter v, p. 16. The usual view, frequent in Lavington; Thomas Green, in his *Dissertation on Enthusiasm* (1755), calls St Francis and St Ignatius Loyola 'ignorant' and 'mad'.

2 Quoted in *Crit. Rev.*, 41 (1776), 214.

3 *Month. Rev.*, VIII (1733), 125.

4 *The Book of Margery Kempe*, modernised by Col. W. Butler-Bowden (1936); E.E.T.S. edn by S. B. Meech and Hope E. Allen (Original Series 212), 1940.

5 *Gent. Mag.*, LIX (1789), 1025.

6 *Crit. Rev.*, 63 (1787), 187.

7 *op. cit.* 44 (1777), 168, quoting John Berkenhout's *Biographia Literaria*, vol. 1 (1777).

8 Stinstra, *Essay on Fanaticism*, p. 177.

9 *ibid.* p. 72.

10 Green, *Dissertation on Enthusiasm*, p. 26.

11 *Crit. Rev.*, 16 (1763), 203.

12 Warburton, *Doctrine of Grace* (1811 edn), p. 272 n.

13 *Month. Rev.*, XXIX (1764), 427.

14 *Crit. Rev.*, n. arr. III (1791), 52.

15 *London Magazine* (1768), p. 55.

16 *A Serious Address to Lay-Methodists, with an Appendix containing an Account of the Fatal, Bloody Effects of Enthusiasm*, 1745 [Zachary Grey].

17 *ibid.* p. 29.

18 *Crit. Rev.*, n. arr. X (1794), 207.

19 *Ann. Reg.*, VII (1764), 112.

20 Sylas Neville, *Diary*, ed. B. Cozens-Hardy (1950), p. 145. Entry for 30 Dec. 1771.

21 Wesley's *Journal*, ed. N. Curnock (1909–16), entry for 25 March 1753.

22 Addison, in *Freeholder*, no. 326 (1716).

23 Thomas Warton, *Observations on the Faerie Queene* (1734), II, 236.

24 David Hume, essay V in *Essays, Political and Moral* (1742).

25 *Ann. Reg.*, XII (1769), quoting William Robertson's *History of the Reign of Charles V* (1769). Cp. Cohn, *Pursuit of the Millennium* (Paladin edn, 1970), p. 270. The Münster sect adopted polygamy, and ended with 'near-promiscuity', the result of John of Leyden's persuasions.

26 *Gent. Mag.*, VII (1737), 458.

27 Richard Baxter, *The Certainty of the Worlds of Spirits* (1691), p. 178.

28 *ibid.* p. 179.

29 Chauncy, *Seasonable Thoughts* (1743).

30 *ibid.* p. vi.

31 *ibid.* p. ii.

32 *ibid.* p. 7.

33 *ibid.* p. 3.

34 Philip Doddridge, *Some Remarkable Passages in the Life of the Honourable Colonel James Gardiner* (1747), p. 137.

35 Richard Hill, *A Lash at Enthusiasm*, quoting from the 2nd edn 'enlarged', 1778.

36 J. W. Fletcher, *Logica Genevensis, or a Fourth Check to Antinomianism* (1772), p. 63 n.

37 John Hildrop, *Reflections upon Reason* (1722), 3rd edn 'corrected and enlarged', 1729, p. 132.

38 Taylor, *Fanaticism*, p. 33. Cp. W. L. Brown, *Essay on the Folly of Scepticism* (1788), p. 91: 'As bigots have cant words and phrases which they continually introduce, so also have infidels.' *Enthusiasm*; *Fanaticism* and *Priestcraft* are his examples.

CHAPTER 6, pp. 62–68

1 Jonathan Boucher, *On Schisms and Sects* (1769), p. 77.

2 Samuel Wesley Jr, verses to Charles Wesley, quoted in Coke and Moore, *Life of Wesley*, p. 62.

3 Green, *Dissertation on Enthusiasm*, p. 41.

4 Daniel Waterland, *Doctrine of the Eucharist* (1737), p. 16.

5 Shaftesbury, *Characteristicks*, I, 18.

6 Lavington, *Enthusiasm*, pref. A1.

7 George, Baron Lyttelton, *Dialogues of the Dead* (1760), no. XXIV, p. 21.

8 Defoe, *The Review*, II, 38.

9 Soames Jenyns, *Works* (1790), IV, 152.

10 *Crit. Rev.*, 15 (1763), 298.

11 *op. cit.* 13 (1762), 270.

12 *Gent. Mag.*, LXIX (1799), 1064.

13 Edwin Honig, *Dark Conceit: The Making of Allegory* (1966), p. 79.

14 Lavington, *The Moravians Compared and Detected* (1755), pp. 37–8.

15 Coke and Moore, *Life of Wesley*, p. 392.

16 Johnson's Dictionary, s.v.

17 Dyche and Pardon's Dictionary, s.v.

18 G. F. Wenderborn, *A View of England* (1791), II, 316, 318.

19 Richard Graves [of Claverton], *Columella* (1779), II, 319.

20 Quoted in *Gent. Mag.*, XXVII (1758).

21 Lyttelton, *Dialogues of the Dead*, no. 1.

22 Orwell, *Nineteen Eighty-Four* (Penguin edn, 1952), pp. 21, 205, 245, 210, 169 *seriatim*.

23 Chauncy, *Seasonable Thoughts*, p. 17.

24 Wharton, *Enthusiasm of the Church of Rome*, unpaginated preface.

25 *An Historical Account of Montanism* (1709), p. 272.

26 *ibid.* p. xviii.

27 Archibald Campbell, *A Discourse Proving that the Apostles were no Enthusiasts* (1730), p. 3.

28 John Douglas, *An Apology for the Clergy* (1755), p. 2.

29 Ralph Heathcote, *A Sketch of Lord Bolingbroke's Philosophy* (1735), p. 21.

30 Robert Adams, *Ikon: John Milton and the Modern Critics* (1955), p. 184.

31 Marjorie H. Nicholson (ed.), *Conway Letters* (1930), p. 421. Cp. Addison, *Remarks on Italy*, p. 293, on Pietism.

32 Thomas Percival, *Moral and Literary Dissertations* (1734), no. IV, p. 124. Cp. Dr Johnson: 'persecutor and enthusiast' (Sermon XXIII, in *Works* (1825 edn), vol. IX).

33 More, *Enthusiasmus Triumphatus*, pref. A3 verso.

34 Burton, *Anatomy of Melancholy*, ed. A. R. Shilleto (1893), p. 393.

35 Sterne, Sermon XXXVII, in *Letters and Sermons*.

36 Lady Sarah Pennington, *An Unfortunate Mother's Advice to her Absent Daughter* (1761).

37 *Crit. Rev.*, n. arr. vol. XXIV (1798). Cp. monument to Margaret, Marchioness of Caernarvon, in Alvington Church, Winchester: 'Her life was one Scene of beneficent actions...Religious without Enthusiasm.' She died in 1768.

38 *Month. Rev.*, LIII (1775), 247.

39 *op. cit.* LXXX (1789), 386.

40 Nathaniel Forster, 'Grace without Enthusiasm: Sermon Preached at All Saints, Colchester, on Trinity Sunday, 1781'.

41 *Month. Rev.*, I (1749), 132.

42 *Brit. Crit.*, VII (1796), 127.

43 *Crit. Rev.*, 6 (1758), 86.

44 Wendeborn, *View of England*, II, 267.

45 Oliver Goldsmith, *Essays, Originally Published in the year 1765* (1854 edn), no. XV. Cp. Horace Walpole's often-quoted comment on Wesley's preaching: that he 'acted very ugly enthusiasm' (letter of 10 Oct. 1766).

CHAPTER 7(i), pp. 69–77

1 Jonathan Swift, *The Mechanical Operation of the Spirit* (1704), 5th edn, 1710, p. 312.

2 *ibid.* pp. 311–12. Cp. William Wotton's comment: 'Enthusiasm with him is an Universal Deception which has run through all

Sciences in all kingdoms and every thing has some Fanatic Branch annexed to it.' (Quoted in Williams, *Swift, The Critical Heritage*, p. 45.)

3   We may think *foible* or *craze* a better word. The poem is based on William Law's *Animadversions upon Dr. Trapp's Late Reply*...(1740).

4   John Byrom, Preface to *Enthusiasm: A Poetical Essay* (1757, but written some years earlier), in Chetham Society edn (1895), vol. II, pt. I, pp. 168–9. *Endemoniasm* is quoted only from Byrom by *O.E.D.* Warburton uses *Demonianism*, which is quoted only from him.

5   A reference to Warburton's *The Divine Legation of Moses*.

6   Byrom, *Enthusiasm*, l. 180.

7   *ibid.* ll. 224–34.

8   Quoted in Chetham Society edn of 1857, XLIV, 366. Warburton is writing to Hurd. Warburton and Byrom discussed the definition in an interchange of letters in 1752. Law joins in: for him, no secular enthusiasm can be innocent (*ibid.* p. 545).

9   Usher, *Clio*, p. 89.

10   *ibid.* pp. 99–100.

11   *ibid.* p. 113.

12   *ibid.* p. 121.

13   *ibid.* p. 127.

14   Jonathan Boucher, *A View of the Causes and Consequences of the American Revolution* (1797), p. 1 (sermons preached between 1763 and 1775).

15   *ibid.* p. liv.

16   Edmund Burke, *Reflections on the French Revolution* (1790), Everyman edn, pp. 316–17.

17   Burke, *Letters* (1797), World's Classics edn (1922), p. 412. It is ironic to find Horace Walpole delighting in the *Reflections*, because it contains 'Logic, wit, truth, eloquence, and enthusiasm in the brightest colours' (letter to Jerningham, 10 Nov. 1790).

Burke seems to have outgrown the views expressed in the essay (no. 16) in his Notebook of forty years earlier. Here Enthusiasm is 'an Instinct preferable to an inferior reason' (Burke's *Notebook*, ed. H. V. F. Somerset (1957), p. 68).

18   Hume, 'Autobiographical Letter of 1784' (in *Letters*, ed. J. Y. T. Grieg (1932), I, 17). The spelling suggests that the philosopher had little concern for convention.

19   Edward Jerningham, *Enthusiasm* (1789).

20 *Brit. Crit.*, IX (1797), 282.

21 *Crit. Rev.*, 67 (1790), 5.

22 John Lawson, *Lectures Concerning Oratory* (1758), 1759 edn, p. 12. Adam Smith agrees: see his *A History of Ancient Physics* in *Works* (1811 edn), V, 233.

23 *Month. Rev.*, LXXII (1785), 538.

24 Martin Madan, *Thelyphthora* (1780), I, 171.

25 *ibid.* p. 178.

26 *ibid.* p. 299.

27 *op. cit.* II, 94 n.

28 Dorothea Herbert, *Retrospections* (*c.* 1806), in reference to 1782.

29 Defoe, *Treatise concerning the Use and Abuse of the Marriage Bed* (1727), p. 2.

30 Francis Hutcheson, *On the Passions* (1728), 1730 edn, p. 98.

31 *ibid.* p. 110. 'Like mad' is now colloquial for 'in a spirit of ardent enthusiasm' (W. H. Collins, *A Third Book of English Idioms* (1960)), but we do not take the madness seriously.

32 Hutcheson, *op. cit.* p. 121.

33 Tobias Smollett, *Peregrine Pickle* (1751), ch. LXII.

CHAPTER 7 (ii), pp. 77–93

1 E. R. Dodds, *The Greeks and the Irrational* (1951), p. 80.

2 Jean Seznec, *Claudel and the Muses* (1950), p. 6.

3 *ibid.* p. 82.

4 Sylvester's list of 'Hardest Wordes' glosses his transliteration of ἐνθουσιασμός as 'poetical fury' (see above, p. 2). The word occurs in *The Furies*, l. 420.

5 James Howell, *Familiar Letters* (1628), 11th edn, 1744, p. 211.

6 Dryden, *Of Heroic Plays* (1672), Everyman edn, p. 90.

7 John Smith, *Select Discourses* (1659), quoting from the 1673 edn.

8 Robert Lowth, *The Sacred Poetry of the Hebrews* (1753), tr. from the Latin by George Gregory (1787), 1847 edn, p. 50. It is to be noted that in Lowth's original Latin text, *enthusiasm* appears in Greek letters. His Latin word is *afflatus*, cp. Ainsworth's English–Latin Dictionary (1773 edn), which gives *numinis afflatus*.

9 Lowth, *op. cit.* pp. 183–4. Wordsworth, *Preface to The Lyrical Ballads* (1815), takes up the same position as Lowth in Hebrew literature, cp. Murray Roston, *Prophet and Poet: The Bible and the Growth of Romanticism* (1965).

10 John Dennis, *Critical Works*, ed. E. N. Hooker, I (1939), 216. Text references refer to vol. I.

11 [J. Newbery] *The Art of Poetry on a New Plan* (1762), II, 357.

12 John Baillie, *Essay on the Sublime* (1749), p. 28.

13 Ruffhead, *Life of Pope*, p. 449.

14 Thomas Belsham, *Essays* (1789), p. 384.

15 *ibid.* p. 397. Cp. 'ardor animi' in D. G. Morhof, *De Enthusiasmo seu Furore Poetico* (1699), p. 76. See above, pp. 51, 66, for the usual connection with melancholy.

16 Lawson, *Oratory*, p. 77.

17 Abraham Rees, *The Cyclopaedia or Universal Dictionary of Arts, Sciences and Literature* (1819), s.v.

18 Zackary Mayne, *Two Dissertations concerning Sense and the Imagination, with an Essay on Consciousness* (1778), p. 197.

19 *Gent. Mag.*, VII (1737), 292.

20 *Month. Rev.*, LXV (1781), 15.

21 *op. cit.* LXXX (1789), 239.

22 West, letter to Walpole, 1 Dec. 1737.

23 Goldsmith, *Essays*, no. XV.

24 Edward Young, *On Lyric Poetry* (1728), see E. J. Morley's edn of *Conjectures on Original Composition* (1918), p. 59.

25 Ruffhead, *Life of Pope*, p. 439.

26 Samuel Parr, *Works*, ed. J. Johnstone (1828), p. 550.

27 Rees, *Cyclopaedia*, s.v.

28 *King Henry V*, III, i, 15–17.

29 Walter Pater, *The Renaissance, Studies in Art and Poetry* (1888), essay on Winckelmann.

30 Usher, *Clio*, p. 99.

31 Snorri Sturluson, *Skáldskaparmál*, ed. F. Jónsson (1900), pp. 71–3.

32 A. Jóhannesson, *Isländisches Etymologisches Wörterbuch* (1956), pp. 102, 288. It is glossed in Ainsworth's Dictionary (1773 edn) as '(1) A prophet or prophetess, (2) a poet or poetess, (3) an interpreter'.

33 Evans, *Modern Enthusiasm*, sect. I, 'Of Natural Enthusiasm'.

34 Richard Glover, *The Athenaid* (c. 1785), in Chalmers's *English Poets*, XVII, 83.

35 Evans, *op. cit.*

36 Casaubon, *A Treatise*, p. 141.

37 *ibid.* p. 203.

38 *ibid.* p. 144.

39 *ibid.* p. 145.

40 *ibid.* p. 187. Pindaric odes were given to enthusiasm. Cp. a note to Cowley's 'The Resurrection' (1700 edn), p. 84: 'This Ode is truly *Pindarical*, falling from one thing into another after his *Enthusiastical manner.*' Maren-Sophie Røstvig, *The Happy Man* (1962), I, 368, refers to Roscommon's 'Ode on Solitude', pointing out that its new enthusiastic manner is a consequence of its Pindaric form.

41 Thomas Rymer, *The Tragedies of the Last Age* (1678), p. 20.

42 Vicesimus Knox, *Essays, Moral and Literary* (1778), II, 380–1, essay CLXXVIII.

43 *ibid.* p. 396, essay CLVII.

44 *ibid.* p. 33, essay CLXVI.

45 *Crit. Rev.*, 68 (1789), 211.

46 Duff, *Original Genius*, pp. 96–7.

47 Graves, *Essay on the Apostles and the Evangelists* (1798), p. 95.

48 Halkett and Laing suggest that Blackmore might be the author; it is surely unlikely that he should have laughed at his own style. See Richard P. Bond, *English Burlesque Poetry, 1700–1750* (1964).

49 *The Flight of the Pretender* (1708), preface.

50 *ibid.* p. 3.

51 *ibid.* p. 7.

52 Whelan, *Enthusiasm in English Poetry of the Eighteenth Century*.

53 Melancholy is not necessarily the effect. Cp. Vicesimus Knox, who in the solitude of a friend's habitation enjoys 'the calm and rational pleasures of philosophy' and becomes 'enthusiastically fond of sequestration' (*Essays*, I, 139, essay XXIX). See also Harth, *Swift and Anglican Rationalism*, ch. 4.

54 Samuel Stennett, *Discourses on Personal Religion* (1709), p. 52.

55 Sir Uvedale Price, *An Essay on the Picturesque* (1794), 1796 edn, p. 115.

56 *Crit. Rev.*, 62 (1786), 321. See the note on 'Enthusiasm for Shakespeare', p. 92 above.

57 Vicesimus Knox, *Essays*, I, 256.

58 *Crit. Rev.*, 45 (1778), 241.

59 Ruffhead, *Life of Pope*, p. 174.

60 *ibid.* p. 15.

61 *ibid.* p. 79.
62 Joseph Spence, *Anecdotes*, ed. S. W. Singer (1820), p. 193.
63 Pope, letter of 5 Feb. 1731/2.
64 *Crit. Rev.*, 40 (1775), 469.
65 *op. cit.* 4 (1757), 166.
66 Nott, *Religious Enthusiasm Considered*, p. 12.
67 *ibid.* p. 39n.
68 Angus Fletcher, *Allegory* (1964), p. 245.
69 Nott, *op. cit.* p. 49n.
70 P. B. Shelley, *Preface to the Revolt of Islam* (1817).
71 William Hazlitt, 'On Poetry in General', in *Lectures on the English Poets* (1802).
72 M. W. England, *Garrick's Jubilee* (1964). The phrase is transferred from *Romeo and Juliet*, II, ii, 114. Cowper, *The Winter Walk at Noon*, applies it to Garrick himself (l. 667).
73 Vicesimus Knox, *Essays*, II, 143, essay CXVIII.
74 Boswell's *Life of Johnson*, II, 470.

CHAPTER 7(iii), pp. 93–106

1   Steffen, *Social Argument against Enthusiasm.*
2   *History of the Three Late Famous Impostors* (1669), pp. 41–2, quoted in Michael Fixler, *Milton and the Kingdoms of God* (1964), p. 247.
3   Hickes, *Ravillac Redivivus*, p. 26.
4   *ibid.* p. 70.
5   Henry Sacheverell, *The Political Union: a Discourse on Dependence of Government on Religion*, in *Sermons* (1702), p. 59. Warburton has similar views on the Methodists: 'But Enthusiasts, hurried on by the fervours of an inflamed fancy, lose the sight of a Christian Land, and a believing Magistrate... Under these delusions, it is no wonder they despise order, insult Government, and set their Rulers at defiance' (quoted in *Works* (1788), IV, 643).
6   D'Urfey, *Modern Prophets*, p. 72.
7   T. E. Owen, *Methodism Unmasked* (1802), pp. 112, 113.
8   Hildrop, *Reflections upon Reason*, p. 61.
9   See for example Evans, *Enthusiasm*, p. 23; cp. John Smith, *Select Discourses*, p. xxi.
10 Green, *Dissertation on Enthusiasm*, p. 44.
11 *ibid.* p. 84.

12 Gilbert Burnet the Younger in Ambrose Philips's *Free Thinker*, p.154. These essays are a detailed analysis of various types of Enthusiasm.

13 *ibid*. p. 157.

14 Sir William Temple, *Upon Heroick Virtue* (4th edn, 1696), sect. v, p. 257.

15 Johnson, *Journey to the Western Highlands*, ed. R. W. Chapman (1924), p. 6.

16 Evans, *Enthusiasm*, p. 55.

17 Pittis, *Trial of Spirits*, p. 138.

18 Warburton, *Doctrine of Grace*, in *Collected Works*, ed. R. Hurd (1811), VIII, 442.

19 'Junius', *Letters*, I, 271, apropos of Wilkes.

20 Burke, *Reflections*, pp. 144–5.

21 *Anti-Jacobin*, II (1798), 562.

22 W. Bagshaw Stevens, *Journal*, ed. Georgina Galbraith (1965), p. 51.

23 Oswald Doughty, *The English Lyric in the Age of Reason* (1922), p. 124.

24 *ibid*. p. 393.

25 Mr Heath received an 'enthusiastic welcome' from the Scottish Tories, according to the B.B.C. of 27 Jan. 1968. It is the normal phrase.

26 Hume, essay x, 'Of Superstition and Enthusiasm'.

27 John Brown, *Estimate of the Manners and Principles of the Times* (2nd edn, 1762), p. 90.

28 John Trenchard, *The Natural History of Superstition* (1709), p. 222.

29 Samuel Johnson, *Irene*, III, viii, 61. Cp. his comment about the 'ravages of religious enthusiasts, and the wars kindled by difference of opinions' (in Sermon XXIII, *Works*, IX, 499).

30 Burke, *Reflections*, p. 69.

31 *ibid*. p. 24.

32 Thomas Paine, speech of 7 July 1795, quoted in *Writings of Thomas Paine*, ed. M. D. Conway, III (1896), 284.

33 Burke, *Reflections*, p. 55.

34 *Month. Rev.*, XXXIV (1766), 22.

35 *Crit. Rev.*, 68 (1789), 114.

36 Boswell, letter of 28 Dec. 1764.

37 *Brit. Crit.*, XI (1798), 28.

38 *Crit. Rev.*, 57 (1784), 227.

39 *op. cit.* 69 (1790), 327.
40 Jerningham, *Enthusiasm*, l. 111.
41 *Lit. Mag.*, VI (1791), 302.
42 Vicesimus Knox, *Essays*, I, 53.
43 Wendeborn, *View of England*, I, 371.
44 *Anti-Jacobin*, II (1798), 31.
45 *ibid.* p. 64.
46 Jenyns, Preface to *Letters*, ed. Charles Nalson Cole (1790), III, 90.
47 John Shebbeare, *Letters on the English Nation* (1756), II, 182.
48 *Ann. Reg.* IX (1766), 174.
49 *Crit. Rev.*, n. arr. III (1791), 2.
50 Paine, *Rights of Man* (1791), Everyman edn, p. 30.
51 *Lit. Mag.*, VI (1791), 267.
52 Edward Gibbon, *Decline and Fall* (1776–8), World's Classics edn, I, 361.
53 *Looker-On*, II (1793), 31.
54 *Gent. Mag.*, LVI (1786), 124.
55 Neville, *Diary*, p. 3.
56 *ibid.* p. 69.
57 L. Dickins and M. Stanton, *An Eighteenth-Century Correspondence* (1910), p. 391.
58 Walpole, *Letters to Conway*, ed. P. Cunningham (1857–9), III, 138.
59 *Anti-Jacobin*, I (1797), 387.
60 *op. cit.* II (1798), 63.
61 *Gent. Mag.*, XXXVII (1768). Some recent research has tried to prove that she may have been an Enthusiast in the sense of a deluded believer in a fake inspiration.
62 Bernard de Mandeville, *Enquiry into the Origin of Honour, and the Usefulness of Christianity in War* (1732), p. 145.
63 Dennis, *Critical Works*, I, 387.
64 Clara Reeve, *The Progress of Romance* (1785), I, 98.
65 Heer, *Intellectual History*, tr. J. Steinberg, p. 450.
66 *ibid.* p. 405. Cp. Burke, p. 99 above.
67 Diana Spearman, *The Novel in Society* (1966), p. 210.
68 Hume, *Essays*, I, 50–1.

CHAPTER 7(iv), pp. 106–109

1 Henry Coventry, *Philemon to Hydaspes* (1736–44), quoting from 2nd edn, 1738.

2 *ibid.* pt. 1, pp. 7–8.

3 *ibid.* p. 41.

4 Orlando, the hero of *Tatler*, nos. 50 and 51 (1709), is described as 'an Enthusiast in Love'. It is obvious from the context that this means he was mad: 'we can't think it wonderful that *Orlando*'s repeated conquests touch'd his Brain' (*ibid.* no. 50).

5 Coventry, *op. cit.* p. 43.

6 *ibid.* p. 45.

7 See Peter Brown, *Augustine of Hippo* (1967), ch. 6. On the subject of Enthusiasm, Love and Religion, William Law is interesting: 'to appropriate Enthusiasm to Religion, is the same Ignorance of Nature, as it is to appropriate *Love* to Religion; for Enthusiasm, a kindled inflamed Spirit of Life, is as *common*, as *universal*, as *essential* to human Nature as *Love*; it goes into *every Kind* of Life as Love does, and has only such a variety of Degrees in Mankind as Love hath' (Law, *Collected Works* (1892–3 reprint), p. 197).

8 Coventry, *op. cit.* p. 55. Cp. Lavington's comments on the Moravians' hymns. According to Warburton, these were 'a heap of blasphemous and beastly nonsense' (*Works* (1788), IV, 626).

9 Coventry, *op. cit.* pp. 56–7.

10 *ibid.* p. 67.

11 *Crit. Rev.*, n. arr. XXVI (1799), 408.

12 *Gent. Mag.*, LXVI (1796), 371.

13 *The Amicable Quixote, or the Enthusiasm of Friendship* (1788), I, 16–17.

14 *ibid.* p. 11.

15 *ibid.* pp. 12–13.

16 *op. cit.* II, 145.

17 *ibid.* p. 197.

CHAPTER 7(v), pp. 110–115

1 *Crit. Rev.*, n. arr. XVI (1796), 257.

2 *Month. Rev.*, LXX (1784), 309.

3 *Gent. Mag.*, LIX (1789), 538.

4 *Month. Rev.*, LXVIII (1783), 232.

5 [J. Stedman] *Laelius and Hortensia* (1782), p. 422.

6 *Crit. Rev.*, 4 (1757), 183.

7   *op. cit.* 9 (1760), 500.
8   William Hogarth, *The Analysis of Beauty* (1753), p. 92.
9   *Crit. Rev.*, 70 (1790), 34.
10 *op. cit.* 28 (1769), 107.
11 *op. cit.* 59 (1785), 9.
12 Shebbeare, *Letters*, I, 19.
13 *Crit. Rev.*, n. arr. XI (1794), 517.
14 Neville, *Diary*, p. 153.
15 *Month. Rev.*, XXV (1762), I.
16 Archibald Alison, *An Essay on Taste* (1790), p. 45.
17 Melmoth, *Letters of Fitzosborne*, letter XX.
18 Note in *Crit. Rev.*, n. arr. IX (1793), 12.
19 *Gent. Mag.*, LXVII (1797), 1033.
20 *op. cit.* III (1733), 469.
21 Quoted in F. W. Hilles, *The Literary Career of Sir Joshua Reynolds* (1936), p. 226.
22 Price, *On the Picturesque*, p. 12.
23 *ibid.* p. 19.
24 Price, *On Architecture and Building* (1796), p. 269 n.
25 Alison, *On Taste*, p. 368.
26 Stedman, *Laelius and Hortensia*, p. 17.
27 Price, *On Architecture*, p. 265. The artist's name was usually half-anglicised at this time.
28 *Crit. Rev.*, 6 (1758), 424.
29 Lyttelton, *Dialogues of the Dead*, no. IX.
30 Lyttelton, *Persian Letters* (1735), letter LXX.
31 *Crit. Rev.*, 69 (1790), 272, quoting from Lavater's *Physiognomy* (1788–9).
32 *Month. Rev.*, LXV (1781), 216, re *Thoughts on Hunting*, in a series of Familiar Letters to a Friend, Salisbury, 1781.

CHAPTER 7 (vi), pp. 115–119

1   Alison, *On Taste*, p. 70.
2   *ibid.* p. 330.
3   Norton Nicholls, letter to Thomas Gray, 27 Nov. 1769.
4   Boswell, letter to John Johnston, 5 Dec. 1764 (quoted in F. A. Pottle, *Boswell, the Earlier Years* (1966), p. 174).
5   Pottle, *op. cit.* p. 47.

6   William Gilpin, *Observations on the Mountains and Lakes in Cumberland and Westmorland* (1786), II, 219, essay XXVIII, 'General Description of the Peak'.

7   Gilpin, *Essay on Picturesque Travel*, 1792). Cp. Smollett in *Humphry Clinker*, 1771 (World's Classics edn, p. 293), where Jery Melford says: 'I feel an enthusiastic pleasure when I survey the brown heath that Ossian was wont to tread.'

8   See Chalmers's *English Poets* (1787), XVII, 465.

9   Young, 'Night Ninth', in *Night Thoughts*, ll. 911–12. How are any sort of Heights *infused*?

10 Graves, *Columella*, II, 178.

11 Samuel Sharp, *Letters from Italy*, quoted in *Ann. Reg.* x (1767), 165.

12 *Crit. Rev.*, 69 (1790), 273.

13 *op. cit.* n. arr. XXII (1798), 375.

14 William Maton, *Observations relative chiefly to the Natural History . . . of the Western Counties . . .* (1797), I, 282–3.

15 Anne Radcliffe, *The Mysteries of Udolpho* (1794), Everyman edn, I, 2, 3, 6, 59, 119 *seriatim*.

16 Anthony Trollope, *The Eustace Diamonds* (1869–70), ch. XXI.

17 Thomas Hardy, 'Aberdeen' (April 1905), in *Time's Laughing Stocks* (1909).

CHAPTER 8, pp. 120–130

1   Glover, *Athenaid*, published 1787, in Chalmers, XVII, 97. It was written earlier, for Glover died in 1785.

2   *ibid.* p. 155.

3   Quoted in G. W. Gignilliat, *The Author of Sandford and Merton* (1952), p. 111.

4   G. W. H. Parker, *The Morning Star* (1965), p. 142.

5   *Anti-Jacobin*, I (1797), 91.

6   *ibid.* p. 196.

7   *ibid.* pp. 325–6.

8   Burke, *Reflections*, p. 70.

9   Adam Ferguson, *Essay on the History of Civil Society* (1767), 1773 edn, p. 127.

10 *Crit. Rev.*, n. arr. IV (1792), 355.

11 William Hayley, *Life of Milton* (1794), I, lxxiii, and *passim*.

12 Henry Fielding, *Joseph Andrews*, ch. 5. Cp. Byrom's use: 'foible' to us. (See p. 71 above.)

13 *Ann. Reg.*, IX (1766), 175, quoting from *Reflections on the general principles of war . . .* 'by a general officer who served campaigns in the Austrian army'.

14 *Crit. Rev.*, 52 (1781), 475.

15 *op. cit.* 64 (1787), 32.

16 Boswell, *Journal of a Tour to the Hebrides* (Chapman edn, 1924), p. 322 n.

17 Bagshaw Stevens, *Journal*, in reference to a concert held on 28 May 1792.

18 Joshua Reynolds, *Fifteen Discourses delivered at the Royal Academy, 1769–97* (Everyman edn), discourse II (1769), p. 19.

19 *ibid.* p. 28.

20 *ibid.* p. 14.

21 *ibid.* discourse VII (1776), p. 100.

22 Sidney Painter, *A History of the Middle Ages, 284–1500* (1953). Page references are given to the Papermac edn of 1964.

23 Cp. modern colloquial 'I've scorched the lawn by being over-enthusiastic with the weed-killer'. Marjorie Nicolson, *Voyages to the Moon* (1960), describes the seventeenth-century Duchess of Newcastle as an 'over-enthusiastic lady'. Her own age saw no need for the *over*. The compound is common enough now.

24 Jane Austen's *Letters* (Chapman edn), p. 135.

25 Burke, *Reflections*, p. 164.

26 *ibid.* p. 154.

27 Cp. Maton, *Observations relative to the Western Counties*, I, 42, where he describes a monastery of immigrant Trappists in Dorset whose situation 'cannot fail to foster that religious enthusiasm under the influence of which alone so singular an institution can continue to gain or preserve votaries'.

28 Burke, *Reflections*, p. 156.

29 F. W. Bradbrook, *Jane Austen and her Predecessors* (1966), p. 65.

30 Jane Austen's *Works* (Chapman edn), VI, 231.

31 *ibid.* p. 371.

32 *ibid.* pp. 429–30.

33 Harry T. Levin, *Christopher Marlowe* (1934), 1967 edn, p. 11.

34 Moody E. Prior, *The Language of Tragedy* (1947), 1960 edn, p. 18.

35 Norman Daniel, *Islam and the West* (1960), p. 301.

36 J. W. Gibbs, *Joseph Priestley* (1965), p. 134.

37 Quoted in *Medieval Miscellany in honour of Eugene Vinaver*, ed. F. Whitehead *et al.* (1965), p. 21.

38 C. Day Lewis, *The Lyric Impulse* (1965), p. 21.

39 Joseph Butler, *Analogy of Religion* (1736), in *Collected Works* (1874), VII, 203.

40 F. T. Wainwright, *Archaeology, Place-Names and History* (1962), p. 101. An early example of the scholarly suspicion of enthusiasm occurs in John Arbuthnot's *Essay in the Usefulness of Mathematical Learning* (1701), pp. 24–5: 'If *Mathematics* had not reduced *Musick* to a regular System, by contriving its *Scales*, it had been no Art, but Enthusiastic Rapture, left to the roving fancy of every practitioner.'

41 Wainwright, *op. cit.* p. 128.

42 W. J. Harvey, *The Art of George Eliot* (1963), p. 9.

43 *Middlemarch*, ch. 37.

44 M. C. Battestin (ed.), *Joseph Andrews and Shamela* (1961), p. xiv.

45 Adams, *Milton and Modern Critics*, p. 202.

46 W. A. Craik, *Jane Austen: The Six Novels* (1965), p. 7.

47 Daniel Waley, *Later Medieval Europe* (1964), p. 280.

48 E. M. W. Tillyard, *The Muse Unchained* (1958), p. 73.

49 Herbert Read, *The Forms of Things Unknown* (1960), p. 76.

50 N. Royde-Smith, *The State of Mind of Mrs Sherwood* (1946), p. 109.

51 Evelyn Underhill, *Worship* (1936), Fontana edn, 1962, p. 332.

52 *Methodist Recorder*, 31 March 1961.

53 J. A. Appleyard, *Coleridge's Philosophy of Literature* (1965), p. 1.

54 Houghton, *Victorian Frame of Mind*, p. 57.

55 G. R. Cragg, *Reason and Authority in the Eighteenth Century* (1964), p. 66.

56 Quoted by Bernetta Quinn, *The Metamorphic Tradition in Modern Poetry* (1955), p. 154.

57 *Anti-Jacobin*, II (1798), 279.

CHAPTER 9, pp. 131–133

1 Nott, *Religious Enthusiasm Considered*, p. 36n.

2 Taylor, *Enthusiasm*, p. iv.

2 *ibid.* p. 6.

4 *ibid.* pp. 16–17.

CHAPTER 10, pp. 134–143

1 A. McIntosh and M. A. K. Halliday, *Patterns of Language* (1966), p. 41.

2 William Morris, Preface to Kelmscott edn of More's *Utopia* (1893).

3 Waley, *Later Medieval Europe*, p. 280.

4 Ernest Bernbaum, *The Drama of Sensibility* (1938), p. 140.

5 René Wellek, *History of Modern Criticism* (1955), vol. I, *The Later Eighteenth Century*, pp. 179, 178.

6 *ibid.* p. 152.

7 Cragg, *Reason and Authority*, p. 66.

8 *ibid.* p. 265.

9 *ibid.* p. 271.

10 *ibid.* p. 242.

11 H. R. Steeves, *Before Jane Austen* (1966), p. 243.

12 Which is the 'peculiar character' of enthusiasm, according to Richard Graves (*Essay*, p. 3).

13 Herbert Read, *Reason and Romanticism* (1926), reprinted in *Poetry and Experience* (1967), p. 100.

14 Contrast Painter, *History of the Middle Ages* and Waley, *Late Medieval Europe*.

15 Germaine Dempster, preface to *Dramatic Irony in Chaucer* (1932), reprint 1959.

16 J. W. Johnson, *The Formation of English Neo-Classical Thought* (1967), pp. 242–3.

17 B.B.C. 'Ten O'Clock', 3 May 1967.

18 *ibid.* 29 September 1967.

19 B.B.C. Home Service talk, 7 September 1967. It does not follow that the teacher would, or should, agree.

20 Donald J. Greene, *The Politics of Samuel Johnson* (1960), p. 17.

21 Review of F. M. Cornford, *The Unwritten Philosophy and Other Essays* (1950) in *The Times Weekly*.

22 Henry James, *Portrait of a Lady* (1887), Penguin Modern Classics edn, pp. 415, 401.

23 J. Wildeblood and P. Brinson, *The Polite World* (1965), p. 47.

24 C. S. Parker, *Sir Robert Peel from his Private Papers* (1899), II, 99.

25 Henry Cockburn, *Memorials of his Time* (1910), p. 227.

26 Shaftesbury, *Characteristicks*, III, 37.

27 See Whelan, *Enthusiasm in English Poetry*, p. 29.

28 William Falconer, 'The Demagogue', 1764, quoted from *Cooke's Pocket Edition of the Original and Complete Works of Select British Poets* (n.d.), p. 93.

29 Hester Chapone, *Miscellanies* (1775), 1807 edn, p. 45.

30 Shaftesbury, *Characteristicks*, I, 55.

31 R. W. Emerson, *Works* (1891), II, 230.

32 B.B.C. 'Today in the West', 12 July 1967.

33 *ibid.* 30 May 1967.

34 B.B.C. 'West of England News', 3 June 1967.

35 *Radio Times*, 4 January 1968.

36 B.B.C. 'Today', 5 May 1965.

37 *ibid.* 6 May 1965.

38 B.B.C. 'West of England News', 24 June 1965.

39 See The Railway Enthusiasts of Great Britain (High Wycombe branch), *The Railway Enthusiast's Guide* (ed. P. M. E. Etwood, 1960); *The Railway Enthusiast's Bedside Book* (ed. H. A. Vaillance, 1966); *The Railway Enthusiast's Handbook* (1967).

40 B.B.C. 'Home This Afternoon', 20 May 1969.

41 Fanny Burney, *Diary*, 3 December 1785.

42 Heer, *Intellectual History of Europe*, p. 378.

43 *ibid.* p. 353.

44 W. F. and E. S. Friedman, *The Shakespearean Ciphers Examined* (1957), p. 154.

45 In *Restoration and Eighteenth-Century Literature*, ed. Carroll Camden (1963), p. 323.

46 Marjorie Nicolson and Nora M. Mohler, 'The Scientific Background', in A. Norman Jeffares (ed.), *Fair Liberty was All his Cry* (1967), p. 250. This collection was published for the Swift Tercentenary.

47 See Camden, *op. cit.* p. 9.

48 In Jeffares, *op. cit.* p. 343.

49 W. F. Wright, *Sensibility in English Prose Fiction, 1760–1814* (1937), p. 32.

50 Samuel Johnson, *Plan of an English Dictionary* (1747), Murphy's edn, 1816, p. 14.

51 I. M. L. Hunter, *Memory* (1957), Penguin edn, 1966, p. 293.

52 For example in F. A. M. L. Cazamian, *The Development of English Humour* (1952), p. 113.

53 Thomas Hardy, *The Dynasts*, pt. I, act I, sc. viii (1894 edn, p. 173).
54 J. V. Logan *et al.*, *Some British Romantics* (1966), p. 163.
55 J. H. Gardiner, G. L. Kittredge and S. L. Arnold, *A Manual of Composition and Rhetoric* (1907).
56 I. A. Richards, *The Philosophy of Rhetoric* (1936), p. 57.
57 W. E. Peck, *Shelley, his Life and Works* (1927), I, 38.
58 J. W. Saunders, *The Profession of Letters* (1964), p. 237.

CHAPTER II, pp. 144–161

1 Common in Rolle of Hampole, though regarded with some reserve by the author of *The Cloud of Unknowing*. See references in Hope E. Allen's edn of *English Writings of Richard Rolle, Hermit of Hampole* (1931), p. 140.
2 John, Earl of Cork and Orrery, *Remarks on the Life and Writings of Dr Jonathan Swift* (1751), 3rd edn, 1752.
3 Paul Fussell, *The Rhetorical World of Augustan Humanism* (1965), p. 107.
4 *Crit. Rev.*, n. arr. III (1791), 300.
5 Lavington, *Enthusiasm of Methodists and Papists*, II, 79.
6 Warburton, *Doctrine of Grace* (1811 edn, p. 272 n.).
7 Trenchard, *Natural History of Superstition*, p. 213.
8 Green, *Dissertation on Enthusiasm*, pp. 28, 43, 58.
9 Douglas, *The Criterion: or, Miracles Examined*, pp. 175, 172.
10 Green, *op. cit.* p. 81.
11 *Reflections upon a Letter Concerning Enthusiasm*, pp. 3, 9.
12 Quoted in *Brit. Crit.*, VIII (1797), 283, from Knox's *Christian Philosophy*.
13 Lavington, *op. cit.* III, 20.
14 Roberts Moss, *Sermons and Discourses on Practical Subjects* (1733), V, 398, sermon XIII, 'The Danger of Quenching the Spirit'.
15 Gibbs, *Joseph Priestley*, p. 80.
16 Joseph Trapp, *The Nature, Folly, Sin and Danger of being Righteous over-much* (1739), 3rd edn, 1739, pp. 39, 65, 61.
17 Taylor, *Enthusiasm*, p. 191.
18 Chauncy, *A Caveat against Enthusiasm*, p. 15.
19 Byrom, *Enthusiasm*, p. 1.
20 Taylor, *op. cit.* pp. 175, 11.
21 Asa Briggs, *Victorian People* (1955), Penguin edn, 1965, p. 108.

22 Evans, *History of Modern Enthusiasm*, p. xxii. She was still 'this enthusiast' for the Chetham Society editor of Byrom in 1854 (*Remains*, vol. I, pt. i, 283 n. 3).

23 Hickes, *Spirit of Enthusiasm Exorcised*, Epistle Dedicatory. Cp. Warburton (*Works*, IV, 703), who notes that 'a Poet is an Enthusiast in jest' and that Law proves that 'an Enthusiast may be a Poet in good earnest'.

24 Green, *op. cit.* p. 57.

25 Thomas Adams, *The Divill's Banket* (1614), p. 328.

26 William Blake, letter to Hayley, 23 Oct. 1804 (in Geoffrey Keynes, Nonesuch edn, 1927, p. 1109, 1957 edn, p. 852).

27 James Downey, *The Eighteenth-Century Pulpit* (1969), p. 13.

28 Morhof, *Dissertationes Academicae* (1699), p. 76.

29 Denis Diderot, *Encyclopédie ou Dictionnaire Raisonné des Sciences, des Arts et des Métiers* (1755), s.v. *Enthousiasme* (in *Philosophie et Belles-Lettres* volume).

30 Jerningham, *Enthusiasm.*

31 Diderot, *op. cit.*

32 Young, *On Original Composition*, p. 23.

33 Gerard, *Essay on Genius* (1758), p. 67.

34 Wesley, Sermon XXXII.

35 *Crit. Rev.*, n. arr. VIII (1792), 260.

36 *op. cit.* VI (1790), 409.

37 [Thomas Mortimer] *Die and be Damned* (1758), 3rd edn, 1761, p. 25. Cp. Thomas Hardy on the crowd's 'hot enthusiasms', *The Dynasts*, pt. I, act I, sc. ii (1894 edn, p. 14).

38 P. Hodgart and T. Redpath, *Romantic Perspectives* (1964), p. 36.

39 Stinstra, *Essay on Fanaticism.*

40 Briggs, *Victorian People*, p. 87.

41 Gibbs, *Joseph Priestley*, p. 12.

42 Trenchard, *Natural History of Superstition*, p. 222.

43 Burke, *On Conciliation with America*, in *Speeches and Letters on American Affairs* (1775), Everyman edn, p. 87.

44 Burke, *Reflections*, p. 267.

45 Quoted from Wrangham, 1879, in Hodgart and Redpath, *op. cit.* p. 215.

46 *Voluspá*, st. 57, aldrnari, quoting from E. V. Gordon's *Introduction to Old Norse* (1956), p. 20.

47 Briggs, *op. cit.* p. 241.

48 Graves, *Essay*, p. 130.

49 E. J. Sweeting, *Early Tudor Criticism* (1940), p. xiii.
50 Parker, *The Morning Star*, p. 134.
51 *Objections to Humanism*, ed. H. J. Blackham (1963), Pelican edn, 1965, p. 27.
52 Sweeting, *op. cit.* p. 171.
53 John Douglas, *An Apology for the Clergy* (1755), p. 34. Cp. the modern contrast between 'true fire' and 'random enthusiasm' in A. W. Hoffman's discussion, *John Dryden's Imagery* (1962), p. 182.
54 Burnet in *Free Thinker*, 96 (coll. edn, 1722), 291.
55 *An Answer to the Letter of Enthusiasm* (1724), p. 29.
56 Trapp, *Of being Righteous over-much*, p. 68.
57 Trenchard, *Natural History of Superstition* (3rd edn, 1739), p. 65.
58 Warburton, *Doctrine of Grace* (1811 edn, p. 259).
59 Green, *Dissertation on Enthusiasm*, p. 118.
60 Wesley, quoted in Coke and Moore, *Life*, p. 454.
61 Burke, *Reflections*, p. 62.
62 R. H. C. Davis, *A History of Medieval Europe* (1938), 1964 edn, p. 353.
63 Pittis, *Discourse concerning Trial of Spirits*.
64 Law, *An Earnest and Serious Answer to Dr Trapp's Late Reply* (1740), in *Works* (1893 edn), p. 199.
65 *Letter of Enthusiasm* (1723), quoted in *An Answer to the Letter of Enthusiasm*, pp. 31–40; see note 55 above. Cp. Edward Stillingfleet, *Irenicon* (1661), 1709 edn, p. 215, which speaks of '*earthquakes* and *convulsions* of enthusiastic origin'.
66 Painter, *History of the Middle Ages*, p. 357.
67 *ibid.* p. 332.
68 Pater, *The Renaissance*, essay on Winckelmann.
69 Doughty, *English Lyric in the Age of Reason*, p. 443.
70 Cockburn, *Memorials*, p. 260.
71 *ibid.* p. 293.
72 Quoted in T. G. Edelstein, *Strange Enthusiasm* (1968), a life of Thomas Wentworth Higginson.
73 C. Winton, *Captain Steele* (1964), p. 41. This lacks the overtones of Cockburn's description of Mrs Grant.
74 M. R. Ridley, *Second Thoughts* (1965), p. 113.
75 *Studies in Honor of T. W. Baldwin* (1958), ed. D. C. Allen, p. 196.
76 Samuel Beckett, *Malone Dies*. The original French is: 'je mourrai tiède, sans enthousiasme' (Les editions de menuit (1951), p. 8).

77 Taylor, *Enthusiasm*, p. 17.

78 *Die and be Damned*, p. 43.

79 Thomas Morgan, *The Absurdity of Opposing Faith to Reason...* (1722).

80 Graves, *Essay*, p. 216. Cp. Irvin Ehrenpreis's comment in 1962 that to Swift the enthusiasms of 'half-baked experimenters' would seem 'a jungle' (*Swift, the Man, his Works and the Age*, vol. 1, *Mr Swift and His Contemporaries* (1962), 85).

81 Evans, *History of Modern Enthusiasm*, p. xiii.

82 Goldsmith, *Essays*, essay XI.

83 Chauncy, *Seasonable Thoughts*, p. 217.

84 Church, *Remarks on Wesley's Last Journal*, p. 4.

85 Chauncy, *A Caveat Against Enthusiasm*, p. 27.

86 B. Blackstone, *The Lost Travellers* (1962), p. 273.

87 A. G. L'Estrange, *Life of Mary Russell Mitford* (1870), I, 257. She is deploring Maria Edgeworth's lack of appreciation for this quality.

88 Nott, *Religious Enthusiasm Considered*, p. 258.

89 *Methodism Vindicated*, p. 45.

90 Parker, *The Morning Star*, p. 115.

91 D. J. Palmer, *The Rise of English Studies* (1965), p. 111. Cp. 'the current of uncritical enthusiasm', R. H. Fletcher, *The Arthurian Material in the Chronicles* (1958), p. 182.

92 John Tulloch, *Rational Theology in England in the XVIIth Century* (1872), p. 17.

93 In *An Account of New England* (1746), quoted by Green, *Dissertation on Enthusiasm*, p. 184.

94 Swift, *Tale of a Tub* (1704), 5th edn, 1710, p. 182.

95 Thomas Taylor, *An Essay on the Beautiful: From the Greek of Plotinus* (1792), pp. xviii, xix.

96 More kindly is the view that we should not be surprised if student enthusiasm sometimes 'bubbles over' into protest (sermon, 1969).

97 Swift's *Works*, ed. Temple Scott (1897–1908), VI, 95.

98 Thomas Sprat, *History of the Royal Society* (1667), 1702 edn, p. 70.

99 Shaftesbury, *Characteristicks*, III, 29.

100 Melmoth, *Letters of Fitzosborne*, letter I.

101 *Crit. Rev.*, 10 (1762), 207.

102 Chapman, Introduction to Jane Austen's *Letters*, p. xiii.

103 *Looker-On* (1793), p. 256.

104 *Methodism Vindicated*, p. 45.

105 Owen, *Methodism Unmasked*, p. 13.

106 Reeve, *Progress of Romance*, I, 52. Cp. *Crit. Rev.*, 12 (1761), 140: 'a mysterious veil of superstition and enthusiasm'.

107 Quoted in Coke and Moore, *Life of Wesley*, p. 345.

108 Quoted in Williams, *Swift: The Critical Heritage*, p. 227.

109 Quoted in F. L. Lucas, *The Art of Living* (1959), p. 263.

110 Warburton, Introduction to *Julian* (*Works*, VII, xiii).

111 Burnet, *Free Thinker* (1722), essay 83, p. 195. On the authorship problems, see Richard P. Bond, *Studies in the Early English Periodical* (1957).

112 Melmoth, *op. cit.* letter I.

113 Chauncy, *A Caveat against Enthusiasm*, p. 14. See C. H. Dodd, *The Epistle of Paul to the Romans* (Fontana edn, 1959), p. 175.

114 Charles Leslie, *The Snake in the Grass* (1696), p. xcvi.

115 John Scott, *The Christian Life* (1681), 3rd edn corrected, 1684, Epistle Dedicatory to Henry, Lord Bishop of London.

116 Douglas, *Apology for the Clergy*, p. 2.

117 George Campbell, *The Spirit of the Gospel Neither a Spirit of Superstition or of Enthusiasm* (1771), p. 24.

118 David Hartley, *Observations on Man* (1749), I, 494.

119 A. Norman Jeffares (ed.), *Swift*, Modern Judgments (1968), p. 50.

CHAPTER 12, pp. 162–165

1 *A Question of Fact*, by Wynyard Browne.

APPENDIX I

1 Brian Vickers, *The World of Jonathan Swift* (1968), p. 4.

2 Moira Dearnley, *The Poetry of Christopher Smart* (1968), p. xiv.

3 *ibid.* p. xxiii.

4 George Watson, *Coleridge the Poet* (1966), p. 51.

5 Heer, *Intellectual History of Europe*, p. 383.

6 B.B.C., 29 Jan. 1967.

7 Hugh Montefiore, *Truth to Tell* (1966).

8 Rosamund E. M. Harding, *An Anatomy of Inspiration* (1940), p. 84.

9 B.B.C. 'Today in the West', 2 May 1969.

APPENDIX 2

1 Quoted in Lucas, *Art of Living*, p. 141.
2 Thomas Carlyle, *Shooting Niagara* (1867), in *Works* (Centenary edn, 1899), xxx, 7. Cp. Coleridge, above, p. 177.
3 I owe these comments to Dr Estelle Morgan of the University of Bristol.

SELECT BIBLIOGRAPHY

Where I have used a later edition than the first, I give both dates, unless the later is an improved version. Place of publication is London, unless otherwise stated. Single works issued anonymously are ascribed to their authors (name in square brackets) where known.

BOOKS AND ARTICLES

Abbey, C. J. and Overton, J. H. *The English Church in the Eighteenth Century*, 1878.

Adams, R. H. *Ikon: John Milton and the Modern Critics*, Ithaca, N.Y., 1955.

Adams, Thomas. *The Divells Banket*, 1614.

Mystical Bedlam, The World of Madmen, 1615.

Addison, Joseph. *Remarks on Several Parts of Italy, etc.*, 1705 (1741 edn).

Aldridge, A. D. *Man of Reason: The Life of Thomas Paine*, 1960.

Alison, Archibald. *An Essay on Taste*, Dublin and Edinburgh, 1790.

Allen, D. C. (ed.). *Studies in Honor of T. W. Baldwin*, Urbana, Ill., 1958.

Allen, Hope E. *English Writings of Richard Rolle, Hermit of Hampole*, Oxford, 1931.

Allen, P. S. and H. M. *Opus Epistolarum Des. Erasmi Roterodami*, Oxford, 1936.

The Amicable Quixote, 1788.

Appleyard, J. A. *Coleridge's Philosophy of Literature*, Cambridge, Mass., 1965.

[Arbuthnot, John] *An Essay on the Usefulness of Mathematical Learning*, Oxford, 1701.

The Art of Poetry on a New Plan, 1762 [J. Newbery, revised by Goldsmith (?)].

Aubin, R. A. *Topographical Poetry in XVIII Century England*, 1956.

Austen, Jane. *Letters*, ed. R. W. Chapman, 1952.

Works, ed. R. W. Chapman, 1954.

Baillie, John. *Essay on the Sublime*, 1749.

Bate, W. J. 'The Sympathetic Imagination in Eighteenth-century Criticism', *E.L.H.*, XII (1945).

Battestin, M. C. (ed.). *Joseph Andrews and Shamela*, Boston, 1961; London, 1965.

Baxter, Richard. *The Certainty of the Worlds of Spirits*, 1691.

Bayley, B. *An Essay on Inspiration*, 2nd edn 'very much corrected and enlarged', 1708.

Beattie, James. *London Diary*, 1773 (ed. R. S. Walker, Aberdeen, 1947). *The Minstrel*, 1771 (printed in A. Chalmers, *English Poets*, vol. xviii, 1810).

Beckett, Samuel. *Malone Meurt*, Paris, 1951.

Beckford, William. *Modern Novel Writing, or The Elegant Enthusiast*, 1796.

Berington, Joseph. *The History of the Reign of Henry the Second*, 1790.

Bernbaum, E. *The Drama of Sensibility*, Harvard Studies in English, iii, Cambridge, Mass., 1915 (1938).

Bessinger, J. H. and Creed, R. P. *Medieval and Linguistic Studies in Honor of Francis Peabody Magoun, Jr.* (British issue of *Franciplegius*), New York, 1965.

Birrell, T. A. (ed.). S[imon] P[atrick], *A Brief Account of the New Sect of Latitude Men*, Augustan Reprints, 100, Los Angeles, 1963. (First published 1662.)

Black, F. G. *The Epistolary Novel in the Late Eighteenth Century*, Oregon Monographs, 2, Eugene, 1940.

Blackham, H. J. *Objections to Humanism*, 1963 (Penguin edn, 1965).

Blackstone, B. *The Lost Travellers*, 1962.

Blair, P. Hunter. *Roman Britain and Early England*, 1963.

Blake, Robert. *Disraeli*, 1966.

Bloch, M. *Feudal Society*, tr. L. A. Manyon, 1961 (1965).

Bond, R. P. *English Burlesque Poets 1700–1750*, Harvard Studies in English, vi, Cambridge, Mass., 1964.
Studies in the Early English Periodical, Chapel Hill, N.C., 1957.

Boswell, James. *Journal of a Tour to the Hebrides*, 1785 (ed. R. W. Chapman, Oxford, 1924).
Life of Samuel Johnson, 1791 (ed. G. B. Hill and L. F. Powell, Oxford, 1934).

Boucher, Johnathan. *On Schisms and Sects*, 1769.
A View of the Causes and Consequences of the American Revolution, 1797 (sermons preached, 1763–75).

Bowden, Muriel. *A Reader's Guide to Geoffrey Chaucer*, 1964 (1965).

Bradbrook, F. W. *Jane Austen and her Predecessors*, Cambridge, 1966.

Brander, L. *George Orwell*, 1954.

Briggs, Asa. *Victorian People*, Chicago, 1955 (Penguin edn, 1965).

Brooke, Henry. *The Fool of Quality*, 1766.

Brown, W. L. *Essay on the Folly of Scepticism*, 1788.

Browne, P. *The Procedure, Extent and Limits of Human Understanding*, 1728.

Buckle, G. E. *Letters of Queen Victoria*, 2nd Series, 1926–8.

Buller, James. *Reply to the Rev. Mr. Wesley's Address to the Clergy*, Bristol, 1756.

Burke, Edmund. *Letters*, ed. H. J. Laski (World's Classics edn, 1922).
Notebook, ed H. V. F. Somerset, Cambridge, 1957.
Reflections on the French Revolution, 1790 (Everyman edn).
Speech on Conciliation with the Colonies, 1775 (in *Speeches and Letters on American Affairs*, Everyman edn).
A Vindication of Natural Society, 1756 (published as 'by a Late Noble Author').

Burnet, Gilbert, the Younger. Papers in *The Free-Thinker*, q.v.

Burney, Fanny (Madame D'Arblay). *Diary*, 1842–6 (Everyman edn).

Burns, Robert. *Letters*, ed. J. de Lancey Ferguson, Oxford, 1931.

Burton, Robert. *The Anatomy of Melancholy*, 1621 (ed. A. R. Shilleto, 1893).

Butler, Joseph. *The Analogy of Religion*, 1736 (Everyman edn).
Sermons (in *Collected Works*, 1874).

Byrom, John. *Enthusiasm, a Poetical Essay*, Dublin, 1757 (Chetham Society, II, 14, Manchester, 1895).

C., M. A. *Enthusiasm not Religion*, 1848.

Calder-Marshall, Arthur. *The Enthusiast*, 1962.

Camden, Carroll (ed.). *Restoration and Eighteenth Century Literature*, Chicago, 1963.

Campbell, Archibald. *A Discourse Proving that the Apostles were no Enthusiasts*, 1730.

Campbell, George. *The Spirit of the Gospel Neither a Spirit of Superstition nor of Enthusiasm*, Edinburgh, 1771.

Carlyle, Thomas. *Montesquieu* (in *Critical and Miscellaneous Essays*, V, Centenary edn, 1899).
Shooting Niagara: and after?, 1867.

Casaubon, Meric. *A Treatise Concerning Enthusiasm, As it is an Effect of Nature*, 1655.

Cazamian, F. A. M. L. *The Development of English Humour*, New York, 1952.

Chalmers, Alexander. *The Works of the English Poets from Chaucer to Cowper*, 1810.

Chambers, Ephraim. *Cyclopaedia*, 1755 (1779).

Chapone, Hester (Mrs Mulso). *Miscellanies, in prose and verse*, 1775 ('New Edition...with author's last corrections and additions', 1806).

Chauncy, Charles. *A Caveat against Enthusiasm: Enthusiasm described and caution'd against, A Sermon*, Boston, 1742.

Seasonable Thoughts on the State of Religion in New England, Boston, 1743.

Church, Thomas. *Remarks on the Revd. Mr. John Wesley's Last Journal*, 1745.

Clarendon, Edward Hyde, Earl of. *History of the Rebellion*, 1702-4 (Oxford, 1888).

Clarke, Desmond. *The Ingenious Mr. Edgeworth*, 1965.

Clarke, Samuel. *A Discourse concerning the Being and Attributes of God*, Boyle Lectures 1704, published 1705 (5th edn, corrected, 1719).

A Discourse concerning the Unchangeable Obligations of a Natural Religion, Boyle Lectures 1705, published 1706 (*see* Selby-Bigge).

Cobbett, William. *Rural Rides*, 1830 (Everyman edn).

Cockburn, Henry. *Memorials of his Time, 1779-1830*, Edinburgh, 1856 (1910).

Cohn, Norman. *The Pursuit of the Millennium*, 1957 (Paladin edn, 1970).

Coke, T. and Moore, H. *The Life of the Rev. John Wesley, A.M.*, 1792.

Coleridge, Samuel Taylor. *Aids to Reflection*, 1825 (in *Complete Works* ed. W. G. T. Shedd, New York, 1853).

Collected Letters, ed. E. L. Griggs, Oxford, 1956 and 1959.

The Friend, 1809-10 (ed. B. E. Rooke, 1969).

Notes on English Divines, ed. Derwent Coleridge, 1853.

Philosophical Lectures, 1818, 1819 (ed. E. J. K. Coburn, 1949).

The Statesman's Manual, 1816 (Shedd, vol. i).

College, Eric. *The Medieval Mystics of England*, 1962.

Collins, Anthony. *Scheme of Literal Prophesy Considered*, 1727 (published at The Hague the year before).

Collins, V. H. *A Third Book of English Idioms*, 1960.

Collins, William. 'Ode on the Poetical Character', in *Odes on Several Descriptive and Allegorical Subjects*, 1747.

[Combe, William] *Original Love Letters* (*Second Journal to Eliza*), 1784.

Congreve, William. *William Congreve's Letters and Documents*, ed. John C. Hodges, 1964.

Cooke's Pocket Edition of the Original and Complete Works of Select British Poets, n.d.

Coventry, Henry. *Philemon to Hydaspes*, 1736-44 (1738).

Cowley, Abraham. *Works*, 1668 (9th edn, 1700).

Cragg, G. R. *Reason and Authority in the Eighteenth-Century*, Cambridge, 1964.

Craik, W. A. *Jane Austen: The Six Novels*, 1965.

Crofts, J. E. V. 'Enthusiasm' in *Eighteenth Century Literature, an Oxford Miscellany*, Oxford. 1909.

Daniel, Norman. *Islam and the West*, Edinburgh University Publications, Language and Literature, 12, Edinburgh, 1960 (1962).

Darrel, William. *A Vindication of Saint Ignatius...*, 1688.

Davis, J. L. 'Mystical versus Enthusiastic Sensibility', *J.H.I.*, 4 (1943), 301–19.

Davis, R. H. C. *A History of Medieval Europe*, 1938 (1964).

Dearnley, Moira. *The Poetry of Christopher Smart*, 1968.

Decarreaux, J. *Monks and Civilisation*, tr. Charlotte Haldane, 1964.

Defoe, Daniel. *The Review*, 1704–13 (facsimile edn by A. W. Secord, New York, 1938).
  Treatise Concerning the Use and Abuse of the Marriage Bed, 1727 (published anonymously).

Delatte, Amand. *Les Conceptions de l'Enthousiasme chez les Philosophes Pre-Socratiques*, Paris, 1934.

Dempster, Germaine. *Dramatic Irony in Chaucer*, 1932 (New York, 1959).

Dennis, John. *Critical Works*, ed. E. N. Hooker, Baltimore, 1939–42.

Dennis, Nigel. *Jonathan Swift*, 1964 (1965).

Derry, Warren. *Dr. Parr: the Whig Dr. Johnson*, 1966.

Dickins, L. and Stanton, M. *An Eighteenth-Century Correspondence*, 1910.

Dickinson, J. C. *Monastic Life in Medieval England*, 1961.

Disraeli, Benjamin. *Coningsby*, 1844 (Chiltern Library edn).
  Sybil, 1845 (World's Classics edn).

Doddridge, Philip. *Some Remarkable Passages in the Life of the Honourable Colonel James Gardiner*, 1747.

Dodds, E. R. *The Greeks and the Irrational*, Berkeley, 1951.

[Dodwell, Henry] *Christianity Not Founded on Argument*, 1741.

Doughty, Oswald. *The English Lyric in the Age of Reason*, 1922.

Douglas, John. *An Apology for the Clergy*, 1755.
  The Criterion: or, Miracles Examined, 1754 (published anonymously).

Dove, John. *A Creed founded on Truth and Common Sense*, 1750.

Downey, James. *The Eighteenth-Century Pulpit*, 1969.

Drake, James. *The Memorial of the Church of England* ,1705

Dryden, John. *Of Heroick Plays*, 1672 (Prefatory to *The Conquest of Granada*, Everyman edn).

Duff, William. *Essay on Original Genius*, 1767.

D'Urfey, Thomas. *The Modern Prophets, or New Wit for a Husband*, 1709.

Echard, Laurence. *A General Ecclesiastical History*, 1702 (6th edn, 1722).

Edgeworth, Maria. *Letters for Literary Ladies*, 1803.

Edwards, Jonathan. *Some Thoughts concerning the Present Revival of Religion in New England*, Boston, 1743.

Ehrenpreis, Irvin. *Swift, the Man, his Works and the Age.* Vol. I, *Mr. Swift and his Contemporaries*, 1962.

Eliot, George. *Middlemarch*, 1871–2 (Zodiac Press edn).

Emerson, Ralph Waldo. *The Oversoul*, 1844 (in *Works*, 1891).

England, M. W. *Garrick's Jubilee*, 1964.

The Enthusiast, or Prejudice and Principle, 1843.

Entwistle, Joseph. *A Letter to the Author of an Anonymous Treatise on Inspiration*, York, 1799.

[Etough, Henry] *A Letter to the Author of Christianity not Founded on Argument*, 1742.

Evans, Theophilus. *The History of Modern Enthusiasm from the Reformation to the Present Times*, 1752 (2nd edn 'with very Large Additions and Amendments', 1759).

Extracts of Letters relating to Methodists and Moravians, 1745.

Falconer, William. *The Demagogue*, 1764 (in *Cooke's Pocket edn of the Original and Complete Works of Select British Poets*).

[Fancourt, Samuel] *A Letter to the Author of the Nature and Consequences of Enthusiasm*, 1719.

Featley, Daniel. *The Dippers Dipt: or the Anabaptists Duck'd and Plung'd*, 1645 (5th edn, 1647).

Fielding, Henry. *Joseph Andrews*, 1742.

Fixler, Michael. *Milton and the Kingdoms of God*, 1964.

Fleishman, A. *A Reading of 'Mansfield Park'*, Minnesota Monographs in the Humanities, 2, Minneapolis, 1967.

Fletcher, Angus. *Allegory*, Ithaca, N.Y., 1964.

Fletcher, John William [Jean Guillaume de la Fléchère], *Logica Genevensis: or a Fourth Check to Antinomianism*, Bristol, 1772.

Fletcher, R. H. *The Arthurian Material in the Chronicles*, Burt Franklin Bibliographical Studies, IX, Franklin, N.Y., 1958.

The Flight of the Pretender, 1708.

[Fowler, Edward] *Reflections upon a Letter concerning Enthusiasm*, 1709.

Fox, Edmond. *Enthusiasm, a poem*, 1758.

Friedman, W. F. and E. S. *The Shakespeare Ciphers Examined*, Cambridge, 1957.

Fussell, Paul. *The Rhetorical World of Augustan Humanism*, Oxford, 1965.

Gerard, Alexander, *An Essay on Genius*, 1774 edn.

An Essay on Taste, 1759.

Gerdes, Henningius J. *de Enthusiasmo schediasma...*, Wittenberg, 1708.

Gibbon, Edward. *The History of the Decline and Fall of the Roman Empire*, 1776–8 (World's Classics edn).

Gibbs, F. W. *Joseph Priestley*, 1965.

Gignilliat, G. W. *The Author of Sandford and Merton*, 1952.

Gilpin, William. *An Essay on Picturesque Travel*, in *A General Essay on the Picturesque*, 1792.

Observations on the Mountains and Lakes of Cumberland and Westmorland, 1786.

Glanvill, Joseph. *Essays*, 1676.

The Vanity of Dogmatizing, 1661.

Glover, Richard. *The Athenaid*, c. 1785 (in Chalmers's *English Poets*, vol. XVII, 1810).

Goldsmith, Oliver. *Essays, originally published in the year 1765* (in P. Cunningham's edn of *Works*, 1854).

Graves, Richard (of Ardagh). *The Whole Works*, ed. R. H. Graves, Dublin, 1840.

Graves, Richard (of Claverton). *Columella*, 1779.

Greaves, Richard. *John Bunyan*, Courtenay Studies in Reformation Theology, Abingdon, 1969.

Green, Thomas. *A Dissertation upon Enthusiasm*, 1755.

[Grey, Zachary] *A Serious Address to Lay-Methodists, with an Appendix containing an Account of the Fatal, Bloody Effects of 'Enthusiasm'*, 1745.

Guthrie, W. K. C. *The Greeks and their Gods*, 1950.

Hammond, Henry. *A Paraphrase and Annotations upon all the Books of the New Testament*, 1653 (1659).

Harding, Rosamund E. M. *An Anatomy of Inspiration*, 1940.

Hardy, Thomas. *Collected Poems*, 1965.

Hare, Edward. *A Refutation of the Charges against the Methodists advanced by the Rev. Doctor Magee*, 1810.

Harth, Philip. *Swift and Anglican Rationalism*, Chicago, 1961.

Hartley, David. *Observations on Man, his Fame, his Duty, and his Expectations*, 1749.

Harvey, W. J. *The Art of George Eliot*, Cambridge, 1963.

Hayley, William. *Edn. of the Poetical Works of John Milton*, 1794.

Hazlitt, William. *Characters of Shakespeare's Plays*, 1817.

    Lectures on the English Poets, 1802 (in A. R. Walker and A. Glover (eds.), *Collected Works*, 1902–4).

Heathcote, Ralph. *A Sketch of Lord Bolingbroke's Philosophy*, 1755.

Heer, Friedrich. *The Intellectual History of Europe*, tr. J. Steinberg, 1953 (1966).

Herbert, Dorothea. *Retrospections*, c. 1806.

Hesketh, Lady. *See* C. B. Johnson.

Hewlett, Ebenezer. *A Letter to Mr. Seagrave*, 1739.

Hickes, George. *Ravillac Redivivus*, 1678 (2nd edn 'very much augmented and enlarged', 1682) [published anonymously].

    The Spirit of Enthusiasm Exorcised, 1680.

Hildebrandt, Franz. *Christianity according to the Wesleys*, 1956.

Hildrop, John. *Reflections upon Reason*, 1722 (3rd edn 'Corrected and Enlarged', 1729).

Hill, Richard. *A Lash at Enthusiasm*, 2nd edn 'enlarged', 1778.

Hill, Rowland. *A Full Answer to...Wesley's Remarks upon a Late Pamphlet*, Bristol, n.d.

Hilles, F. W. *The Literary Career of Sir Joshua Reynolds*, Cambridge, 1936.

Hilles, F. W. and Bloom, Harold. *From Sensibility to Romanticism*, New York, 1965.

Hirsch, Eric Donald. *Innocence and Experience: An Introduction to Blake*, New Haven, 1964.

Hodgart, P. and Redpath, T. *Romantic Perspectives*, 1964.

Hoffman, A. W. *John Dryden's Imagery*, Gainesville, Fla., 1962.

Hogarth, William. *The Analysis of Beauty*, 1753.

    Works, ed. Thomas Clerk, 1810.

Holcroft, Thomas. Tr. of Lavater's *Physiognomy*, 1789.

Home, John. *Works*, ed. Henry Mackenzie, Edinburgh, 1822.

Honig, Edwin. *Dark Conceit: The Making of Allegory*, New York, 1966.

Hopkins, M. A. *Hannah More and her Circle*, New York and Toronto, 1947.

Hornbeeck, Johannes. *Summa Controversiarum Religionis*, Utrecht, 1653.

Houghton, Walter E. *The Victorian Frame of Mind, 1837–1870*, New Haven, 1957.

Howe, Irving. *Politics and the Novel*, 1961.

Howell, James. *Familiar Letters*, ed. Joseph Jacobs, Oxford, 1892.

Hubbard, W. *The Present State of New England*, pt. II, 1677.

Hume, David. *Essays, Political and Moral*, 1742.

　Letters, ed. J. Y. T. Greig, 1932.

Hunter, Ian M. L. *Memory*, 1957 (Penguin edn, 1966).

Hutcheson, Francis. *On the Passions*, 1728 (1730).

Impartial Reflections on what are termed Revivals of Religions, 1816, by 'a member of the Church of England'.

James, Henry. *Portrait of a Lady*, 1881 (Penguin edn).

Jeffares, A. Norman (ed.). *Fair Liberty was All his Cry*, 1967.

　Swift (Modern Judgments), 1968.

Jensen, H. James. *A Glossary of John Dryden's Critical Terms*, Minneapolis, 1969.

Jenyns, Soame. *A Free Enquiry into the Origin of Evil*, 1757.

Jerningham, Edward. *Enthusiasm, a Poem*, 1789.

Johnson, Catherine B. *Letters of Lady Hesketh to John Johnson*, 1901.

Johnson, J. W. *The Formation of English Neo-Classical Thought*, 1967.

Johnson, Samuel. *Irene* (produced at Drury Lane in 1749 but written in great part by 1737), in *The Poems of Samuel Johnson*, ed. D. N. Smith and E. L. McAdam, Oxford, 1941.

　Journey to the Western Islands, 1775 (ed. R. W. Chapman, Oxford, 1924).

　Works, 1825 edn.

'Junius' (pseud.). *Letters*, 1768–71 (1796).

Knox, Ronald A. *Enthusiasm*, Oxford, 1950.

Knox, Vicesimus. *Christian Philosophy: Cautions Concerning Enthusiasm*, 1795.

　Essays, Moral and Literary, 1778.

Lackington, James. *Memoirs*, 1791 (13th edn, 1810).

Langhorne, John. *Letters on Religious Retirement, Melancholy and Enthusiasm*, 1762.

Lavington, George. *The Enthusiasm of Methodists and Papists Compar'd*, 1749–51.

　The Moravians Compared and Detected, 1755.

Law, Edmund. *Considerations on the State of the World with regard to the Theory of Religion*, Cambridge, 1745.

Law, William. *Collected Works*, 1762 (reprint, Canterbury, 1892–3).

Lawson, John. *Lectures concerning Oratory*, Dublin, 1758 (1759).

Leland, John. *A View of the Principal Deistical Writers*, 1754–6.

Leslie, Charles. *The Snake in the Grass*, 1696.

L'Estrange, A. G. *The Life of Mary Russell Mitford*, 1870.

A Letter to the Rev. Mr. Whitefield...to prevent his doing Mischief to the Common People, 1739.

The Letter of Enthusiasm, 1723 (*An Answer to The Letter of Enthusiasm* was published in *British Journal*, 1724).

Levin, Harry T. *Christopher Marlowe: The Overreacher*, Cambridge, Mass., 1934, British edn, 1954 (1967).

Lewis, C. Day. *The Lyric Impulse*, 1965.

Lichtenstein, Aharon. *Henry More: The Rational Theology of a Cambridge Platonist*, Cambridge, Mass., 1962.

Litz, A. Walton, *Jane Austen: A Study of her Artistic Development*, 1965.

Locke, John. *Essay concerning Humane Understanding*, 1690, Part IV. 19 added in 1700 (1823).

Logan, J. V., Jordan, J. E., and Frye, N. *Some British Romantics*, Columbus, 1966.

Lowth, Robert. *The Sacred Poetry of the Hebrews*, 1753 (Latin), tr. George Gregory, 1787.

Lucas, F. L. *The Art of Living: Four Eighteenth-Century Minds, Hume, Horace Walpole, Burke, Benjamin Franklin*, 1959.

Ludlam, Thomas. *Four Essays*, 1797.

Lyles, Albert M. *Methodism Mocked*, 1960.

Lyttelton, George, First Baron. *Dialogues of the Dead*, 1760–5.
Observations on the Conversion of St Paul, 1747.
Persian Letters, 1735.

M[adan], M[artin]. *A Full and Compleat Answer to the Capital Errors, Contained in the writings of the late Rev. William Law...*, 1763.
Thelyphthora, 1780 (2nd edn enlarged, 1781).

Magee, William. *Discourses*, Dublin, 1809.

Mandeville, Bernard de. *Enquiry into the Origin of Honour, and the Usefulness of Christianity in War*, 1732.

Manuel, F. E. *The Eighteenth Century Confronts the Gods*, Cambridge, Mass., 1959.

[Mason, William] *Methodism Displayed and Enthusiasm Detected*, by a member of the Church of England, Liverpool, 1813 (a slightly modernised version of Mason's tract of 1756).

Maton, W. G. *Observations relative chiefly to the Natural History...of the Western Counties...*, 1797.

Mayne, Zackary. *Two Dissertations concerning Sense and the Imagination, with an Essay on Consciousness*, 1778.

McIntosh, A. and Halliday, M. A. K. *Patterns of Language*, 1966.

Melmoth, William. *Letters of Sir Thomas Fitzosborne on Several Subjects*, 1737.

Methodism Vindicated from the Charge of Ignorance and Enthusiasm, 1775.

Milton, John. *Defensio Prima*, 1650–1.

    Defensio Secunda, 1653.

    Prose Works, ed. M. L. Y. Hughes, New York, 1957.

Montagu, Richard. *Acts and Monuments of the Church*, 1642.

Montefiore, Hugh. *Truth to Tell*, 1966.

[Moor, James] *Essays Read to a Literary Society. . .at Glasgow*, Glasgow, 1759.

More, Henry, *Enthusiasmus Triumphatus*, 1656 (1662).

    An Explanation of the Grand Mystery of Godliness, 1660.

    A Modest Enquiry into the Mystery of Iniquity, 1664.

Morgan, Thomas. *The Absurdity of Opposing Faith to Reason . . .*, 1722.

    Enthusiasm in Distress, 1722.

Morhof, D. G. *Dissertationes Academicae*, Hamburg, 1699 (delivered 1661).

Morris, William. *Preface to Kelmscott 'Utopia'*, 1893.

[Mortimer, Thomas] *Die and be Damned*, 1758 (1761).

Moss, Roberts. *Sermons and Discourses on Practical Subjects*, 1733.

Neville, Sylas. *Diary*, ed. Basil Cozens-Hardy, Cambridge, 1950.

Nicholson, Henry. *The Falsehood of the New Prophets*, 1708.

Nicolson, Marjorie H. (ed.). *Conway Letters*, 1930.

    Voyages to the Moon, New York, 1960.

Nott, George F. *Religious Enthusiasm Considered*, Oxford, 1803 (8 sermons preached at Oxford in 1802).

Orrery, John Boyle, 5th Earl of Cork and. *Remarks on the Life and Writings of Dr. Jonathan Swift*, 1751 (3rd edn corrected, 1752).

Orwell, George. *Nineteen Eighty-Four*, 1949 (Penguin edn, 1952).

Owen John. Πνευματολογία: *or, a Discourse Concerning the Holy Spirit*, 1674 (written in 1651).

Owen, T. E. *Methodism Unmasked*, 1802.

Paine, Thomas. *Writings*, ed. M. D. Conway, 1894–6.

Painter, Sidney. *A History of the Middle Ages, 284–1500*, New York, 1953 (1964).

Palmer, D. J. *The Rise of English Studies*, 1965.

Parker, C. S. *Sir Robert Peel from his Private Papers*, 1899.

Parker, G. H. W. *The Morning Star*, Exeter, 1965.

Parker, Samuel. *A Discourse of Ecclesiastical Politics. . .* 1670.

Parr, Samuel. *Works*, ed. John Johnstone, 1828.

Pater, Walter. *The Renaissance: Studies in Art and Poetry*, 1888.

P[atrick], S[imon], *see* T. A. Birrell.

Peck, W. E. *Shelley, his Life and Works*, 1927.

Pennington, Lady Sarah. *An Unfortunate Mother's Advice to her Absent Daughter*, 1761.

Percival, Thomas. *Moral and Literary Dissertations*, Warrington, 1734.

Pinto, V. de Sola. *Enthusiast in Wit: A Portrait of John Wilmot, Earl of Rochester*, 1962.

Pittis, Thomas. *A Discourse Concerning the Trial of Spirits*, 1682.

Plato. *Ion*, Loeb edn, 1925.

Polwhele, Richard. Edn of Lavington's *Enthusiasm*, 1819 (1833).

Pope, Alexander. *Letters*, ed. John Butt, World's Classics, 1960.

Pottle, F. A. *Boswell, The Earlier Years*, 1966.

Price, Sir Uvedale. *On Architecture and Building*, 1796 enlarged edn.
    An Essay on the Picturesque, as Compared with the Sublime and Beautiful, 1794 (1796).

Priestley, Joseph. *Institutes of Natural Religion*, Birmingham, 1772–4 (2nd edn, 1782).

Prior, Moodie E. *The Language of Tragedy*, New York, 1947 (1960).

Pyper, J. Tr. of Urfé, *The History of Astraea*, 1620.

Quinn, Bernetta, *The Metamorphic Tradition in Modern Poetry*, New Brunswick, 1955.

Radcliffe, Anne. *The Mysteries of Udolpho*, 1794 (Everyman edn).

Read, Sir Herbert. *The Forms of Things Unknown*, 1960.
    Poetry and Experience, 1967.

Reason opposed to some Popular Errors ('by Mr. L.'), 1763.

Reeve, Clara. *The Progress of Romance*, 1785.

Reynolds, Sir Joshua. *Fifteen Discourses delivered at the Royal Academy, 1769–97*, Everyman edn.

Richards, I. A. *The Philosophy of Rhetoric*, New York, 1936.

Richardson, Samuel. *Clarissa*, 1747–8 (Everyman edn).
    Selected Letters, ed. John Carroll, Oxford, 1964.

Ridley, M. R. *Second Thoughts*, 1965.
    Studies in Three Literatures, 1962.

Rogers, P. G. *The Fifth Monarchy Men*, 1966.

Rohde, Erwin. *Psyche*, 1903 (tr. from 8th edn by W. B. Hills, 1925).

Roston, Murray. *Prophet and Poet: The Bible and the Growth of Romanticism*, 1965.

Røstvig, Maren-Sophie. *The Happy Man, Studies in the Metamorphosis of a Classical Ideal*, vol. I, Oslo Studies in English, 1954 (2nd edn revised, 1962).

Royde-Smith, Naomi. *The State of Mind of Mrs Sherwood*, 1946.

Ruffhead, Owen. *The Life of Alexander Pope, Esq.*, 1769.

Rust, George. *A Discourse on the Use of Reason in Matters of Religion* (Latin), tr. and annotated by Henry Halliwell, 1683.

Ryan, Edward, *The History of the Effects of Religion on Mankind*, 1788 (3rd edn 'corrected and enlarged', Edinburgh, 1806).

Rymer, Thomas. *The Tragedies of the Last Age*, 1678.

Sacheverell, Henry. *The Perils of False Brethren*, Oxford, 1709.
   The Political Union: a Discourse on the Dependence of Government on Religion, Oxford, 1702.

Saunders, J. W. *The Profession of Letters*, 1964.

Scott, John. *The Christian Life*, 1681 (3rd edn corrected, 1684).

Selby-Bigge, Sir Lewis A. *The British Moralists*, Oxford, 1897.

Seznec, Jean. *Claudel and the Muses*, Perspectives in Criticism, Harvard Studies in Comparative Literature, 20 (ed. Harry Levin), 1950.

Shaftesbury, Anthony Ashley Cooper, Third Earl of. *Characteristicks of Men, Manners, Opinions, Times*, 1711 (2nd edn corrected, 1714–15).
   Works, ed. J. M. Robertson, 1900.

Shaw, M. R. L. *Laurence Sterne: Second Journal to Eliza*, c. 1929 (*see* William Combe).

Shebbeare, John. *Letters on the English Nation*, 1756.

Shelley, Percy Bysshe. *Preface to The Revolt of Islam*, 1817.

Smith, Adam. *A History of Ancient Physics*, 1795 (in *Works*, ed. Dugald Stewart, 1811, vol. v).

Smith, Haddon. *Philalethes: The Methodists Vindicated*, 1771.

Smith, John. *Select Discourses*, 1659 (3rd edn corrected, Cambridge, 1673).

Smith, Patrick. *A Preservative against Quakerism*, 1732.

Smollett, Tobias. *Humphry Clinker*, 1771 (Everyman edn).
   Peregrine Pickle, 1751 (Everyman edn).

Southam, B. C. *Jane Austen's Literary MSS.*, 1964.

Spearman, Diana. *The Novel in Society*, 1966.

Spence, Joseph, *Anecdotes*, ed. S. W. Singer, 1820.

Spinckes, N. *The New Pretenders to Prophecy examined*, 1709.

Stacey, John. *Wyclif and Reform*, 1964.

Starr, G. A. *Defoe and Spiritual Autobiography*, Princeton, 1965.

[Stedman, J.] *Laelius and Hortensia*, 1782.

Steeves, H. R. *Before Jane Austen*, 1966.

Steffen, T. G. *The Social Argument against Enthusiasm*, Texas Studies in English, 1941.

Stennett, Samuel. *Discourses on Personal Religion*, 1709.

Sterne, Laurence. *Letters and Sermons* (*Works*, ed. David Herbert, Edinburgh, 1872).

Stevens, William Bagshaw. *The Journal*, ed. Georgina Galbraith, Oxford, 1965.

Stillingfleet, Edward. *Irenicon*, 1661 (1709).

Stinstra, Johannes. *An Essay on Fanaticism*, tr. from the French version of the Dutch by Isaac Subremont, Dublin, 1774.

Stukeley, William. *Stonehenge*, 1740.

Sturluson, Snorri. *Skáldskaparmál*, ed. F. Jónsson, Copenhagen, 1900.

Sweeting, E. J. *Early Tudor Criticism*, Oxford, 1940.

Swift, Jonathan. *The Mechanical Operation of the Spirit* (*A Tale of a Tub*), 1704 (5th edn, 1710).

Sylvester, Joshua. Tr. of Du Bartas, *La Semaine*, 1592–9.

Taylor, Isaac. *The Natural History of Enthusiasm*, 1829 (published anonymously).

   The Natural History of Fanaticism, 1833.

   Spiritual Despotism, 1855 (published anonymously).

Taylor, Thomas. *An Essay on the Beautiful: From the Greek of Plotinus*, 1792.

Temple, Sir William. *Of Heroick Virtue*, in *Miscellanea* (two parts, 1680 and 1692), 4th edn, 1696.

Thomson, J. A. K. *Classical Influences on English Prose*, 1956.

Tillyard, E. M. W. *The Muse Unchained*, 1958.

Tindall, William York. *John Bunyan: Mechanick Preacher*, 1934 (Columbia University Studies in English and Comparative Literature, New York, 1964).

[Tong, William] *The Nature and Consequences of Enthusiasm Consider'd*, 1720 (2nd edn).

Trapp, Joseph. *The Nature, Folly, Sin and Danger of being Righteous over-much*, 1739 (3rd edn, 1739).

Trenchard, John. *The Natural History of Superstition*, 1709.

Trenchard, J. and Gordon, T. *The Independent Whig*, 1720–1 (coll. edn, 1732).

Trollope, Anthony. *The Eustace Diamonds*, 1869–70.

SELECT BIBLIOGRAPHY

Tulloch, John. *Rational Theology in England in the XVIIth Century*, Edinburgh, 1872.

Underhill, Evelyn. *Worship*, 1936 (Fontana Library, 1962).

Usher, James. *Clio*, 1767 (4th edn enlarged, 1778).

Vallins, G. H. *The Wesleys and the English Language*, 1937.

Vickers, Brian. *The World of Jonathan Swift*, Cambridge, 1968.

Wainwright, F. T. *Archaeology, Place-Names and History*, 1962.

Waley, Daniel. *Later Medieval Europe*, 1964.

Walker, E. C. (ed.). *The History of 'Enthusiasm' as a Factor in Religious and Social Problems of the Eighteenth Century*, Institute of Historical Research, Toronto, 1932.

Walpole, Horace. *Correspondence*, ed. W. S. Lewis (Yale edn); London and New Haven, 1937–67.

Letters to Conway, ed. P. Cunningham, 1857–9.

Walsh, James (ed.). *Pre-Reformation Spirituality*, 1966.

Walzer, Michael. *The Revolution of the Saints*, 1966.

Warburton, William. *The Doctrine of Grace*, 1762 (in *Works* (1788), IV, 535–723 and in *Collected Works*, ed. R. Hurd (1811), vol. VIII).

Warton, Thomas. *Observations on the Faerie Queene*, 1734.

Waterland, Daniel. *Doctrine of the Eucharist*, 1737.

Watson, George. *Coleridge the Poet*, 1966.

Watts, Isaac. *A Guide to Prayer*, 3rd edn 'corrected', 1743.

Weatherley, E. H. *The Correspondence of John Wilkes and Charles Churchill*, New York, 1954.

Webster, Clarence M. 'Swift and Some Modern Satirists of Puritan Enthusiasm', *P.M.L.A.*, vol. XLVIII (1933).

'Swift's *Tale of a Tub* compared with Earlier Satires on the Puritans', *P.M.L.A.*, vol. XLVII (1932).

Wellek, René. *History of Modern Criticism*, 1955. Vol. I, *The Later Eighteenth Century*.

Wendeborn, G. F. *A View of England*, 1791.

Wesley, John. *An Answer to the Rev. Mr. Church's Remarks*, 1745.

Journals, ed. N. Curnock, 1909–16.

Letter to the Author of the Enthusiasm of the Methodists and Papists Compar'd, 1750.

Sermon on Enthusiasm, 1750 (Sermon XXXII in *Standard Sermons*, ed. E. H. Sugden, 1921, vol. II).

Wharton, Henry. *The Enthusiasm of the Church of Rome demonstrated in some Observations upon the Life of Ignatius Loyola*, 1688.

Whelan, M. K. *Enthusiasm in English Poetry of the Eighteenth Century*, Texas Studies in English, 1935.

Whichcote, Benjamin. *Moral and Religious Aphorisms*, 1703 (ed. W. R. Inge, 1930).

Whitehead, F., Diverres, A. H. and Sutcliffe, F. E. *A Medieval Miscellany in Honour of Eugene Vinaver*, Manchester, 1965.

Wildeblood, J. and Brinson, P. *The Polite World*, 1965.

Williams, Kathleen (ed.). *Swift: The Critical Heritage*, 1970.

Winton, C. *Captain Steele*, 1964.

Wood, Paul Spenser. 'Native Elements in English Neo-Classicism', *M.Ph.*, XXIV (1926–7).

Wood, Robert. *Strictures on a Recent Publication entitled The Support of our Established Church...by Robert Moore, D.D.*, 1815.

Woodward, Josiah. *Remarks on the Modern Prophets*, 1708.

Wordsworth, William. *The French Revolution as it Appeared to Enthusiasts at its Commencement*, 1815.

Preface to The Lyrical Ballads, 1815.

Wright, W. F. *Sensibility in English Prose Fiction, 1760–1814*, Illinois Studies in Language and Literature, 22, Urbana, 1937.

Young, Edward. *Conjectures on Original Composition*, 1759 (ed. E. J. Morley, 1918).

On Lyric Poetry, 1728.

Night Thoughts, 1742–5 (1758).

PERIODICALS

Periodicals quoted, with abbreviated titles where used after the first references or where they are the conventional mode of reference.

The Annual Register: 1758–	*Ann. Reg.*
The Anti-Jacobin: 1797–8	
The British Critic: 1793–1826.	*Brit. Crit.*
The British Journal: 1722–31 (?)	
The Critical Review: 1756–1817.	*Crit. Rev.*
(New Arrangement volumes from 1791 = n. arr.)	
English Literary History: Baltimore, 1934–	*E.L.H.*
The Freeholder: 1715–16.	
The Free Thinker: 1718–23.	
The Gentleman's Magazine: 1731–1922.	*Gent. Mag.*
The Independent Whig: 1720 (coll. edn, 1732).	
The Journal of the History of Ideas: New York, 1940–	*J.H.I.*

SELECT BIBLIOGRAPHY

The Literary Magazine: 1788–94.   *Lit. Mag.*
The London Magazine: 1736–85.
The Looker-On: 1792–4.
Modern Philology: Chicago, 1902–   *M. Ph.*
The Monthly Review: 1749–1845.   *Month. Rev.*
Publications of the Modern Language Association of
    America: Baltimore, and Menasha, Wis.: 1880–   *P.M.L.A.*
The Review (see Defoe): 1704–13.
The Spectator: 1711–12 (no. 201 quoted from 12th edn,
    1739).
The Tatler: 1709–11 (quoted from coll. edn of 1710–11).
The World: 1753–6 (quoted from 1776 edn Edinburgh).

WORKS OF REFERENCE

Ainsworth, Robert. *Dictionary, English and Latin,* 1736 (1773, with
    additions by Thomas Morell) [originally *Thesaurus Linguae Latinae*
    Compendarius].
Annals of English Literature, 1473–1925, Oxford, 1935.
Bailey, Nathaniel. *Universal Etymological English Dictionary,* 1721 (1731).
Blount, Thomas. *Glossographia: or a dictionary listing all such hard words of*
    whatever language, now used in our refined English tongue, 1656.
The Cambridge Bibliography of English Literature, 1940–57.
Chambers, Ephraim. *Cyclopaedia,* 1755 (1779).
Cocker, Edward. *English Dictionary,* 1704.
Coles, Edward. *English Dictionary,* 1696.
Concise Oxford Dictionary (C.O.D.), 1964.
A Dictionary of American English on Historical Principles, ed. W. A. Craigie
    and J. R. Hulbert, Chicago and London, 1938–44.
The Dictionary of National Biography, 1885–1901, Supplement, 1949.
Dictionnaire de Théologie Catholique, Paris, 1930–68.
Diderot, Denis, and Alembert, le Rondet. *Encyclopédie ou Dictionnaire*
    Raisonné des Sciences, des Arts et des Métiers, Paris, 1751–76.
Dyche, Thomas and Pardon, William. *A New General English Dictionary,*
    1702, and many later edns (4th edn, 1744).
Glossographia Anglicana Nova, 1707.
Halkett, S., Laing, J. *et al. The Dictionary of Anonymous and Pseudonymous*
    Writings, Edinburgh, 1926–34, Supplement, 1962.
Jóhannesson, Alexander. *Isländisches Etymologisches Wörterbuch,* Bern,
    1951–6.

Johnson, Samuel. *Dictionary of the English Language*, 1755 (5th edn, 1784).

Martin, Benjamin. *Lingua Britannica Reformata, or A New English Dictionary*, 1749.

The Oxford Companion to English Literature, 1932.

The Oxford Dictionary of the Christian Church, 1957.

The Oxford Dictionary of Current English, 1969.

The Oxford Dictionary of English Etymology, 1966.

The Oxford Dictionary of English Proverbs, 1935.

The Oxford English Dictionary (O.E.D.), reissue, 1933.

Penguin English Dictionary, 1965.

Phillips, Edward ['E.P.']. *The New World of Words*, 1658, 1662, 1671, 1720.

Rees, Abraham, *et al. The Cyclopaedia or Universal Dictionary of Arts, Sciences, and Literature*, 1819.

Sheridan, Thomas. *Dictionary of the English Language*, 1780.

The Stanford Dictionary of Anglicised Words and Phrases, Cambridge, 1892, reissue, 1965.

[Wesley, John] *The Complete English Dictionary*, Bristol, 1753 (2nd edn, 1764).

The Catalogues of the Bodleian Library, the British Museum and the Library of the University of Bristol.

INDEX

Pater, Walter 154
Paul, St 40, 139
Peel, Sir Robert 137
Penguin English Dictionary, The 166
Percival, Thomas 66
Philemon to Hydaspes 106–8
Phillips, Edward 15
Pindar 184n
Pitt, William, Earl of Chatham 137
Plato 21, 78
Plotinus 139, 158
Plumier, Charles 112
Plutarch 3, 22
Polwhele, Richard 35
Pope, Alexander 51, 82, 90, 106, 110
Porphyry 139
Poussin, Nicolas 113
Prester John 152
Price, Richard 153
Price, Sir Uvedale 113
Priestley, Joseph 36, 127, 147, 150–1
Puritans 8, 10, 52, 56–7

Quakers 29, 33, 47, 52, 58, 139, 148, 156
Quintana, Ricardo 141
Quintilian 86

Radcliffe, Anne 118
Reed, Sir Herbert 129, 136
Rees, Abraham 17, 81, 83–4
Reeve, Clara 159
Reynolds, Sir Joshua 113, 124
Richards, I. A. 142–3
Rogers, P. G. 7–8
Rolle of Hampole, Richard 195n
Rossetti, Gabriele 141
Rousseau, Jean-Jacques 100, 141
Rubens, Peter Paul 76–7
Ruffhead, Owen 51, 81, 83, 90

Ryan, Edward 36
Rymer, Thomas 86–7

Sacheverell, Henry 32, 94
Salmasius, Claudius (i.e. Claude Saumaise) 26
Schiller, F. W. J. von 91
Scott, John 161
Scott, John, of Amwell 116
Scott, Sir Walter 137, 143
Seneca, Lucius Annaeus 86
Shaftesbury, Anthony Ashley Cooper, Third Earl of 14, 21, 51, 63, 138, 139, 158
Shakespeare, William 84, 92–3, 114, 128
Sharp, Archbishop James 94
Shaw, George Bernard 92
Shebbeare, John 102, 111
Shelley, Percy Bysshe 77, 92
Sheridan, Thomas 159, 172n, 174n
Sherwood, Mary Martha 129
Siddons, Sarah 140
Smith, John 78–9
Smollett, Tobias 76–7, 190n
Spectator, The 52, 151
Spinkes, N. 169n
Sprat, Thomas 158
Stanford Dictionary of Anglicised Words and Phrases, The 168
Sterne, Laurence 9–10, 66
Stevens, W. Bagshaw 98, 123–4
Stillingfleet, Edward 197n
Stinstra, Johannes 18, 53, 150
Stork, Nicholas (properly Niklas Storch) 15
Stukely, William 30–1
Swedenborg, Emanuel (properly Swedberg) 53, 139
Sweeting, E. J. 152
Swift, Jonathan 9, 69, 145, 157, 161